FAST FACTS® ON THE MIDDLE EAST CONFLICT

Randall Price

HARVEST HOUSE™ PUBLISHERS

EUGENE, OREGON

All Scripture quotations are taken from the New American Standard Bible ®, © 1960, 1962, 1963, 1968, 1971, 1972, 1973, 1975, 1977, 1995 by The Lockman Foundation. Used by permission.

Cover by Terry Dugan Design, Minneapolis, Minnesota

FAST FACTS is a registered trademark of The Hawkins Children's LLC. Harvest House Publishers, Inc. is the exclusive licensee of the federally registered trademark, FAST FACTS.

FAST FACTS® ON THE MIDDLE EAST CONFLICT

Copyright © 2003 by Randall Price
Published by Harvest House Publishers
Eugene, Oregon 97402
www.harvesthousepublishers.com

Harvest House Publishers, Inc. is the exclusive licensee of the trademark, FAST FACTS.

Library of Congress Cataloging-in-Publication Data

Price, Randall.
    Fast facts on the Middle East conflict / Randall Price.
        p. cm.
    Includes bibliographical references.
        ISBN 0-7369-1142-1
    1. Arab-Israeli conflict. 2. Arab-Israeli conflict—Causes. 3. Arab-Israeli conflict—1993—Peace.
    4. Zionism—History 5. Palestinian Arabs—Social conditions—20th century. 6. Palestinian Arabs—Ethnic identity. 7. Israel—Ethnic relations. I. Title.
        DS119.7.P739 2003
        956.04—dc21   2003002359

Printed in the United States of America

04   05   06   07   08   09   10   / BP-CF /   12   11   10   9   8   7   6   5   4

In Memory of

John F. Walvoord

Professor and Friend

Who taught his students to view the confounding problems of the Middle East conflict in light of the comforting promise of Messiah's coming.

Dedicated to

Terry Norris

My brother in the journey whose servant heart glorifies the Father and gratifies his friends. *"He is no fool who gives what he cannot keep to gain what he cannot lose"* (Jim Elliot).

Acknowledgments

I wish to give special thanks to Zachary Vandermeer, an International Relations graduate of the James Madison College at Michigan State University, who served as a research intern with World of the Bible Ministries, Inc. during the fall of 2002. Zack gathered essential resources, provided chapter outlines, and prepared the various sidebars for this book. Thanks, Zack, for a job well done!

I also wish to thank my mother, Maurine Price, for her devotion and gentle reminders to "get to the writing," and the board and congregation of Grace Bible Church, San Marcos, Texas, who understands their pastor's ministry outside their walls and faithfully prays for its success.

Appreciation is also expressed to the fine staff of Harvest House Publishers and especially Bob Hawkins, Jr. (president), Carolyn McCready (vice president of editorial), and Terry Glaspey for their vision and encouragement to write this book; to Steve Miller, LaRae Weikert, and Betty Fletcher (all editorial) for their outstanding work with the text; and to Corey Fisher (design and layout) for producing the superb graphics.

As in each previous book I've written, I want to express my love and gratitude to my wife Beverlee and my children Elisabeth, Eleisha, Erin, Jonathan, and Emilee, and my son-in-law Eric, whose encouragement and support in the task of writing is worth more than words can tell.

CONTENTS

SECTION IV:
WAR IN THE MODERN MIDDLE EAST

SECTION V:
THE BATTLE FOR JERUSALEM

SECTION VI:
THE PURSUIT FOR PEACE IN THE MODERN MIDDLE EAST

SECTION VII:
THE PALESTINIAN UPRISINGS

SECTION VIII:
THE THREAT OF GLOBAL TERRORISM

SECTION IX:
THE IRAQI CONFLICT AND ITS AFTERMATH

EXPLANATION OF TERMINOLOGY

Words have become a part of the Middle East warfare. Each side in the conflict has chosen terminology that best supports their interpretation of events and that can be used in media references to propagate their cause. For example, the Arab world refers to Israel as "Palestine" and biblical Judea and Samaria as "the West Bank." Even though Jerusalem has been a united city since 1967, Arabs continue to speak of it as divided, and of "East Jerusalem" as their particular possession. Because this terminology, though disputed, has become accepted by political scientists and is used almost universally by the media, it has been retained here where necessary for clarity. Such use should not be construed as an indication of the author's political views.

EXPLANATION OF "FAST FACT" SIDEBARS

In order to highlight certain facts, figures, and features we have created user-friendly sidebars that will enable you to quickly locate specific information. There are several kinds of sidebars, as follows:

Fast Focus—provides a timeline of key dates related to the questions considered in the text of that section of the book.

Fast Facts—provides essential information on key actions, events, ideologies and organizations.

Fast Features—provides a short overview of important topics and connections between key figures and facts.

Fast Figures—provides a brief biographical sketch of significant personalities.

Fast Quotes—provides quotes by political and/or religious representatives and commentators, illustrating the facts presented in the surrounding text.

For a complete index of all sidebars (except for Fast Focus) please see pages 191-193.

WHAT IS HAPPENING
IN THE MIDDLE EAST?

The Middle East today is in a conflict that now spans three centuries and threatens to engulf the modern world in a new war of apocalyptic proportions. Since the events of September 11, 2001, the West has awakened to the realization that it must assert itself in a more aggressive manner in the Middle East. Although for decades it influenced affairs in the region and suffered terrorist attacks on its foreign embassies, until al-Qaeda's assault on the United States, the West had been able to maintain a comfortable distance from the conflict. Yesterday, it was "the problem in the East." Today, a Maginot line has been crossed and it has become "the problem of the West." This "problem" has led the United States and its allies into bitter debate over the Arab states, presaging a greater confrontation between the West and the East. It has also moved the local conflict between the Israelis and Palestinians into the global arena, forging fervent alliances between Middle Eastern countries while creating new complexities and compromises for the foreign policies of Western nations.

All of this has forced Westerners to become more aware of the history and the forces that have brought them into such dire confrontation with certain militant ideologies and organizations. Moreover, Westerners have puzzled over the seemingly illogical mindset that has kept the Middle Eastern parties at an impasse, despite dedicated diplomacy, and prevented a peaceful resolution. Why has it been so difficult to bring peace? What keeps this conflict going?

There's a well-worn story from the Middle East that aptly portrays the confusing and contradictory nature of the conflict. A desert scorpion came to the bank of the Nile River and, finding a crocodile sunning himself, approached him and asked, "Brother crocodile, let us form an alliance to cross to the other side of the river." Whereupon the crocodile replied, "Do you think this sun has baked my brain? As soon as we start to cross you will sting me and kill me! What guarantee could you give that I would be safe?" The scorpion answered, "I promise I will not sting you! After all, if I were to sting you, I would drown too!" The crocodile thought about this and, deciding it made sense, took the scorpion upon his back. However, just as the two came to the middle of the Nile the scorpion became agitated and stung the crocodile. As they sank beneath the water, the crocodile said to the scorpion, "Why did you break your promise? Now both of us will die. What explanation is there for what you have done?" "There is none," answered the scorpion, "this is the Middle East!"

As this story reveals, the cause of the Middle East conflict cannot be rationally explained. Even so, political analysts have sought to offer explanations based on the historical rivalry between competing forces in the region. One such analyst defined the cause of the conflict in this way: "The independent Arab states [recent creations formed largely by the whims of the imperial powers after World War I] have fought with Israel [the only non-Arab, non-Muslim democracy in the Middle East] and among themselves, struggling with the conflicting influences of Pan-Arabism, the desire to create a unitary Arab state, Pan-Islamism, the motivation to reconstitute the Islamic empire, nationalistic movements to create independent states [such as the Palestinians], and the dictatorial and imperial designs of individual Arab leaders."[1]

Given such complex and uncompromising factors, we can begin to see why conflict continues. However, it *is* possible to break down the various elements of the present struggles and gain a clearer understanding of their origin and why they continue. That's the purpose of this book.

Fast Facts on the Middle East Conflict has been written to provide a concise explanation of the historical events that have produced the conflict in the Middle East and which at present are shaping the larger conflict between the East and the West. It has been written in a question-and-answer format to help make these facts more accessible, and you'll find sidebars along the way that highlight essential information concerning important events and individuals.

This book is brief by design, and was written to provide as concise an overview of the Middle East conflict as possible in a user-friendly format. The book's brevity, however, requires that some significant material be excluded. While I have attempted to present facts as objectively as possible, the selection of facts to be included or excluded is a subjective matter, and although unintended, may reflect an interpretive bias. For a more in-depth analysis that includes my views on some of these issues, the reader may consult my book *Unholy War: America, Israel, and Radical Islam* (Harvest House Publishers, 2001). In addition, you can also acquire other works mentioned in this book that will help you gain a more complete picture of the problems in the Middle East.

SECTION I:

CAUSES OF THE CONFLICT
IN THE MODERN MIDDLE EAST

Fast Focus

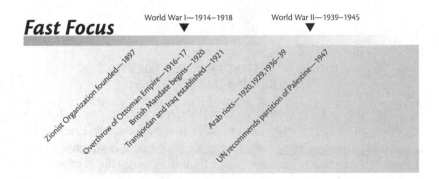

World War I—1914–1918 ▼

World War II—1939–1945 ▼

Zionist Organization founded—1897

Overthrow of Ottoman Empire—1916–17

British Mandate begins—1920

Transjordan and Iraq established—1921

Arab riots—1920,1929,1936–39

UN recommends partition of Palestine—1947

FOR GENERATIONS THE MODERN MIDDLE EAST has been a cauldron of unceasing conflict. For as long as most of us can remember, our newspapers and news programs have headlined the continuing struggle between Israel and the Arab world. In recent years, as Western powers have asserted their influence in the Middle East to mediate peace, a backlash of terrorism has emerged. This wave of terrorism swept the shores of the United States in September 2001, launching a U.S.-led "War on Terrorism." Ever since, militant forces in the Middle East have turned their attack against the West as well as against democratic regimes in their own region. Israel and its Western allies now face a mounting crisis of global proportion that may well have a dramatic effect on the economic and domestic security of every person on earth. What started this conflict, and why has it continued to escalate? Why has peace been so elusive, and is there any hope of ever resolving it?

Complicating the answers to these questions are factors seldom mentioned by the media—factors that we will consider within these pages. Moreover, through the years the media has presented the facts of

11

the conflict to the Western world in isolated sound bites, in such a way that it has been difficult to understand how the pieces of the Middle Eastern puzzle fit together. Only when we are able to see the historical picture from its inception, tracing its outline through time, can we realize the reasons behind the conflict and begin to comprehend what has happened and why. In the upcoming pages we will set the pieces in place and offer a clearer perspective of the puzzle by considering the words and actions of those on both sides of the conflict. We'll start by asking the most obvious question first: "How did the conflict begin?"

1

In short, what brought about the Arab-Israeli conflict?

Beginning in the late nineteenth century, Jewish Zionists immigrated to Palestine to join Jewish communities that had existed in the Land since biblical times. They lived alongside Arabs who had come to the country during the Islamic invasion of A.D. 638 and with the Ottoman Turks, whose homeland had maintained control of Palestine and the region for 400 years. Following the collapse of the Ottoman Empire in 1918, the League of Nations placed Syria-Palestine under separate French and British Mandates. Now separated from one another, the Arab people in these regions developed independent nationalistic ambitions and, with the Jews, received conflicting promises of independence from British officials. In order to resolve the growing number of clashes between the Arab and Jewish communities, the United Nations put forth a partition plan to create Jewish and Arab states in Palestine. The Jews accepted the partition plan and declared their independence in 1948.

The Arabs rejected partition and went to war to destroy the newly announced Jewish state. As a consequence of this war and another Arab invasion and war in 1967, the West Bank, Gaza Strip, and Golan Heights became occupied by Israel and a Palestinian refugee people was created. Prior to the 1967 war a Palestinian organization, the Palestine Liberation Organization (PLO), was founded to represent the Palestinian people and provoke the Arab world to destroy Israel. In 1987, the PLO started a popular uprising (Intifada) against Israel, employing terrorist tactics designed to force Israel to retaliate and gain international recognition of the Palestinian plight. In 1993, international mediation brought Israeli

Important Dates in the History of the Middle East Conflict

B.C. 2000	Abraham—Beginning of Jewish and Arab Lines
1406	Jews enter Canaan (Israel)
1000–925	Kingdom Established, First Temple Built (Jerusalem)
63	Roman Occupation of Israel
A.D. 70	Jerusalem Temple Destroyed by Romans
135	Jewish Nationalism Ends, Jewish Exile
613	Mohammed Forms Religion of Islam
638	Muslim Conquest of Holy Land, Al-Aqsa Mosque Built
691	Dome of the Rock Built in Jerusalem on Temple Mount
1897	First Zionist Congress
1916	Tripartite (Sykes-Picot) Agreement—Creates Borders of Modern Middle East
1918	British Mandate over Palestine Begins
1922	Britain Creates Transjordan (for Arabs)
1929	Arab Riots in Palestine
1933–1947	Jewish Flight from Persecution
1937	Peel Partition Plan of Palestine
1939	British White Papers Restrict Jewish Immigration
1947	United Nations Partition Plan
1948	Declaration of Jewish State, Arab-Israeli War Begins
1950	Jewish Law of Return Enacted, Jordan Cedes West Bank
1956	Sinai War
1967	Six-Day War
1973	Yom Kippur War
1979	Egyptian-Israel Peace Agreement (Camp David)
1987	Intifada Begins
1989	Mass Exodus of Soviet Jewry Begins
1991	Gulf War (Alliance of Iraq, Jordan, and PLO against Israel)
1993-2000	Oslo Accords (peace negotiations between Israel and Palestinians)
1994	Peace Treaty with Jordan
2000	Intifada Renewed ("Battle of Al-Aqsa" or "Oslo War")
2001	Terrorist Attack on America America and Allies Launch War on Terrorism
2002	U.S. War in Afghanistan, Escalation in Israeli-Palestinian Conflict
2003	U.S.–led war against Iraq Aqaba Summit on Road Map to Peace in the Middle East

and PLO leaders together at Oslo, Norway in an attempt to resolve the conflict. On September 13, both sides negotiated an interim peace agreement known as the Oslo Peace Process by signing a Declaration of Principles. However, during the five years of the interim agreement, even though the PLO had become the Palestinian National Authority (PA), and had received autonomy in Jericho, Gaza, and much of the West Bank, Palestinian acts of terrorism continued. In May 1999, the interim phase outlined in the Oslo Agreement ended and, despite attempts at mediation by the United States and other countries, the Intifada was resumed in September 2000.

These historical events must be considered within the larger context of the crisis that has been taking place within the Islamic world. With the decline of Islam and the rise of the West to superpower status and the intrusion of the non-Islamic westernized democracy of Israel into the Islamic-dominated, largely nondemocratic Middle East, Islamic doctrine and values have been "violated." Radical Islamic groups, using the Palestinian cause as a means to destroy Israel and restore Arab unity and Islamic dominance, have furthered the conflict as a means of forcing a final confrontation between the East and the West. The U.S.-led War on Terrorism, which was precipitated by the September 11, 2001 attack by Arab Muslim radicals, may be the beginning of such a confrontation, although it has been tempered by the constraints of U.S. foreign policy, Arab alliances, and the opinions of the European Union and the international community. In concert with this escalating conflict has been an arms race in the Middle East that has often pitted suppliers from democracies in the West against communist powers and Arab dictators in the East. This arms race has today reached a terminal point, with opposing Middle Eastern powers possessing weapons of mass destruction and threatening to use them regionally as well as in terror attacks against the West. Therefore, for the first time in history, the Middle East conflict has the potential of becoming a global struggle.

2

WHAT IS ZIONISM?

Arab sources have blamed Zionism as the major cause for the conflict in the Middle East. They state that they are not opposed to a Jewish presence in the Middle East or to the religion of Judaism, but to the political ambitions of Zionism, which are believed to be imperialistic. For example, one militant Palestinian source states: "The idea of creating a nationalist nation for the Jews was a dream of many of the most influential Jews and Jewish thinkers. The suggestion of Palestine as this nation springs from their religious belief—as they claim— that this is the Promised Land, and the temple of God was in it. However, this belief is no more than a cover for the bringing together of the Jews. The new goal for choosing Palestine as a country for the Jews springs from a strategic and economic objective and not from a religious objective at all.... Palestine forms the point of concentration of all the world powers, because it is the strategic center for controlling money" (reported in "Hamas, the Historical Roots and the

Fast Quote

Zionism as defined by the PLO
"Zionism is a political movement organically related to world imperialism and hostile to all movements of liberation and progress in the world. It is a racist and fascist movement in its formation; aggressive, expansionist, and colonialist in its aims; and fascist and Nazi in its methods. Israel is the tool of the Zionist movement...."

Article 22 of the Palestine National Charter

Pact," p. 16).[1] However, Dr. Kamel el Baker, president of Om Dorman Islamic University in the Sudan, contends that Zionism is a religious entity: "Judaism is a 'religion' in which the believers follow a certain creed. Zionism is the same as Judaism, but seeks to achieve the end sought by Judaism through political action....This, then, is the essence of the Palestinian problem—and religious Jewish state founded by Zionists—even though it may appear in the form of political implications [dis]guised by the successors of the Crusaders in modern garb."[2] According to such Arab Muslim authorities, there is no such thing as a secular Jewish state; rather, there is a Zionist state that's on a religious quest to destroy Islam and occupy Muslim lands. These authorities say it is the existence of this Zionist state that is the cause of the modern conflict, and why Israel cannot continue to exist in the heart of the Muslim Middle East.

With similar sentiment, at the World Council against Racism in Durban, South Africa, representatives of the Arab states and the Palestinians, along with many European countries, collectively called for a declaration of "Zionism as racism."[3] Zionism is also blamed for the impasse in the political peace process as the cause of the pro-Israel bias in U.S. foreign policy. According to General Mousa Arafat, the Palestinian Authority chief of military intelligence: "There is no

Contributing Factors & Issues
in the Middle East Conflict

Issues

Territory
- Golan Heights
- Gaza Strip
- West Bank
- Jerusalem

Immigration
- Settlements
- Refugees

Security
- Lebanese Security Zone
- Terrorism
- Arms Control

Others
- Trade
- Water
- International Recognition

Religious

Islam — *Unifies Arabs, promotes jihad against Jews*

Judaism — *Isolates Jews, promotes return to Land*

Political

- Arab Brotherhood
- Zionism
- Pledges of other nations
- Pogroms and Holocaust against Jews, creating need for homeland and immigration

Economic

Arabs — *Petroleum wealth, renewed influence and power, nuclear capability/threat to West*

Israelis — *Only democracy in Middle East, surveillance and intelligence, nuclear arsenal*

Sociological

Palestinian Problem
- Creation of a refugee people
- Demand for statehood
- Revisionist history

Settlement Problem
- Increased Jewish immigration
- Settlement in West Bank areas

difference between Zionism and any U.S. administration, because U.S. administrations are elected primarily by the Zionist body operating in the U.S."[4]

Having heard from the Arab perspective, let's now ask, What are the facts about Zionism, the political factor stated by the Arab states to be the central cause of the Middle East conflict?

The Concept of Zionism

The concept of Zionism is a return to Zion, the ancient and biblical homeland of the Jewish people. This understanding was inherent in the first use of the term by Austrian journalist Nathan Birnbaum in 1886, who derived it from the biblical word that symbolized God's eternally chosen city Jerusalem (Psalm 132:13-18) and, by extension, the whole Jewish nation. As a concept it expresses the hope of national Jewish liberation in its political and religious dimensions (national independence and spiritual renewal). As such, its origin may be traced to the call by Joseph in Egypt for a Jewish return to the Land promised to Abraham (Genesis 50:24-25; cf. 15:13-21) and embodies every desire for return from the beginning of Jewish nationalism at the foot of Mount Sinai to the prayers of the Jewish exiles to be restored to Zion (Daniel 9:16-20; cf. Jeremiah 30:3,18-24; 31:23; Ezekiel 36:24) to the Jews in the Land and in the Diaspora over the past 2,000 years to recover the Jewish national independence lost to the ancient Romans. It should be recognized that Jewish *existence* in the Land of Israel has remained unbroken since ancient times, with remnant Jewish communities maintaining residence especially in cities of historical significance. Therefore, the concept of Zionism is not simply the return of Jewish people themselves to the Land, but the return of Jewish sovereignty to the ancestral homeland, in keeping with the Abrahamic Covenant and the biblical prophecies of universal spiritual blessing in the Land (Zechariah 8:1-8,11-13). However, this understanding of Zionism was not universally accepted by early Zionists.

Fast Fact

The Aims of Zionism as adopted by the 27th World Zionist Congress (June 1968). 1) The unity of the Jewish people and the centrality of Israel in Jewish life. 2) The ingathering of the Jewish people to their historic homeland *Eretz Yisrael* through *aliyah* from all countries. 3) The strengthening of the identity of the State of Israel, founded on the prophetic ideals of justice and peace. 4) The preservation of the identity of the Jewish people through the fostering of Jewish and Hebrew education and of spiritual and cultural values. 5) The protection of Jewish rights everywhere.

Revisionist Zionists, who called for the establishment of a Jewish state on both sides of the Jordan, accepted the biblical concept described above. Bi-nationalist Zionists, those who sought the co-existence of the Jewish community (the Yishuv) with the Arab community in Palestine without the formation of an independent state, advocated a more humanistic concept of Zionism, and their aims were simply the creation of a world where Jewish culture could exist.

Fast Figure

Theodor Herzl
Known as the founder of modern Zionism, the Viennese journalist traveled to Paris in 1893 to cover the Dreyfus affair. After witnessing the event, Herzl wrote "The Jewish State," which concluded that the Jews would never be safe without a state of their own. He died in 1904 after many fruitless efforts at gaining a homeland for his people.

The Zionist Movement

As a secular, political movement, Zionism was formulated in modern times by Moses Hess (1812–1875), refined by Leo Pinsker (1821–1891), and finally organized by Theodor Herzl (1860–1904) in response to anti-Semitism and Jewish persecution. Pogroms (organized attacks) on the Jewish communities of Russia in the 1880s and later in Eastern Europe (which climaxed in the Nazi Holocaust) threatened Jewish existence and demanded a safe refuge for the preservation of the Jewish people. Theodor Herzl, considered the father of modern Zionism, realized this growing threat to the Jewish community in 1893 when, as a journalist, he witnessed the anti-Semitic demonstrations that accompanied the "Dreyfus Affair."

Alfred Dreyfus, an officer in the French army, was convicted and imprisoned for treason simply because he was Jewish. Though Dreyfus was later proven innocent and pardoned, initially the real traitor (another French officer) was

Fast Figure

Chaim Weizmann
Widely looked at as Herzl's successor, Weizmann earned the gratitude of the English government through his scientific discoveries, which proved helpful during World War I. Weizmann lobbied the British government to endorse the establishment of a Jewish state in Palestine, and the Balfour Declaration, which supported this goal, can be attributed to Weizmann, since the British signed it primarily to reward him for his services.

acquitted and Dreyfus was re-convicted in the new trial. The anti-Semitic demonstrations in France against the Jewish community over the Dreyfus case convinced Herzl that centuries of Jewish assimilation to other cultures had not (and would not) protect Jews from persecution. He reasoned that the only refuge for the Jewish people would be in a Jewish state where Jews could preserve and defend their national existence. To implement this goal, Herzl founded the World Zionist Organization and convened the First Zionist Congress in 1897. At that time, he stated his vision that a Jewish state would exist within 50 years. Herzl and his successors agreed that only the ancestral home of the Land of Israel (then called Palestine) could ultimately fulfill the Jewish dream,[5] and this reality was fulfilled to the year of Herzl's prediction with the announcement of the United Nation's resolution to partition Palestine (November 29, 1947).

The Factions of Zionism

Although Herzl's Zionism was introduced as a secular political movement, various ideological groups soon developed within it. The first group was the "political Zionists," who negotiated with the imperial powers for a Jewish homeland and eventually secured a Jewish state through the United Nations. The second group was the "practical Zionists," who saw immigration and settlement in Palestine as a means to secure a Jewish cultural revival, and worked to increase the Jewish population and its territorial holdings and build a solid economic base. The third group was the "labor Zionists," who worked toward the establishment of a socialist state. The fourth group was the "religious Zionists," who envisioned a Jewish state governed strictly by Jewish law.

The Spiritual Aim of Zionism

Despite these differences and the eventual opposition of ultra-Orthodox Judaism, the political Zionism that finally established a secular

Fast Fact

The Ingathering of the Exiles

The Romans suppressed two Jewish revolts in A.D. 70 and 132, and afterward renamed Jerusalem and its surrounding countryside Aelia Capitolina and Syria Palaestina, respectively. Jews were also exiled from Jerusalem and Judaism became an illegal religion. The Roman victory was complete and the Jews were dispersed throughout the world. Though the Jews suffered much at the hands of Gentiles (both Christian and non-Christian alike) throughout the following centuries, they would find that they had not been abandoned by God. The Lord gathered them in the Land of Israel once again after nearly 2,000 years in the Diaspora and through hard work and many trials their state was reborn. Many wonder how the Jewish people have survived their tumultuous history. The only explanation is that they remain the Lord's people and a major part of His plan today!

state was not without a religious motivation. Joseph Heller (1888–1957), who published his book *The Zionist Idea* in 1947, wrote:

> The aim of Zionism is not merely the establishment of a Jewish Commonwealth in the Land of Israel, but to pave the way for a rebirth of the spirit of the Prophets and for a revival of Judaism....The highest value of Zionism lies, however, not in the material and political sphere, but in its spiritual meaning for Jews and for the world. It is this moral and spiritual effect of the development of a free Jewish community in the land of the Prophets which paves the way for the final settlement of the Jewish question....Zionists believe that the land of Israel will again become a source of spiritual life for the Jews and for the non-Jewish world alike.[6]

Those who support this objective, whether Jew or Gentile, may be called "Zionists." In this regard, Christians who recognize the biblical basis of the Jewish claim to the Land of Israel and uphold the right of the Jewish return to establish an independent state may be considered "Christian Zionists."

Zionism and Immigration

The practical application of Zionism for Jews has been the performance of *aliyah* (Hebrew "to go up"), or immigration to Israel. Originally immigration was in waves—for example, the first *aliyah* (1880–1900) brought some 20,000 Jews, and the second *aliyah* (1900–1914) settled approximately 40,000 more.

The kibbutz movement, which established communal settlements to work the Land, was initially a central feature of Zionism in concert with the pioneering efforts of the new immigrants. The Arabs considered Jewish immigration and settlement as a threat to their culture and brought the initial opposition to Zionism as a movement. This fear was based on the belief that an increase in the Jewish population would displace Arabs from the land. Moreover, the political

Fast Fact

Kibbutzim

The original kibbutzim (and moshavim—farming collectives) were founded in the early twentieth century and were primarily agricultural. During the growth of the state, the focus on agriculture remained though expanding to the fields of tourism, technology, and industry. However, in the twenty-first century, the kibbutz movement has declined, with the majority of Israelis living in cities.

Jewish Settlements

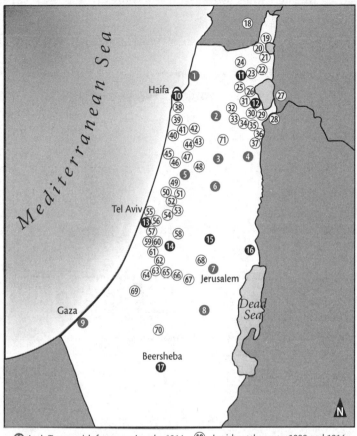

🔟 Arab Towns with few or no Jews by 1914   🔟 Jewish settlements, 1880 and 1914
🔟 Towns with Jewish and Arab people

1. Acre	15. Ramallah	28. Deganya	43. Givat Ada	58. Ben Shemen
2. Nazareth	16. Jericho	29. Kinneret	44. Karkur	59. Rishon le Zion
3. Jenin	17. Beersheba	30. Poriya	45. Heftzibah	60 Beer Yakov
4. Beisan		31. Mizpah	46. Hadera	61. Nes Ziona
5. Tulkarm	18. Metulla	32. Sejera	47. Gan Shmuel	62. Rehovot
6. Nablus	19. Yesod Hamada	33. Sharona	48. Nahliel	63. Ekron
7. Jerusalem	20. Ayelet Hashahar	34. Beit Gan	49. Kfar Sava	64. Gedera
8. Hebron	21. Mishmar	35. Yavneel	50. Kfar Mahal	65. Hulda
9. Gaza	Hayarden	36. Beltanya	51. Ein Hal	66. Kfar Uriya
	22. Mahanayim	37. Menahemya	52. Petah Tikvah	67. Hartuv
10. Haifa	23. Rosh Pina	38. Atlit	53. Ein Ganim	68. Motza
11. Safed	24. Ein Zeitim	39. Tantura	54. Mahane Yehuda	69. Beer-Toviya
12. Tiberias	25. Migdal	40. Zikhron Yaakov	55. Tel Aviv	(Kastinia)
13. Jaffa	26. Kfar Hittim	41. Shefeiya	56. Mikve Israel	70. Ruhama
14. Ramla	27. Bnel Yehuda	42. Bat	57. Nahalat Yehuda	71. Merhavya

goal of Jewish independence, based on the principle of self-determination, influenced Muslim Arabs to think of Zionism as religious imperialism and to view it as a continuation of the Western crusade against Islam.

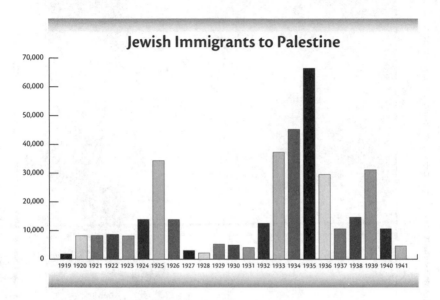

Jewish Immigrants to Palestine

3

WHAT IS ARAB NATIONALISM?

Unlike Zionism, Arab nationalism did not emerge from an ancient concept or a religious motivation. Nationalism is the desire for a government that embodies the spirit of its people and is primarily a secular, Western concept. Islam conquered much of the Middle East in the seventh to fifteenth centuries and conformed Arab culture to its theocratic form of government, in which there can be no fidelity to a political system apart from the religion. The religious centers of Islam have long been in Mecca and Medina, and therefore throughout the Muslim world Arabs have expressed no allegiance to local rulers and showed no interest in identifying with a particular land, including Palestine, until recently. Rather, united with their co-religionists, Arabs were content to live in adherence to the *umma*, or greater Islamic community.

In regard to Palestine, the concept of a single Arab nation precluded any nationalistic ambition to create separate Arab states. Until 1918, Palestine was part of the Ottoman Empire and had been under the Turkish feudal system for hundreds of years. There was no national "Palestine" nor were there "Palestinians" who had a distinct identity or private ownership of "Palestinian" land. A census conducted in 1882 revealed that fewer than 250,000 Arabs were living in the entire country.[7] Most of these were Bedouin (nomadic desert dwellers) or fellahin (peasant-migrant laborers) existing under harsh and primitive conditions because the Ottomans had never sought to colonize or develop the country. Instead, they had focused their attention solely on Jerusalem for bureaucratic purposes, abandoning the rest of the land to desolation.

Aside from the nomadic Bedouin, who claim no nationality, the majority of the Arabs in the 1882 census were either descendants of Arabs who had immigrated in the previous 70 years or immigrants who had recently arrived to work for the Zionist settlers who had begun settlements some five years earlier. Though there were no nationalistic feelings among the Arab population, a separatism existed based on the Qur'anic regulations concerning treatment of *dhimmi* (Jews and Christians), who are considered inferiors in Muslim religion. Further, the increase in population and prosperity by the Jewish minority threatened this position of Arab (Muslim) dominance that, according to Islamic law, once established, could not be surrendered to non-Muslims. In addition, the influence of the Zionist's Western, European culture was viewed as a threat to Arab culture and seventh-century Islamic values. These factors created the climate for an awakening nationalism based on changing political realities.

Fast Fact

Condition of Pre-Mandate Palestine

"We found it [Palestine] inhabited by fellahin who lived in mud hovels and suffered severely from the prevalent malaria....Large areas... were uncultivated....The fellahin, if not themselves cattle thieves, were always ready to harbor these and other criminals. The individual plots [of land] changed hands annually. There was little public security, and the fellahin's lot was an alternation of pillage and blackmail by their neighbors, the Bedouin."

Lewis French, British Director of Development, 1913

4

WHAT BROUGHT ABOUT THE RISE OF ARAB NATIONALISM?

The scenario just described continued largely unchanged until the last half of the nineteenth century, when a number of factors combined to provoke a new nationalism among the Arabs. One of these factors was the opening of the Middle East to Western travelers and Christian missionaries, as well as intellectual and cultural forces from Europe. These outside influences began having an impact on younger Arabs. Another factor was the oppression of Arabs under the Ottoman (Turkish) Empire, which had dominated the Middle East for 200 years, extending from Hungary to Yemen and from the Crimea to the Sudan. Yet another factor was the reforming revolution known as Wahhabism, which arose within Islam in the eighteenth century. Still, the Arab minority that championed a nationalistic revolt against the Turks was unstable and unorganized, according to T. E. Lawrence, the British officer who led the Arab revolt (1916–17) to overthrow the Ottoman Empire. Also, from the Arab perspective, the fight for independence was not a *political* revolt but a cultural revolution to remove Turkish oppression and reconnect Palestine with Arab Syria. However, after the First World War the Sykes-Picot Agreement (signed by the imperial powers in 1916) divided the territory of the former Ottoman Empire. The League of Nations created the mandate system to allow its member nations to rule over the former German colonies (the Ottoman Empire had been allied with Germany in the war and was also subject to the mandate system). Consequently, Palestine was separated from Syria and put under British mandate while

Fast Fact

Arab Nationalism and Islamic Fundamentalism

Many people do not realize there is a major difference between these two philosophies and that each sees Israel in a different light. Arab nationalism is largely secular and its goals are based on gaining and maintaining Arab power in the Arab lands of the Middle East. It uses Islam to pacify the religious crowds of the land and unite all Arabs under one common banner. Israel is looked at as a cancerous tumor in the heart of Arab land. Islamic fundamentalism, however, is a religious philosophy with different goals than Arab nationalism. This radicalism seeks to establish Islamic dominance in the Middle East and eventually spread to the rest of the world. Israel is the symbol of Jewish power in the Middle East, which is an insult to the Islamic god, Allah, and can never be allowed to exist peacefully with the Islamic world.

Syria was placed under French mandate. These acts created the conditions for a new local Arab nationalism that sought independence from colonial control and, as a result, a distinct identity in Palestine.

5

HOW DID ARAB NATIONALISM BEGIN IN PALESTINE?

In March 1919, at the Paris Peace Conference, an agreement was signed between Zionist leader Chaim Weizmann and Arab leader Emir Faisal that promoted the development of a Jewish homeland. The language of this document spoke of "the Arab state and Palestine," clearly reflecting the understanding that Palestine was that part of the Middle East designated for the Jewish homeland and separate from that part claimed by the Arabs. However, a different opinion had been expressed in February 1919, shortly before the conference convened. At the first congress of the Muslim-Christian Association, which had met in Jerusalem to choose its representatives for the Paris Peace Conference, the following resolution was adopted: "We consider Palestine as part of Arab Syria, as it has never been separated from it at any time. We are connected with it by national, religious, linguistic, natural, economic, and geographical bonds."[8] Both opinions, then, indicated that Arabs did not view Palestine as having an independent Arab status.

This thinking changed the next year when the British began to delineate Palestine and the French overthrew the Hashemite king Amin Husseini, thereby abolishing the notion of a Southern Syria. Isolated by these events, the Muslims of Palestine had to make the best of a bad situation and a prominent Jerusalemite declared at that time that "after the recent events in Damascus, we have to effect a complete change in our plans here. Southern Syria no longer exists. We must defend Palestine."[9] To what extent this thinking may have been shared by other Arabs is unclear, but when the Peel Commission in 1936 proposed the partition of Palestine, another local Arab leader, Auni Bey Abdul-Hadi, told the commission: "There is no such country [as Palestine]! Palestine is a term the Zionists invented! There is no Palestine in the Bible. Palestine is alien to us; it is the Zionists who introduced it. Our country was for centuries part of Syria."[10]

However, a non-Jewish Palestine has existed in modern times and was created by the British in 1922 when they separated the land east of the Jordan, which forms the present-day country of Jordan. Indeed, the majority of Jordan's population and army are Palestinian, and most of the Palestinian Arabs in the West Bank region hold Jordanian passports. Even though this "Palestine" has been said to have ceased to exist as a political entity when the State of Israel and the Hashemite kingdom of Jordan were established, there remained an Arab recognition that Jordan was the Palestinian state. For example, in interviews with the Arab press in 1981 and 1984, the late King Hussein (grandson of Abdullah) stated, "The truth is that Jordan is Palestine and Palestine is Jordan."[11] Yasser Arafat has stated the same thing: "What you call Jordan is actually Palestine."[12] Even the war between the PLO and Jordan was considered a "civil war," and Arafat and Hussein joined forces with Saddam Hussein in 1991 to liberate Palestine, the West Bank of which Jordan still thought of as its possession.

Arab nationalism in Palestine developed as a result of the outcome of the war to prevent the formation of a Jewish state in 1948. Tareq Y. Ismael explains this when he states,

> So traumatic to the Arab masses was the loss of Palestine and the alien cleavage of the Arab homeland that it fostered a transformation of Arab nationalism. This transformation shifted the emphasis from the glories of the past to the failures—particularly the failure in Palestine—of the present....The Palestine defeat, then, sounded the death-knell of liberal nationalism in the Arab world, and with it has come the growing rejection of Western models of government. The Palestine defeat sparked the reevaluation of Arab society; and from this has arisen what may be called radical Arab nationalism—a nationalism dedicated to fundamental social change to achieve the objectives of freedom and unity.[13]

Fast Figure

The Hashemite Family

Believed to be direct descendants of the Prophet Muhammad, Hussein ibn 'Ali was named the Sherif of Mecca in 1908 and became one of the more powerful Muslim leaders in Arabia. The English led him to inspire the revolt of 1916 against the Ottoman Empire. In return he was to receive independence for much of the Middle East. The English would place Hussein's sons, Abdullah and Feisal, on the thrones of Transjordan and Iraq respectively. Modern-day Jordan continues to be ruled by the Hashemite line today.

Furthermore, the concept that Arab unity superceded individual Arab nationalism, originally promoted by Egyptian president Abdel Nasser, rallied the Arab states to eliminate the Jewish state, which was seen as the principal obstacle to achieving this comprehensive Arab unity.

6

HOW DID THE CONFLICT BETWEEN THE JEWS AND ARABS BEGIN?

For 400 years, Ottoman rule in Palestine had been one of recurring warfare between local pashas (Turkish provincial governors). These conflicts brought military recruitment and forced labor on the locals, while the political instability allowed Bedouin robber bands to terrorize the country. Government corruption also permitted tax-farmers, which collected monies on behalf of equally corrupt landlords (effendis), to extort poor Arab farmers. Added to these dreadful conditions were those of frequent famine and drought that kept the land in a barren state. Into this situation came the Zionists, who purchased property from the effendi and employed fellahin Arabs to help develop the land. Most of the land, especially that developed by the kibbutz movement, was purchased by the Jewish National Fund (later to be owned by the government of Israel). As a result of these operations the wealth of the land increased and the Jews (and Arabs) prospered. For example, the higher standard of living introduced by the Jewish settlements more than doubled the per-capita income of Arabs in Palestine and improved health standards decreased the rate of Arab infant mortality (from 19.6 percent in 1922 to 14 percent in 1939). The Ottoman government, recognizing the economic potential of Jewish settlement, initially permitted increased immigration to Palestine. However, as the Zionist population increased, local Arabs grew fearful that the balance of power would shift from the Muslim authorities to the Jews. This concern was fueled by the Islamic teaching that the Jews, as *dhimmi*, were inferior to Muslims and would corrupt Arab culture with their Western value system. On these grounds, later Palestinian nationalists objected to the existence of any Jewish settlement in Palestine that might lead to the creation of a Jewish state, and therefore rejected any benefits brought by Jewish settlement. One Palestinian nationalist, Musa Alami, stated this position clearly when he declared, "I prefer that the country remain impoverished and barren for another hundred years, until we ourselves are able to develop it on our own."[14]

Thus the Arab leaders protested to the Ottomans that the Jews had cheated the fellahin out of their land and that the expanding Jewish settlement would eventually crowd out the resident Arab population. In response, the Ottoman government deported the Jewish population in the city of Jaffa, which led to more than 30,000 Jews leaving the country between 1914 and 1918. The fact, however, was this: It was Arab effendi families such as the Husseinis, the Nashashibis, and the Khalidis who had large land holdings and who were exploiting the Arab peasant-migrants. It was from these families that the Jewish immigrants bought small and inferior tracts of land, usually paying exorbitant sums. In fact, as Mitchell G. Bard points out, "more than 90% of the land Jews had purchased by 1936 had been bought from land owners, nearly 40% of whom lived in Egypt and Syria. Less than 8.7% of the Jews' land was purchased from the fellahin. In addition, of the 370,000 acres in Jewish hands, 87,500 acres were swampland and 125,000 acres were lands never before cultivated. Jews, who comprised 29% of the population, held only 5.5% of the land area west of the Jordan and only 11% of the area defined as 'arable.'"[15]

With respect to Jewish immigration and settlement in Palestine, between the first two world wars the non-Jewish population increased by 75 percent, surpassing any increase in Jewish population. This fact was substantiated by the Peel Commission, which carried out an investigation appointed by the British government in 1936. The commission determined that the shortage of land was "due less to the amount of land acquired by Jews than to the increase in the Arab population."[16] Despite these facts, the British authorities in Palestine dissuaded Arabs from negotiating with Jews, and Jews, in turn, wanting to preserve their relations with the British, refrained from making their case to the Arabs. These unchecked problems, coupled with the new Arab nationalism introduced to the region, made it clear to political observers that a conflict was inevitable. As early as 1905, Neguib Azoury, in the French publication *Le Reveil de la Nation Arabe* ("The Revival of the Arab Nation"), had predicted, "The reawakening of the Arab nation, and the growing Jewish efforts at rebuilding the ancient monarchy of Israel on a very large scale—these two movements are destined to fight each other continually, until one of them triumphs over the other."

7

WHAT WERE THE CONFLICTING POSITIONS OF JEWS AND ARABS OVER PALESTINE?

In response to both religious and nationalistic concerns, as well as conflicting territorial promises made by Great Britain, Jews and Arabs developed opposing arguments for their demand of sovereignty in the Land. These views, as declared in 1947 to the United Nations Special Committee on Palestine by the Arab Higher Committee and Menachem Begin, chief of the Irgun (a paramilitary organization set up to help defend the Jewish population), can be outlined as follows:

Jewish Position	Arab Position
1. Israel is the land of the Jewish people	1. Palestine belongs to the Arabs
2. Israel includes both sides of the Jordan, including Transjordan (as promised in the Balfour Declaration)	2. Arabs never accepted the Balfour Declaration
3. Immediate repatriation of all Jews wishing repatriation	3. Jewish immigration to Palestine (which does not concern European refugees) and land purchase must be stopped
4. Jews and Arabs can share the country*	4. Unpartitioned independence under an Arab majority
5. Continued mandatory control by force of arms requires an armed response to achieve independence	5. Arabs will forcefully resist any unfavorable decision

* The Jewish Labor party did not support shared existence with the Arabs, but demanded a transfer of the Arab population from the country.

In 1947, neither Jews nor Arabs were in favor of partition. The Jews argued on biblical grounds that the entire country was the Jewish national home and that no arbitrary boundaries could effectively separate the two peoples. As a result of the Holocaust, the expulsion of Jewry in Eastern Europe, and the British blockade, the Zionists had demanded complete control over Jewish immigration. The Arabs, by contrast, argued on the

Fast Figure

Menachem Begin

A Russian Jew educated in Poland who fought the Nazis in a unit of the Polish army, Begin came to Palestine in the 1940s. From there he became the leader of the Irgun and dedicated himself to the removal of the British and the creation of a Jewish state. After the War of Independence, Begin moved into the political realm and became not only the first Likud prime minister, but also the first Israeli leader to negotiate a peace treaty with an Arab state (Egypt). He and Anwar Sadat shared the Nobel Peace Prize in 1978; however, he resigned in 1983 after becoming mired in controversy over the Lebanon War.

grounds of Arab and Islamic unity that the Jewish immigration was imperialistic in nature and was an intrusion to the region that destroyed Arab unity. They threatened war if any type of partition plan was implemented. As David Ben-Gurion stated at the time, "There is no solution. We want the country to be ours and they want the country to be theirs."

These intractable positions have continued to represent the Jewish and Arab communities up to the present day. Revisions have been made on both sides, such as Israeli acceptance of a homeland on only one side of the Jordan and Arab acceptance of Jewish immigration and settlement, though not to areas considered occupied by Israel and destined for a Palestinian state. The moderate Palestinian position, growing out of the Oslo Accord and the Declaration of Principles (1993) and the Saudi Peace Proposal (2002), accepts in principle a Jewish state (after withdrawal to pre-1967 borders) and an independent Palestinian state with a shared capital in Jerusalem. (However, the Palestinian Authority's continued ascription to the PLO's Phased Plan, which calls for the elimination of the Jewish state, qualifies this moderate position.) The militant Palestinian position rejects any recognition of Israel and demands an independent state from the Jordan River to the Mediterranean Sea (including Jerusalem) under exclusive Arab sovereignty.

8

HOW DID THE "GREAT POWERS" BECOME INVOLVED IN THE CONFLICT?

When World War I broke out, it was clear to the British government that the significant Arab presence in the Middle East was of strategic advantage to their military campaigns against the Ottoman Empire, as

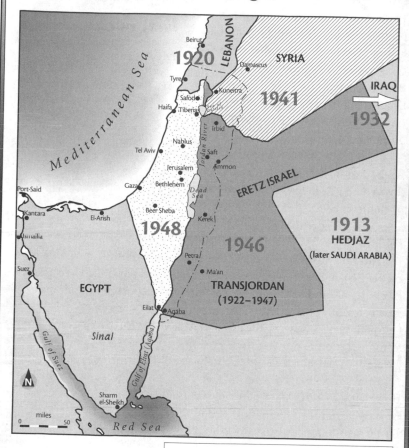

Britain and the Jewish National Home:
Pledges and Border Changes, 1917–1923

Map labels: LEBANON · SYRIA · IRAQ · 1920 · 1941 · 1932 · 1913 HEDJAZ (later SAUDI ARABIA) · ERETZ ISRAEL · 1948 · 1946 · TRANSJORDAN (1922–1947) · EGYPT · Sinal · Gulf of Suez · Gulf of Eilat (Aqaba) · Red Sea · Mediterranean Sea · Jordan River · Dead Sea

Cities: Beirut · Damascus · Tyre · Kuneitra · Safed · Haifa · Tiberias · Irbid · Nablus · Tel Aviv · Saft · Jerusalem · Ammon · Gaza · Bethlehem · Port-Said · Kantara · El-Arish · Beer Sheba · Kerek · Ismailia · Petra · Suez · Ma'an · Eilat · Aqaba · Sharm el-Sheikh

Legend:

- – – – Approximate boundary of the area in which the Jewish people hoped to set up their national home
- The Palestine Mandate, granted to Britain at the San Remo Conference in 1920, as the region of a Jewish national home.
- Separated from Palestine by Britain in 1921 and given to the Emir Abdullah. Named Transjordan, this territory was at once closed to Jewish settlement.
- Ceded by Britain to the French Mandate of Syria, 1923.
- **1948** Year of independence, present borders.

miles 0 — 50

N

well as to their goal of colonial expansion. In Palestine, however, it was not only the Arabs, but also the Jews, who could offer assistance in over-throwing Ottoman rule. So as the Arabs joined with British officer T.E. Lawrence to revolt against the Turks, Jewish volunteers fought separately under the British from 1915–1918. Both the Jews and Arabs hoped their contribution to the British offense would be rewarded with some form of national independence in Palestine. The basis for these aspirations was two documents issued by the British during the war years. In 1915, the Arabs had been given written assurance by the British High Commissioner for Egypt, Sir Henry MacMahon, that Britain would cede to them Turkish territories after the war. In 1917, the British government offered the Zionist movement the Balfour Declaration, which expressed official recognition of the right of the Jewish people to establish a national home in Palestine.

The next year, American president Woodrow Wilson further fanned the flame of Arab and Jewish nationalism in his proposal of self-determination for all nationalities as part of a peace settlement to follow the war. The condition for self-determination was a demonstration of national autonomy, with candidate nations existing under a mandate system until they achieved this status. However, it became clear that the great powers (especially Great Britain and France, both of whom had vital interests in the Middle East) were more interested in their own empire-building than helping the Arabs and Jews achieve national autonomy. This was evidenced by a secret pact made by the British with the Russians and French in 1916 (and made public only after the British issued the Balfour Declaration) known as the Sykes-Picot Agreement. The terms of this arrangement betrayed the promises made to the Arabs and Jews by promising (in exchange for political favors) control of Syria and Lebanon to the French and Armenia to the Russians, while Britain would maintain control over Palestine and Iraq.

After World War I, this agreement was implemented at the San Remo Conference (1920) and ratified by 52 governments in the League of Nations (1922). Thus the former Ottoman Empire was divided among the European powers, leaving the Arabs and Jews of Palestine under mandatory governments. As the British Mandate went into effect, Arabs and Jews were angered over Britain's refusal to honor what they separately recognized as agreements to create independent Arab and Jewish states. Officially, Palestine had been not included in the MacMahon correspondence,

Palestine—The Jewish National Home

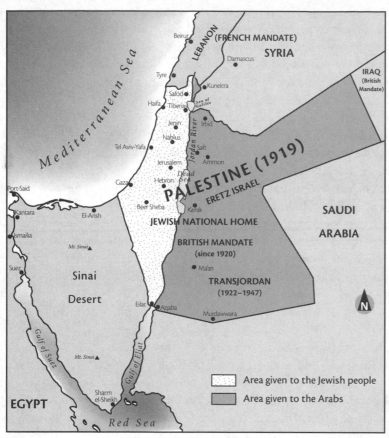

The whole country on both sides of the Jordan was destined to be the Jewish National Home according to the Balfour Declaration of 1917 and the negotiations of the Paris Peace Conference in 1919 and the Palestine Mandate to Britain in 1920. In 1922 Britain redivided the Jewish National Home and gave 77 percent of the mandate to the Arabs as Transjordan. The area to the left of the Jordan River is the portion that was allocated to the Jewish people.

though the Arabs had understood it to be. With respect to the Jews, the Balfour Declaration was included in the British Mandate, formalizing for the Jewish people the boundaries that would comprise their future national home. This resulted in a third *aliyah* or wave of immigration (from 1918–1924), which doubled the Jewish population. So while Arab resentment to the West and nationalistic ambitions continued to grow, the Arabs also protested that Zionist settlement was threatening "the traditional Arab position" (i.e., Islamic social and cultural dominance) in Palestine.

Despite Britain's betrayal of the Arab nationalist cause, the British favored the Arab position over that of the Jews because they felt an Arab alliance was more to their advantage (in case another war erupted in the region).

This favoritism revealed itself in the British military administration's prevention of negotiations between Arab leaders and the Jewish Agency (see sidebar) and in the fact that British Arabists incited Arab nationalists to revolt against the Jewish community. A case in point is that of Colonel Waters Taylor, the financial advisor to the British military administration. Knowing that tensions between Arabs and Jews were greatest at the shared holy sites, he went to the mufti of Jerusalem, Haj Amin al-Husseini, the most influential Arab religious leader in Palestinian affairs, and counseled the mufti to stage a riot in the city during the Easter season to show the world that Palestinian Arabs would not permit the Jews to dominate Palestine. Haj Amin, who had that same year been appointed by the British as mufti, devised a program of pogroms against the Jewish community and organized homicide squads known as the *fedayeen* to launch terror attacks in cities with significant Jewish populations.

Fast Fact

The Arab Legion
Upon the creation of Transjordan in 1921, the British recruited and trained Palestinian Arabs (now Jordanians) to become the Arab Legion. This was the most powerful and effective armed force in the Middle East for some time and was even led by British officers throughout Israel's War for Independence.

Fast Fact

The Jewish Agency
Established in 1929 as the formal representative of the Jews to the British government in Palestine. This agency was the precursor to the future Israeli government and th primary Jewish group in Palestin After the establishment of Israel 1948, the Jewish Agency would on as a liaison between the Jew Israel and the world.

In one riot spearheaded by the mufti in 1929, which began at the Western Wall in Jerusalem and spread to the Tomb of the Patriarchs in Hebron and finally as far as Safed in the north, Arabs set fire to Jewish synagogues and murdered 135 Jewish men, women, and children and wounded almost 350 other Jews.

In an effort to appease the anger of Arab leaders, the British, in 1921, made generous new arrangements with the Arab sheikhs Faisal and his brother Abdullah, giving the former rule over Iraq and creating for the latter the new emirate of Transjordan. This act took some 80 percent of the land recognized historically as Palestine—and considered by Jews to be part of their promised homeland—and transferred it to Arab control (though still under control of the British Mandate). The Jews were then prohibited from settling in Transjordan by Abdullah, a policy that has been maintained by each successive Hashemite ruler. In 1923, the British ceded the area known as the Golan Heights to the French mandatory government of Syria. These moves established the British government's pro-Arab bias and were viewed by Zionists as a severe reduction (if not contradiction) of the rights established by the Balfour Declaration (which had called for the establishment of a Jewish homeland in all or any part of Palestine) and the League of Nations.

Then, in 1922, when mufti Haj Amin wrote to then-colonial secretary Winston Churchill insisting that restrictions be placed on Jewish immigration and land acquisition, Churchill responded favorably with the first of a number of "White Papers." These were official statements of British policy,

Fast Figure

Haj Amin al-Husseini

A Palestinian radical who was named the mufti of Jerusalem by the British in 1921, he became the most powerful Palestinian Arab during the British Mandate. Known for his role in many of the Arab riots, he was interested only in Arab dominance of Greater Syria (Palestine, Transjordan, and Syria) and had no desire to make peace with the Jews and even refused to negotiate or come to any agreement with them.

Fast Fact

The Fedayeen

Arab Muslim suicide squads. Haj Amin al-Husseini organized the first groups back in the 1920s. Egyptian president Gamel Abdel Nasser equipped and trained more of these terrorists in the 1950s to carry out attacks on Israel from Egypt, Jordan, Syria, and Lebanon. Israel responded to the *fedayeen* with its own secret squad, Unit 101, which was led by Ariel Sharon and specialized in preemptive strikes against *fedayeen* bases.

usually issued at the conclusion of investigations in the aftermath of Arab rioting, that limited Jewish immigration. In the first White Paper, Churchill sought to "clarify" for the Arabs the Balfour Declaration, explaining that Britain's intent had not been to recognize Palestine as the Jewish national homeland but only to acknowledge that a home for Jews should be established there. Interestingly, a little more than a decade later, the British-appointed Peel Commission would clarify Churchill's words, concluding that "the field in which the Jewish National Home was to be established was understood, at the time of the Balfour Declaration, to be the whole of historic Palestine, including Transjordan."[17]

Despite these attempts to pacify the Arab community, the terrorist acts which British Arabists had initiated under the mufti increased over the next two decades, crushing any attempts at peaceful settlement, and creating, as Colonel Taylor had predicted, an international problem that forced Britain to find a solution to the mounting conflict. In the history of the pogroms against the Jews, the British military authorities had not acted to prevent Arab rioting (although they attempted to arrest the riot leaders) or to protect the Jewish population. In fact, Britain's own Peel Commission, launched to investigate Arab complaints associated with the Arab riots of 1936, reported, "If one thing stands out clearly from the record of the Mandatory Administration, it is the leniency with which Arab

Fast Fact

The British White Papers

These were statements of British policy in the Middle East. They came in response to Arab-Zionist violence and were meant to alleviate the situation, though they were aimed at pacifying and appeasing the Arabs. They came in 1922, 1929, and 1939, and all placed strict controls on the Jewish population while conceding more and more to the Arabs of Palestine.

Fast Fact

Jewish and Arab Immigration to Palestine During the British Mandate

No one disputes that Arabs have lived in Palestine for many centuries; rather, the controversial issue is that of immigration. In 1915, there were 590,000 Arabs in Palestine and only 83,000 Jews. By 1922, a census recorded 84,000 Jews and 643,000 Arabs in the land. Between the world wars, 588,000 more Arabs and 470,000 more Jews made their way to Palestine. The Arab population would increase by 120 percent between the creation of Transjordan in 1921 and the United Nations decision to partition the land in 1947. Why did the Arabs immigrate to Palestine? To take advantage of the higher standard of living the Jews of Palestine provided to the community.

political agitation, even when carried to the point of violence and murder, has been treated."[18] The Peel Commission even furthered British favoritism by proposing a partition plan that, although it created separate Arab and Jewish states, gave most of the land to the Arabs, with Jerusalem remaining under British rule. The Jews rejected this plan as an attempt to isolate them within an Arab state, while the Arabs rejected it because some Arabs would end up living within a Jewish state—a state they did not want in the Middle East, let alone in Palestine.

In a further attempt to appease the Arabs and quell violence, the British restricted Jewish immigration for six months in 1938, and in 1939, issued the most restrictive White Paper yet, which called for the establishment of an Arab state (incidentally, *not* a Palestinian state) to which no Jewish immigration would be permitted without Arab authorization. However, this action did not lessen the Arab rioting, and the Arabs rejected the British proposal of an independent Arab state, maintaining with the Syrians (who had received their independence from the French Mandate in 1941) that Palestine was inseparable from Greater Syria.

Jewish desperation increased as World War II broke out and Jews learned of the Nazi invasion of Czechoslovakia, the systematic attacks against the Jewish communities of Eastern Europe, and the atrocities of the Holocaust. Jews in Palestine wanted to join the Allied Powers and fight against the Axis Powers that were persecuting their people, but the British, fearing a Jewish brigade would also fight for the creation of an independent state, prevented Jewish participation in the war effort until 1944. Moreover, the Arab Higher Committee, headed by the Palestinian mufti Haj Amin al-Husseini, supported the Nazis and sought assistance from Hitler to intercede for the Arabs against the Jews in Palestine. The Arab nations joined in this effort by forming an Arab boycott against the Jews. Worse yet, during the war years, a British blockade prevented Jews

Fast Fact

The Arab Boycott

The Arab nations formally declared a boycott against Palestinian Jews in 1945, three years before Israel became a nation. This boycott, which is still in effect, has three facets: 1) No direct trade with Israel; 2) no business with companies that do business with Israel; and 3) no business with companies that trade with other companies that do business with Israel. Sound confusing? It should. The Arab nations covered all of their bases in order to have a maximum negative effect on Israel. But the boycott never hurt Israel as the Arabs had hoped, and the restrictions are somewhat relaxed today due to Israel's peace treaties with Egypt and Jordan, though there is still very little direct trade between Arabs and Israelis today.

seeking refuge from the Nazi persecution from entering Palestine. This resulted in untold thousands of Jews being left with no avenue of escape and thus being forced to perish in the German concentration camps. Some 70,000 European Jewish refugees attempted to get by the British blockade, but most of them were fired upon and forced back to sea, and 50,000 were captured and placed in internment camps in Cyprus (28,000 until 1948).

Fast Fact

The Bombing of the King David Hotel

On July 22, 1946, the Irgun smuggled bombs into the King David Hotel in Jerusalem. This was the headquarters of the British Mandate in Palestine. In the weeks that had passed, the British considered all Jews to be accomplices to terror and had attacked the Jewish Agency and arrested over 1,000 Jews throughout Palestine. The Irgun wanted the retribution to equal the magnitude of the original attack. Later that day, calls were made to warn the British to evacuate the hotel, but they were not heeded. When the bombs exploded, over 90 people were found dead in the rubble, 15 of whom were Jews. About 45 others were injured from the blast. The bombing was denounced around the world, casting the Jews as accomplices and masterminds of terror. With the Holocaust still fresh on people's minds, however, the hotel bombing did not provide as much of a setback to Jewish hopes as the British would have liked.

These actions brought the Jews to realize that if the same British government that had promised them a homeland was now denying them entry, especially at a time when their very existence was being threatened, then there would never be a time under British rule when a Jewish state could be established. Thus the Jewish Agency had to defend the Jewish community against *both* the Arab rioters and the British government in Palestine.

By 1941, this defense necessitated the creation of an underground armed resistance, which took the form of paramilitary organizations that were united in purpose though different in the degree of tactics employed to achieve independence. The first of these organizations was known as the Haganah, within which was the Palmach, an elite strike force developed to defend the Jewish community in event of an emergency. A more militant group, the Irgun, which broke off from the Haganah, used Arab terrorist tactics against the Arab community and restricted British military targets. A still more militant group, the Stern Gang, aimed terrorism against all Englishmen in order to remove the British presence from Palestine. By 1946 the country had become a combat zone entrenched in guerilla warfare, with frequent Jewish raids, sabotage, bombings (such as that of British headquarters at the King David Hotel in Jerusalem), kidnappings, and attempted assassinations of British officials.

Zionists were divided on the appropriateness of these terrorist tactics, with leaders such as Ben-Gurion siding with the British security forces and against the Jewish extremists. Even so, the British government (headed by the less-sympathetic prime minister Clement Atlee) reacted with severe reprisals against the Jewish community. Curfews were imposed on Jewish cities and mass arrests were made. Carrying weapons brought the death penalty, resistance leaders were imprisoned, and some were publicly executed. On May 14, 1946 the British, in a decisive move against the Jewish ambition to establish a Jewish state east of the Jordan, granted independence to the emirate of Transjordan, creating the Hashemite kingdom of Jordan. Thus, the eastern four-fifths of the land promised by the Balfour Declaration as the Jewish national home, and the area later intended for the resettlement of Palestinian Arabs (*not* to become an Arab state) by the League of Nations, became an independent Arab state.[19] And the Jewish population, which by 1946 had increased to 1.9 million, continued its fight against British rule to gain independence in the 23 percent of the land left to them.

Fast Fact

Jewish Defense: The Haganah, Irgun, and Stern Gang

The Jews had hoped to come to Palestine and live peacefully with their Arab neighbors. When they realized that would not be possible, they began to organize defense groups for their kibbutzim and towns. The Haganah was made up of small, armed groups in the settlements and larger towns until 1929, when the Arab riots made Jews realize they needed a larger force. The Haganah grew into a militia that recruited and trained Palestinian Jews to combat violence, and later, this evolved into the Israel Defense Forces. Later, some Jews would say that the Haganah was not answering the Arab and British violence with enough force. These dissidents went on to create a more militant group known as the Irgun, led by future Israeli prime minister Menachem Begin. As the violence between the Jews and British continued to escalate, Irgunist Abraham Stern went on to create the Stern Gang, an even more militant group that concentrated solely on undermining and attacking the British in Palestine.

9

HOW DID THE UNITED NATIONS GET INVOLVED IN THE CONFLICT?

By 1947, the British government, reeling from its struggle to manage the conflict in Palestine and criticized domestically for the increasing violence and internationally for its handling of Jewish refugees in light of the Holocaust, decided to appeal to the United Nations for a recommendation on how to further administer their mandatory plan that would be acceptable to both Jews and Arabs. This fell short of what the British public had expected: giving up the mandate and allowing the Jews and Arabs to fight to the finish. It appears the British move was simply political posturing designed to alleviate public criticism and permit their military to enforce greater control without censure. The British scheme reasoned that a peaceful solution was impossible and once the United Nations failed to achieve a recommendation it would back off, and Britain could then secure colonial control over Palestine as desired.

In response to the British appeal, the UN General Assembly set up a multinational council known as UNSCOP (the United Nations Special Committee on Palestine) to investigate the causes of conflict in Palestine and recommend a solution. The Arab Higher Committee rejected UNSCOP and demanded unpartitioned independence under an Arab majority. The Jewish Irgun cooperated with UNSCOP and, in their demands, expressed a willingness to share Palestine with the Arab population. Ultimately, one thing became clear in the investigation: any solution recommended by the UN could not include a continuation of the British Mandate, since this would only perpetuate the conflict.

The UNSCOP report to the UN General Assembly negated the Jewish claim that immigration had been beneficial, and blamed Arab hostility on the increase in the Jewish population, even though at this time Jews owned only 6 percent of the land and constituted only 30 percent of the population. However, the report also refuted the Arab belief that Palestine had been promised as an Arab state by British High Commissioner Henry MacMahon during the First World War. UNSCOP contended that the MacMahon Correspondence (with Sherif Hussein of Mecca) had not contained an "unequivocal agreement according to which it was possible to determine whether Palestine was included in the territory promised independence." Indeed, the wording had only mentioned "Syria," even though the Arabs considered Palestine a part of Greater Syria. The committee's recommendation to replace British mandatory rule offered two alternatives: a minority proposal in which Jews would remain a minority under Arab rule in a federal state, and a majority proposal of partition.

The United Nations Partition Plan, 1947

LEBANON

SYRIA

Hanita

Matzuva · *Eilon*
Nahariya · *Gaaton*
Acre · *Safed*

Yeham
Kfar Hahoresh

Haifa

Sea of Galilee

Mediterranean Sea

Hadera

Jenin

Tel Aviv
Jaffa

Nablus

TRANSJORDAN

Ben Shemen

Jordan River

Atarot
Neve Yakkov
Bet Haarava

Nitzanim *Kfar Menachem* *Hartuv* *Kalia*
Yad Mordecai *Kedma* *Revadim* *Galon*
Gat *Massuot Yitzhak* *Ein Tzurim* *Gush Etzion*

Dead Sea

Kfar Darom

Hebron

Beersheba

Nirim

· **El Arish**

Negev

On November 29, 1947, the General Assembly of the United Nations voted to set up both a Jewish and an Arab state, and determined their borders. The city of Jerusalem was to be an international zone. The Jews accepted the plan, but Arabs not only rejected it, but immediately attacked Jewish settlements in every part of Palestine.

EGYPT

Sinai

— ·· — ·· — Boundary of the British Palestine Mandate, 1922–1947

▨ The proposed Jewish state

☐ The proposed Arab state

⊙ Jewish settlements to be included in the Arab state

▩ Jerusalem and suburbs an international zone

N

0   miles   20

Eilat
Aqaba

The partition plan, adopted as part of UN General Assembly Resolution 181, carved up the land based on the demographic arrangement of the Jewish and Arab populations to create two separate states. However, Jews had settled throughout the land and their prosperity had attracted large numbers of Arabs to Jewish cities. Segregating the two peoples was therefore impossible and no matter how the UN drew the borders for a Jewish state, it would still contain an Arab population. In the end, the Jewish state ended up having a slightly *greater* Arab population than Jewish (509,780 Arabs to 499,020 Jews), while the Arab state with 749,101 Arabs had only 9,520 Jews! Furthermore, 60 percent of the land given to the Jewish state was comprised of the barren Negev Desert (where some 40,000 Bedouin Arabs lived) and the demographically determined borders were not drawn with a concern for security and were practically indefensible. Moreover, the city of Jerusalem, which stood at the center of the conflict, would belong to neither state, but become an "international zone" with a population of more than 100,000 Jews in the midst of an Arab state.

Despite the disadvantages of this plan for the Jewish people, which caused the Labor Zionists to urge its rejection, the Jewish authorities in the Irgun leadership accepted the proposal. The Arab leaders, however, completely rejected it, believing they were the disadvantaged party and that the United Nation's decision was made merely to assuage guilt feelings over the Holocaust. To make matters worse, the Arab League secretary, Abd al-Rachman Azzam Pasha, declared in September 1947 that it was too late for a peaceful solution and that the Jews would be expelled as were the Crusaders. Jamal Husseini, the spokesman for the Arab Higher Committee, told the United Nations that Arabs would fight for every inch of what they believed to be their territory and drench "the soil of our beloved country with the last drop of our blood."[20]

Even so, on November 29, 1947 the UN General Assembly approved the partition plan 33 to 13. The outcome of this vote was influenced largely by the pressure exerted on UN member nations by the United States—or, more specifically, President Harry Truman. Retired Hebrew University of Jerusalem Professor Ory Mazar, a personal friend of Truman, stated that Truman acted independently of his administration, especially his defense secretary and Joint Chiefs of Staff (who were opposed to partition on the grounds of U.S. oil interests and having a strategic military position in the region and a possible Arab alliance with the then-U.S.S.R. against the

West). According to Mazar, Truman announced the United States's intent to support the resolution in the press in advance of consulting his administration, thus committing the administration to uphold the president's decision![21] The UN vote was also influenced by the surprising support of the Soviet Union, who wanted the British out of Palestine and also believed the new Jewish state, under the influence of social Zionism, would become a Socialist state.

After the voting, the British government initially announced an end to the mandate over Palestine, but later reneged, stating that the original requirement that all parties must accept the UN recommendation had not been achieved because the Arab League had pledged to go to war to prevent partition. Further, the British argued that the United Nations had failed to include a provision for military implementation, making it impossible to enforce the plan. But the UN's involvement had set the course for the turbulent events that followed, which included Israel's declaration of independence and the first Israeli-Arab war, which ended in the establishment of the Jewish state. The State of Israel was admitted to the United Nations as its fifty-ninth member on May 11, 1949 and has since played a role in the support of UN-related organizations, such as the UN Relief and Works Agency (UNRWA), designed to dispense foreign aid to the Palestinians, and worked with the UN peacekeeping forces stationed in the region.

Fast Fact

The Arab League

Formed in Cairo, Egypt in 1945, the Arab League was designed to unify the Arab nations. However, because of certain inter-Arab rivalries, the Arabs have rarely agreed on anything other than opposition to the existence of Israel. When Egypt made peace with Israel in 1979, even that issue brewed a strong controversy among members of the League that was not alleviated until the signing of the Declaration of Principles in 1993 between the Palestinians and Israel. Today, the League still stands but has little power over its members, for they each go their own way when they do not agree with the League's decisions.

Fast Feature

The United Nations, Israel, and the Palestinians

The United Nations is believed by many to be the most legitimate and fair mediator between the Israelis and Palestinians. The facts say otherwise. The United Nations gave its best contribution to the peace process in late 1967 through UN Resolution 242, which calls for a peaceful and fair settlement of the issues. Depending on how you interpret it, the resolution calls for the Arabs to make peace with the Jews, for the return of most of the territory captured in the Six-Day War, and for the affirmation of the right of every state involved to live in peace and security with Israel. However, the Arabs interpret the resolution in such a way that all concessions are to be made by the Israelis, while the Arabs do nothing. Although this attitude is to be expected from the Arab nations, it has not been expected that the United Nations would consistently undermine its own resolution over the last 35 years. The United Nations has routinely tried to impose solutions on Israel in favor of the Palestinians even though Resolution 242 was adopted to find a fair solution to *both* parties. One instance of this occurred in 1975, when the United Nations declared Zionism as racism. The decision was repealed in 1991 (at the disapproval of many Arab nations), but only after the United Nations had condemned Israel for its role in the first Intifada, its treatment of the Palestinians, its declaration of Jerusalem as its capital, and its control over the Golan Heights, and demanded its withdrawal from the Occupied Territories! It is also important to note that the Palestinians have more power in the United Nations than any other people without a state. They have non-voting status in the General Assembly of the United Nations, have a UN-sponsored International Day of Solidarity with the Palestinian People (November 29), and are even designated by the UN as "Palestine." Israel, by contrast, has only recently been able to participate in a regional group of the United Nations and has constantly had its UN-member status undermined and attacked by the Palestinians.

Section II

Conflicting Claims
to the Land

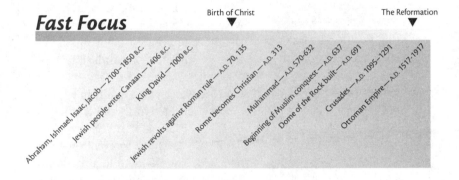

Fast Focus

Birth of Christ ▼   The Reformation ▼

Abraham, Ishmael, Isaac, Jacob—2100–1850 B.C.
Jewish people enter Canaan—1406 B.C.
King David—1000 B.C.
Jewish revolts against Roman rule—A.D. 70, 135
Rome becomes Christian—A.D. 313
Muhammad—A.D. 570–632
Beginning of Muslim conquest—A.D. 637
Dome of the Rock built—A.D. 691
Crusades—A.D. 1095–1291
Ottoman Empire—A.D. 1517–1917

10

What is the basis of
the Jewish claim to the Land?

The Jewish people's claim to the Land of Israel as a national home is based on four historical facts, two of which are from the past and two of which are from the present, giving a continuity to their claim from ancient to modern times.

1. *The biblical covenant with the Jewish patriarch Abraham included a promise of the Land of Israel to the Jewish people.* Assuming the chronology of the Bible, this Abrahamic Covenant was established around 2100 B.C. and re-established with three succeeding generations. This is an important point in that Abraham was not only the father of the Jewish people (through Isaac) but also of the Arab people (through Ishmael). However, the Bible states that the covenant was re-established not with Ishmael, but

45

only with Isaac and his descendants (see Genesis 17:18-21). This means that the Abrahamic Covenant and the land promise contained within it (Genesis 15:18-21) is exclusive to the Jewish people as the sole descendants of Isaac. This promise, in turn, was selectively passed on to Isaac's son Jacob (who was renamed "Israel") rather than his son Esau (Genesis 28:13-15; 35:12). Esau and his descendants, the Edomites, were rejected with respect to the covenant and therefore appointed land outside of the covenanted boundaries (see Malachi 1:3-4). That the covenant of God is with a chosen family line is frequently repeated in the Bible, such as in Psalm 105:8-11: "He has remembered His covenant forever, the word which He commanded to a thousand generations, the covenant which He made with Abraham, and His oath to Isaac. Then He confirmed it to Jacob for a statute, to Israel as an everlasting covenant, saying, 'To you I will give the land of Canaan as the portion of your inheritance.'"

Moreover, the Abrahamic Covenant was made unilaterally and unconditionally, which means that its fulfillment depends upon God, not man. The biblical prophets emphasized this aspect of the Abrahamic Covenant to Israel when, as a result of violations of the Mosaic Covenant (which was multilateral and conditional), the nation was punished by exile from the Land (see Deuteronomy 4:26-27,40; Jeremiah 7:3-7). There are certainly conditional aspects in unconditional covenants, but the conditions (such as obedience) relate to the temporal fulfillment of the covenant by man, not the ultimate and eternal fulfillment by God. This is because, as Deuteronomy chapters 29–30 explain, in God's plan the Land and Israel are joined in final fulfillment. Israel's disobedience and exile is predicted (Deutero-

Fast Quote

Land Given to the Jews by God

"On that day the Lord made a covenant with Abram, saying, 'To your descendants I have given this land. From the river of Egypt as far as the great river, the river Euphrates.... I will establish My covenant between Me and you and your descendants after you throughout their generations for an everlasting covenant, to be God to you and to your descendants after you. I will give to you and your descendants after you, the land of your sojournings, all the land of Canaan, for an everlasting possession..."

Genesis 15:18; 17:7-8

Fast Quote

Covenental Conditions

"So you shall keep His statutes and commandments...that it may go well with you and your children after you, and that you may live long on the land which the Lord your God is giving you for all time."

Deuteronomy 4:40

nomy 30:2-4), but will be followed with an equally predicted return and restoration (Deuteronomy 30:1-10).

To reiterate, the Abrahamic Covenant is unconditional because God initiated it and has personally assumed the obligation for its fulfillment. Restoration to the Land was therefore possible, for even sin on the part of the Jewish people cannot keep the promise of God's own covenant from being fulfilled (see Deuteronomy 4:29-31; Isaiah 41:8-9; Jeremiah 30:2-3,8-11; 31:35-37; 33:23-26; Ezekiel 36:18-28). These texts reveal that Israel will fulfill the conditional terms of the covenant because in the Last Days, every Israelite will know the Lord (Jeremiah 31:34), for God will have given them a new heart and a new spirit and put His Spirit within them and caused them to walk in His ways (see Ezekiel 36:25-28). According to the prophets, it will be at this time (the Last Days) that the territorial aspects of the Abrahamic Covenant (such as possession of the full extent of the promised boundaries and the universal blessing of all mankind) will find fulfillment (Isaiah 2:2-4; Hosea 3:4-5; cf. Ezekiel 37:24-28; Zechariah 8:7-8,11-13).

This is in concert with the statements made concerning the duration of the covenant as "everlasting" (Genesis 17:8) and "for all time" (Deuteronomy 4:40). This would mean that Israel's possession of the Land was not meant for a limited period, ended by sin, as Muslims understand the teaching of the Qur'an, or by spiritual substitution, with Israel being replaced by the church, as some Christians interpret certain statements in the New Testament. At any rate, Judaism has understood the Abrahamic Covenant to be perpetually in force and to have never been rescinded, so their modern claim to the Land rests on an ancient and unchanging divine promise.

2. *The Jewish people settled and developed the Land and have maintained a continuous existence in (as well as a historic tie with) the Land for the past 3,500 years.* The Jewish people took possession of Canaan through military campaigns under Joshua beginning around 1406 B.C. Settling throughout the Land in tribal allotments, the Jewish people established a national existence with a distinct culture, language, and civilization. Despite an exile of the northern kingdom by the Assyrians (721 B.C.) and an exile of the southern kingdom by the Babylonians (605–596 B.C.), a remnant of the Jewish people returned to the Land to re-establish their national existence even though, more importantly, a remnant of the Jewish population was *not* exiled and remained resident

in the Land during the exilic period. Too, the large Diaspora Jewish communities that existed in Egypt and Babylon during this time adapted, grew, and flourished for centuries thereafter, always maintaining a vital link with the Land (for example, through the payment of the Temple tithe, and later through religious and cultural connections). Though the Romans exiled large numbers of Jews as a punishment for the First Jewish Revolt (A.D. 66–73), a Jewish population continued to exist in the Land and even staged a Second Jewish Revolt against the Romans (A.D. 132–135), temporarily re-establishing national sovereignty. The Romans soon ended this Jewish rule and imposed greater restrictions, yet Jews continued to live in parts of the Land and under pagan Roman rule (A.D. 135–391) and then Roman Byzantine Christian rule (A.D. 391–636). When Islam invaded the Holy Land in A.D. 638, Jews helped the invaders in their conquest, and then lived under Muslim rule up until the creation of the modern State of Israel. A number of historical resources refer to large Jewish communities in Palestine and reveal a continuous Jewish presence in the Land for the past 19 centuries.

The Jewish religion continued as well, though without a Temple (since A.D. 70), and was reformulated as Rabbinic Judaism at Yavne (ca. A.D. 90). Through the production of Oral Law, such as the Palestinian Talmud (edited in Palestine by rabbis around A.D. 400), the Jewish people maintained their distinct identity and unity through the following centuries. A central focus of this Judaism has been the eternal relationship between the Jewish people and the Land. This is evident in the fact that Jews direct their prayers toward Jerusalem and express the hope of a universal return of Jewry to the Land as stated in the Passover Haggadah's closing words, "Next Year in Jerusalem!"

Also, when the first Zionist pioneers made *aliyah* to Palestine (1882–1903), they found that the Land was not empty, nor exclusively Arab, but contained established Jewish communities that had been in existence from antiquity. On this basis, the Jewish people claim an uninterrupted settlement in the Land from the time of Joshua onward, and Zionism set out to develop this existence in nationalistic terms in the nineteenth century.

3. *The international community recognized the Jewish claim to the Land and granted the Jewish people political sovereignty in Palestine.* Once Zionism emerged as a political movement in response to anti-Semitism in Europe, the Jews began to receive international recognition

of their need for a secure homeland for those Jews suffering persecution. Great Britain responded to this need with the Balfour Declaration in 1917, and based on this declaration, the United Nations voted to partition Palestine and create a Jewish state in 1947. While statehood came by an independent Israeli declaration in 1948 and an Israeli victory in a war with the Arabs, international recognition followed with the admission of Israel to the United Nations in 1949, as well as by most nations of the world since. Today there is no question that the six million Jews living in the State of Israel constitute a distinct nation defined within historic borders.

4. *The State of Israel has a right to claim historic land captured as the result of fighting defensive wars.* In 1948, the Arab nations attempted to destroy Israel, only to lose territory offered them for an Arab state under the UN partition resolution. Israel had hoped to negotiate with the Arabs for a peaceful settlement, which would have included withdrawal from captured lands, but the Arabs rejected any recognition of the Jewish state. When Israel's security was provoked by Egypt in 1967 and it launched a pre-emptive strike to protect itself from an Egyptian air assault, Arab nations again attempted to destroy Israel. Again, Israel emerged the victor, now controlling three times the amount of land it formerly held. At this time Israel unified its capital city of Jerusalem, but it did not annex the West Bank (even though it comprises the biblical territories of Judea and Samaria), fully expecting that the negotiation of peace with the Arabs would involve territorial concessions. However, the Arabs issued a statement at Khartoum in August 1967 that stated unequivocally that Arabs would still not recognize nor negotiate with the Jewish state, so the West Bank became a military administration.

When Egypt recognized Israel in 1979 and negotiated a cold peace, Israel returned the Sinai to Egypt as part of the treaty. Further territorial concessions were made as a result of the Oslo Peace Process, returning to the Palestinian Authority most of the Gaza Strip and significant portions of the West Bank. Much of the Golan Heights was offered to Syria as part of a peace package, but was rejected by the Syrians. In fact, Israel has returned more than 90 percent of the land captured in defensive wars, but was never obligated to do so in light of the historical precedent set by most all nations of the world. However, UN Resolution 242, adopted on November 22, 1967, stated the "inadmissibility of the acquisition of territory by war" and called for the "withdrawal of Israeli armed forces from the territories occupied in the recent conflict." Israel has interpreted the reference to "war" in the first statement as referring only to "offensive war," which Israel does not believe applies in the case of the 1967 Six-Day War. With respect to the call for withdrawal from occupied territories, Israel points out that the resolution does not say from "all territories," and that this wording was deliberately excluded after debate by the UN Security Council.

Israel also notes that its withdrawal from 91 percent of captured territory with the return of the Sinai to Egypt partially, if not wholly, fulfills the intention of the resolution's statement. What additional land must Israel withdraw from to further satisfy this statement? Since the Palestinians are not even mentioned in the resolution, can they demand withdrawal from territory they today wish to control? Even so, Resolution 242 also declares that "every State in the area" has the "right to live in peace within secure and recognized boundaries free from threats or acts of force." It has long been recognized that Israel's withdrawal to pre-1967 lines would not constitute secure boundaries and that the return of this territory would not secure peace, because when this territory was under the control of the Arabs, they still attacked Israel. Therefore, Israel claims possession of the land captured in defensive wars as necessary for its continued security and survival as a nation.

11

What is the basis of the Arab claim to the Land?

The Arab claim is based on their own historical, but primarily religious, relationship to the Land. Like the Jewish claim, two of these claims are rooted in the past and two are based on interpretations of modern political agreements or events.

1. *The Arabs claim an ancestry with Abraham and a promise of the Land through his son Ishmael.* This claim is made on religious grounds based entirely on the Qur'anic teaching that the Arabs are descendants of Abraham through Ishmael: "Abraham in truth was not a Jew, neither a Christian; but he was a Muslim...and we made a covenant with Abraham and Ishmael" (*Sura* 3:60; 2:110). However, based on the Bible, Abraham

was neither a Jew, Christian, Muslim, nor an Arab, but a Mesopotamian pagan. The historical origin of the Arabs is debated, but a connection with biblical Ishmael appears doubtful historically. As Semitic specialist S.D. Goiten affirms, "there is nothing in the Bible to indicate that Ishmael was the forefather of the Arabs, nor was this a belief of the ancient Arabs."[1] The historical uncertainty arises from the fact that the proper noun *Ishmael* later became used as a common noun to describe desert tribes in general, such as the Midianites (Judges 8:24; cf. 7:12), whose lineage is traced to a *different* son of Abraham through his second wife, Keturah (Genesis 25:2). In addition, even though the "sons of Ishmael" listed in Genesis 25:12-17 can be traced to Arabian desert tribes, the expression may here be used simply to describe a Bedouin-like existence and not to indicate relation to the biblical Ishmael as a forefather. Moreover, the term *Arabian* in the Old and New Testaments indicates an *inhabitant* of Arabia, and is not necessarily synonymous with *Arabs*.

Fast Fact

Islamic View of the Old Testament

"No copy of the original Taurat ["Torah"] granted by Allah to Musa is extant. As a matter of fact, during their long and chequered history, the Jews repeatedly lost their revealed books...the Bani Isra'il ["children of Israel"] failed to act up to the Taurat, they made it into (separate) sheets for show and concealed much of its contents...and they distorted and perverted Allah's word and changed its meaning (*Sura* 2:75,213; 4:46; 5:14,44; 6:91; 7:169; 10:93; 11:110; 16:124; 41:45; 45:17). The Old Testament in the Bible cannot, for these reasons, be regarded as the book revealed by Allah to Musa."

Altaf Ahmed Kherie,
Islam: A Comprehensive
Guide-Book (Pakistan, 1993), p. 28.

Muslims, of course, do not consider the interpretation of history, secular or biblical, but only that which is preserved in the Qur'an. They regard the Jews as having forfeited their chosen status and right to the Land through sin, and the Jewish Torah (and the New Testament of the Christians, which agrees with the Abrahamic account in the Jewish Torah), as having been lost and corrupted. This agrees with Islam as a supercessionist religion, replacing previous religions as the final and complete revelation. As Stanley Ellisen points out: "By any evaluation, the Koran is a revision of the Bible with Arabic overtones. It reinterprets and revises both the Old Testament stories of Abraham and Ishmael and the New Testament stories of Jesus. Abraham is transformed into an Arabic sheikh; Jesus' birth and death are completely recast with a bedouin touch...."[2] Therefore, the Muslim Arab identification with

Ishmael was the result of Muhammad taking over the original tradition from Judaism and Christianity.

2. *The Arabs claim a long and continuous residency in the Land.* When the British ended 400 years of Ottoman Turkish rule in Palestine in 1917, Arabs comprised the majority population. The British accepted the Wilsonian doctrine of "self-determination" as the basis for post-World War I settlements, and therefore favored the Arab population as the rightful heirs of the Land (even though they had lived under foreign rule!).

Fast Fact

Islamic View of the New Testament

"Allah took a covenant from those who call themselves Christians but they forgot a good part of the message that was sent to them" (*Sura* 5:15). "The Injil ['Gospel'] mentioned in the Holy Qur'an is not the New Testament or the four Gospels; but refers to the book revealed by Allah to His prophet, 'Isa, son of Maryam.'" "By the time of Muhammad all of the books revealed up to that time had either been totally lost, or their original contents and the true message had been grossly perverted and distorted."

Altaf Ahmed Kherie,
Islam: A Comprehensive
Guide-Book (Pakistan, 1993), p. 28.

The claim of long and continuous residency from the Muslim conquest has been a chief argument of Arabs, but recently the Palestinians have argued continuous residency going back 5,000 years. There is no historical basis for this specific Palestinian claim, and more importantly, history does not support the general Arab claim.

Arab Muslims came to Palestine in A.D. 638 as the latest in a line of conquerors following the Persians and Romans. Jewish communities had remained in the Land from antiquity, even though Christianity had been the dominant religion for the three centuries leading up to A.D. 638. Islam established itself as the conqueror's religion, and Muslims began to take up residence in Palestine. However, most of the Muslim rulers during the 1,174 years of Islamic dominance were *not* Arab. Consider the historical succession of Islamic rulers: The Seljuks, whose rule lasted from 1071–1099, were Turkish mercenaries. The Muslim commander Saladin, whose defeat of the Crusaders began the Ayyubid period (1187–1260), was a Kurd. The Mamluks (1260–1516) were descendants of Turkish and Caucasian slave soldiers from the Caucasus. And Suleiman the Magnificent, whose capture of Jerusalem began the last period of Islamic rule, the Ottoman period (1516–1917), and who rebuilt the walls of the Old City to their modern appearance, was a Turk. Historian David George Hogarth stated the fact of the brevity of Arab rule: "When we look back at the history of the early Caliphate, we find the period of genuine Arab empire extraordinarily short....Arabs governed Arabs, though Arabs on an imperial scale for much less than a century, just the Umayyad Damascus period and no more."[3]

In addition, many of the Arab states didn't receive their independence until the twentieth century (as did Israel): Saudi Arabia (1913), Lebanon (1920), Iraq (1932), Syria (1941), Jordan (1946), and Kuwait (1961). None of these Arab states can make historical claims to certain borders on the basis of antiquity in their own regions.

Moreover, while the Druze (a Muslim sect), the Bedouin, and various Christian sects have inhabited the Land for thousands of years, they never made a claim to all of the Land based on their historic habitation. Therefore, no Arab people can make a historic claim to the Land based on long residency, since during this time they shared the Land with others (who have equal claim on this basis) and were scarcely in political control of the Land.

Fast Quote

Arab Control of the Land
"The only Arab domination since the Conquest in 635 A.D. hardly lasted, as such, 22 years."

*Chairman of the Syrian delegation
to the Paris Peace Conference (1919)*

3. *The British MacMahon-Hussein Agreement promised the Land to the Arabs.* During World War I, the Sherifians of the Hejaz, and especially Hussein ibn 'Ali, Sherif of Mecca, custodian of the Islamic shrines in the Hejaz, were central figures in the new Arab nationalism. As one of Islam's spiritual leaders, he was sent a letter on October 24, 1915 by the British High Commissioner for Egypt, Sir Henry MacMahon. The letter outlined the terms for Arab participation in the British war with the Ottoman Empire and particularly the territory that would be given to the Arabs for their cooperation. After the war, the Arabs claimed that the MacMahon-Hussein correspondence promised them independence in Palestine as a spoil of war. However, the language of the letter was deliberately obscure and MacMahon explicitly denied ever offering Palestine and said that King Hussein had understood that to be the case.

In truth, the correspondence does not mention Palestine, although it also does not state what would become of it. Today, the Arabs contend that the omission was intentional so that Great Britain would have an "out" when it reneged on its promise, and the Arabs state the British pledge still remains as a legal basis for their claim to the Land. However,

Britain's belief at the time of the war's end was that the Arabs would establish a pan-Arab state over the whole eastern Levant and that the Balfour Declaration's unambiguous promise of a homeland in Palestine for the Jews might then be fulfilled. This perspective is evident in this statement from the British Royal Commission (1937): "If King Hussein and Emir Faisal [Hussein's son] secured their big Arab State…they would concede little Palestine to the Jews."[4]

4. *The Palestinian refugee crisis demands repatriation to the Arab homeland in Palestine.* After the 1948 war, during which hundreds of thousands of Arabs had abandoned their lands and property in the wake of the invading Arab army, UN General Assembly Resolution 242 required a "just settlement of the refugee problem." A further resolution spoke of "compensation" by "the governments or authorities responsible." It has been estimated that some 60 percent of Israel's total land area consisted of abandoned Arab land (though mostly wasteland) and that by 1954 more than a third of Israel's Jewish population lived on "absentee property."[5]

Fast Quote

Palestine Not Included

"I feel it my duty to state, and I do so emphatically, that it was not intended by me in giving this pledge to King Hussein to include Palestine in the area in which Arab independence was promised. I also had every reason to believe at the time that the fact that Palestine was not included in my pledge was well understood by King Hussein."

Sir Henry MacMahon

Based on these facts and the UN resolutions, Palestinian Arabs have claimed that the only just settlement for the Palestinian problem is repatriation to the lands and homes confiscated by Israel after the war and that this constitutes recognition of Palestine as their land. However, while the Arab population may certainly make this claim, the displaced Jewish population may also make such a claim. The Balfour Declaration contained provisions to protect "the civil and religious rights of existing non-Jewish communities in Palestine," as well as "the rights and political status enjoyed by Jews in any other country." These provisions were violated by both parties. In 1948 those Jewish communities in the eastern part of Jerusalem (a majority of the population) and throughout Judea and Samaria (the West Bank) had to flee from their homes and possessions in wake of the invading Jordanian army, which captured this area. During the 19 years those areas were under Jordanian rule, Jews were not offered any opportunity to return nor reparations of any kind. They were barred from even visiting the 58 historic synagogues of the Jewish Quarter or the Western Wall in Jerusalem or Rachel's Tomb near Bethlehem or the Tomb of the Patriarchs in Hebron and Joseph's Tomb in Nablus (all Jewish religious sites).

It is important to note that the number of Jews that were forced out of Arab countries as refugees during World War II is about equal to the number of Arabs who suffered similarly in the 1948 war. These Jews left, in most cases, with only the clothes on their backs, and no Arab country has since offered repatriation or reparations. The difference today is that there are no Jewish refugees, while there are still Palestinian Arab refugees. The explanation for this is that the Jewish refugees were absorbed into the Jewish state, while the Arab states mostly refused to accept the Palestinian refugees. Another key reason for this difference is that the Israeli government *did* make reparations to those Arabs who fled in 1948, offering both Israeli citizenship for those who would live within Israeli borders or monetary compensation for those who could prove claim of dispossession, while Arab governments did not offer such to any Jews. No doubt, historic injustices have occurred with respect to refugees, but they have occurred for both peoples sharing the same Land. Therefore, the claim of one people to the Land on this basis cannot be made in exclusion of the other.

Fast Feature

Conflicting Claims to Religious Sites

Complicating territorial disputes between Israelis and Arabs is the conflict over religious sites claimed by both Jews and Muslims as exclusive to their religions. Two of the most important religious sites, located in the two most ancient and traditionally "holy cities," are, in order of sanctity: 1) *Har Habayit* ("the Temple Mount"—Jewish) or *Harem es-Sharif* ("the Noble Enclosure"—Muslim) in Jerusalem, and 2) the Tomb of the Patriarchs (Jewish) or the Ibrahim Mosque (Muslim) in Hebron. Jews (both religious and secular) accept the Temple Mount as the site of the first (960–586 B.C.) and second (538 B.C.–A.D. 70) Jewish Temples and most religious Jews believe it will be the site of a future third Temple, fulfilling biblical prophecies concerning Israel's promised time of redemption and restoration to the Land of Israel. Muslims believe that the *Harem* is the site of the ascension to heaven of the prophet Muhammad during his Night Journey from Mecca to *al-aqsa* ("the far

Continued on page 56

Fast Feature

Continued from page 55

corner"—interpreted as Jerusalem). According to tradition, the Caliph Omar in A.D. 638 identified these sites and the Caliph 'Abd al-Malik built the Dome of the Rock in A.D. 691, with the Al-Aqsa Mosque being completed A.D. 715.

In 1996 the Palestinian Authority began a public disinformation campaign to deny that a Jewish Temple had ever existed on the site. Although the site has been under the sovereignty of the State of Israel as part of Jerusalem's united capital since 1967, Muslim officials banned Jews from the site at the beginning of the Al-Aqsa Intifada (September 28, 2000). In opposition, Israeli authorities, and especially Orthodox Jewish activists, have declared their right of access to the holy site for Jewish prayer, a right Muslims contend violates Islamic law, which forbids non-Muslims to exercise religious expression at an Islamic holy place.

Islam on Israel and the Jews

The conflict between Israelis and Arabs is, at its core, a religious conflict. This conflict may express itself in terms of Arab and Palestinian nationalism, but it is rooted in the concept of Arab unity (*umma*) and teachings concerning Israel and the Jews in the Islamic holy books: the Qur'an and Hadith. Even for the minority of Arabs who are non-Muslim, Islam's dominance in Arab countries for 1,400 years has created a cultural bias against Israel and Jews. However, with the return of Jews to the Holy Land, the establishment of an independent (non-Muslim) Jewish state (on land previously conquered by Muslims), and the defeat of Arab armies by Jewish soldiers, there occurred an affront to Islam and an irreconcilable disgrace to the Arab and Muslim world. Arab representative Hashim Jawad stated at the United Nations in 1960, "Israel, being an alien body in the Arab homeland, has no right whatsoever to continue to exist in the territories of the Arab East" (*Middle East Record,* October 6, 1960, p. 174a). This fundamental Islamic perspective continues to control the agenda of every Arab ruler and Palestinian leader today. Given the supreme position of the Qur'an and of imams in Islamic society, it is evident that neither western-style diplomacy nor regional military action will be able to resolve the religious nature of the conflict.

SECTION III
THE PALESTINIAN PROBLEM

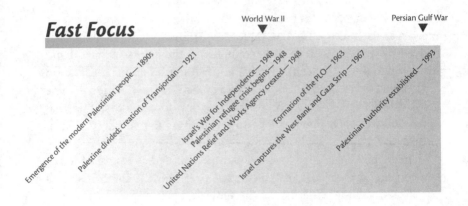

Fast Focus

World War II ▼

Persian Gulf War ▼

Emergence of the modern Palestinian people—1890s

Palestine divided; creation of Transjordan—1921

Israel's War for Independence—1948

Palestinian refugee crisis begins—1948

United Nations Relief and Works Agency created—1948

Formation of the PLO—1963

Israel captures the West Bank and Gaza Strip—1967

Palestinian Authority established—1993

12

WHO ARE THE PALESTINIANS?

The Arabs in Palestine who originally sought national independence never thought of themselves as Palestinians. In fact, as Daniel Pipes, a writer for the Middle East Forum, explains, "Some said the residents of the Levant are a nation; others said Eastern Arabic speakers; or all Arabic speakers; or all Moslems. However, no one suggested 'Palestinians,' and for good reason. Palestine, then a secular way of saying *Eretz Yisra'el* or *Terra Sancta*, embodied a purely Jewish and Christian concept, one utterly foreign to Moslems, even repugnant to them.... Instead, Moslems west of the Jordan directed their allegiance to Damascus, where the great-great-uncle of Jordan's King Abdullah II was then ruling; they identified themselves as Southern Syrians."[1]

The term *Palestinian* was used in antiquity to describe the inhabitants of Syria Minor and may have designated the Jews in particular (through a Greek word play on the Hebrew word *Israel*).[2] It also was the Greek and Latin term for the Philistines, the ancient enemies of the Israelites. Because of this connection it was officially made the name of the country as a punishment by the Roman emperor Hadrian after suppressing the Second Jewish Revolt (A.D. 135). Before Crusader rule, Arabs used the term *Filastin* for the Roman division of "first Palestine" (which included Judea and Samaria) to distinguish it from *Urdunn* ("Jordan"). Yet throughout the entire period of Islamic dominance (A.D. 638–1918), the terms *Palestine* and *Palestinian* do not appear to have been used of any Muslim peoples, Arab or otherwise. Though the term was never used in the Hebrew Bible nor Arabic Qur'an, its usage was revived by the British and applied equally to the country's Jewish and Arab populations. In fact, the British government's Balfour Declaration (1917) referred to the land of Palestine as the place for a "national home for the Jewish people." Arabs reacted to the document, stating that "there was no such thing as Palestine except as the southern part of Greater Syria."

Under the British Mandate, the name *Palestine* was restricted to the land on the western side of the Jordan River because the British had established, on the eastern side, the emirate of Transjordan. Interestingly, the Arabs in Palestine had immigrated primarily from Egypt, Syria, and Transjordan, and they shunned the name *Palestinian*, which had no reference to their Arab identity. Thus the British were careful to refer to the Jews alone as Palestinians, while referring to the Arabs as simply "Arabs." Therefore, at this time the Arab leadership in the area did not refer to itself as the "Palestinian Authority" but as the "Arab Higher Committee." This terminology prevailed even when consideration was given to separating Palestine into Jewish and Arab states. When the Anglo-American Committee of Inquiry convened in Jerusalem in 1946, the distinguished Arab historian Professor Philip Hitti testified, "There is no such thing as Palestine in [Arab] history, absolutely not."[3] He likewise opposed the use of the name Palestine on area maps because it was "associated in the mind of the average American, and perhaps the Englishman too, with the Jews."[4]

The use of the term *Palestinian* in reference to the Arab population west of the Jordan River cannot be found in any dictionary, encyclopedia, or history book until after the creation of the State of Israel in 1948. Although before 1948 both Jews and Arabs, as inhabitants of

Palestine, could have been called "Palestinian Jews" and "Palestinian Arabs," once the State of Israel was established, Jews were identified as "Israelis." This left available the name Palestinian for the non-Israeli Arab population. Even so, it was not immediately adopted by the Arab population. In 1947, when UNSCOP was investigating the cause of violence in Palestine and listening to the demands of Arab leaders, there was never any mention of "Palestinians" nor a demand for the establishment of a Palestinian state, nor was this ever made a part of any debate in the United Nations. The plain reason for this is that there was no Palestinian nationalism at this time. Palestinians did not have a separate identity from the Arab culture and accepted the Arab goal in Palestine, which was not political independence in the Land, but an Arab state that would be reunited to the Arab Islamic world. This was explained a few years later by Ahmed Shuqeiri (later the chairman of the PLO) to the UN Security Council: "It is common knowledge that Palestine is nothing but southern Syria."[5]

Fast Fact

The PLO

Created in 1963 by the Arab League, the Palestine Liberation Organization was to be the primary Arabian vehicle for the destruction of Israel. It was little more than a terrorist organization until it came under the full control of Yasser Arafat, who eventually steered the group away from being a purely terrorist organization and made it into a sort of political organization with a legitimate cause in the eyes of the world. Over the years, the PLO has become less and less violent in order to establish relations with the United States and Israel, and as a result, it has lost much of its former legitimacy with the Palestinian people.

The term *Palestine* does not appear with reference to Arab nationalist goals until the formation of the Palestine Liberation Organization (PLO) in 1963. During the mid-1960s, the primary goal of the PLO was the destruction of the Jewish state in Palestine. There was no thought of establishing an independent Palestinian state, but rather, the plan was to replace the Jewish state with an Arab state in concert with the goal of the Arab states in the region since 1948. When the Six-Day War erupted in 1967, the struggle was about the survival of the Jewish state, not about "Palestinian" land. The territories captured by the Israelis in 1967 (now claimed by the Palestinians as their occupied homeland) did not constitute Palestine or belong to Palestinians, but belonged to Egypt (Gaza Strip), Syria (Golan Heights), and Jordan (West Bank). After the Six-Day War, these Arab countries sought the recovery of these territories for *themselves* and not as a homeland for the "Palestinians." There were no negotiations with Palestinians after the Arab wars with Israel. For this reason the term "Palestinian(s)" does not appear in any of the foundational documents related to resolving the Arab-Israeli conflicts of the 1967 Six-Day War, the 1973 Yom Kippur War, or UN Security Council Resolutions 242 and 338. Such an omission can be explained only by the recognition that the Arabs described in these resolutions were not then thought of as "Palestinians." What's more, the Arab nations thought of the Hashemite kingdom of Jordan (which had annexed the West Bank in 1950) as Palestine. Jordan's King Hussein made a declaration of this a year after the Six-Day War (in which he lost the West Bank territory): "Jordan is Palestine and Palestine is Jordan."[6] As late as 1974, Yasser Arafat was saying the same thing: "What you call Jordan is actually Palestine."[7]

The current usage of the term "Palestinian(s)" became prominent in the mid-1970s when it became politically expedient for the PLO to distinguish residents of the Israeli-occupied territories and refugee Arab population. The PLO leadership realized that it would be much better to describe their effort to destroy Israel in nationalist terms as a struggle for freedom from occupation than as a pan-Arabic effort (as it had been expressed since 1948). Since the formation of the Palestinian Authority in 1993, the term "Palestinian" has become the official name of those Arabs outside Israel's pre-1967 borders. Israeli-Arabs (those living inside Israel proper as Israeli citizens) also changed their identity in a show of solidarity and now identify themselves as Palestinians.

13

FROM WHERE DID THE PALESTINIANS ORIGINATE?

The approximately three million modern Palestinians in East Jerusalem, the West Bank, and Gaza Strip claim to be the descendants of the ancient natives of Palestine. For example, Tad Szulc, writing in *National Geographic* magazine, stated, "The ancestors of today's Palestinians appeared along the southeastern Mediterranean coast more than five millennia ago and settled down to a life of fishing, farming and herding."[8] In like manner, the report *The Arab Case for Palestine*, which was submitted by the Arab Office, Jerusalem, to the Anglo-American Committee of Inquiry in March 1946, says this: "The Arabs of Palestine are the indigenous inhabitants of the country, who have been in occupation of it since the beginning of history."[9] Recent Palestinian authors have identified these "Arab" ancestors of the Palestinians as Canaanites, Jebusites, and Philistines.

These claims stand in contrast to archaeology and history, which are united in the fact that the Philistines and the Jebusites were non-Semitic peoples. Furthermore, the Bible distinguishes the "Arabs" from the Philistines (2 Chronicles 17:11). The Jebusites disappeared from history by the end of the tenth century B.C. The last historical mention of the Philistines dates to about 600 B.C., when they were taken into captivity by the Babylonian ruler Nebuchadnezzar.[10] Moreover, Arab heritage is traceable in secular history no earlier than references in the Neo-Assyrian annals of the ninth to seventh centuries B.C. However, Palestinian historians claim that the present-day Palestinian people are descendants of the Canaanites through the Muslim invaders of the seventh century who intermarried with the Canaanite remnant *still living* in the Land. Some scholars have traced Canaanite artistic traditions (through the Phoenicians) in script, pottery designs, and cultic motifs of the Punic culture in Carthage to as late as 149 B.C.[11] Yet even this preserved influence of Canaanite art still leaves another 1,000 years until the coming of the Arabian nomads of Islam to the Land. There is simply no trace in any historical document from this long period that indicates any of the Canaanite peoples continued to exist in the Land. Perhaps it is for this reason that the Qur'an (as well as any Muslim writing after the Muslim conquest) makes no ancestral connection going back to the Canaanites (or to the Philistines or Jebusites).

Fast Quote

Palestine According to the Palestinians

"Palestine, the land of the three monotheistic faiths, is where the Palestinian Arab people was born, on which it grew, developed and excelled. Thus the Palestinian Arab people ensured for itself an everlasting union between itself, its land, and its history. Resolute throughout that history, the Palestinian Arab people forged its national identity, rising even to unimagined levels in its defense, as invasion, the design of others, and the appeal special to Palestine's ancient and luminous place on the eminence where powers and civilizations are joined. All this intervened thereby to deprive the people of its political independence. Yet the undying connection between Palestine and its people secured for the land its character, and for the people its national genius."

Palestinian Declaration of Independence
(November 15, 1988)

The actual origin of the modern Palestinians begins in the closing decades of the Ottoman Empire in Palestine in the late nineteenth century. During that time, most of the agricultural land was owned by large-scale landowners that had existed in a feudal system for hundreds of years. The fertile coastal plain was worked by poor tenant farmers and laborers imported from other countries. While most of the country was desolate, Arab villages existed in parts of the land alongside Jewish communities that had long existed in cities of religious importance such as Jerusalem, Hebron, and Safed. Ottoman bureaucrats resided only in Jerusalem, and Arab Bedouin occupied the desert regions, tending their animals. Therefore, while Palestine was not an "empty land," its general desolation was inhospitable to life and it was sparsely populated. Starting about 1878 harsh conditions forced many groups to immigrate into Palestine, where work was available. According to historical surveys, these migrant workers, from which the Palestinians of today are descended came from many nationalities: "Balkans, Greeks, Syrians, Latins, Egyptians, Turks, Armenians, Italians, Persians, Kurds, Germans, Afghans, Druzes, Turks, Circassians, Bosnians, Sudanese, Samaritans, Algerians, Motawila, Tartars, Hungarians, Scots, Navarese, Bretons, English, Franks, Ruthenians, Bohemians, Bulgarians, Georgians, Persian Nestorians, Indians, Copts, Maronites, and many others."[12] Of the non-Jewish population surveyed in 1882, at least 25 percent of the people were newcomers (mostly from non-Arab countries),[13] the rest being Bedouin nomads and the descendants of previous immigrants (within the previous 70 years). Moreover, according to former prime minister Binyamin Netanyahu, this group "came to the West Bank just prior to the Six Day War."[14] These, then, are the indigenous Palestinian people claimed by the Palestinian Authority to have existed throughout Palestine from antiquity.

Fast Fact

Tactical Fabrication

"The Arabs learned their disinformation tactic from the Nazis: If you repeat the lie long enough, and loud enough, people will actually believe you. As a result, most people now believe there is something called the 'Palestinian' people, a total fabrication, complete with a phony history and a phony culture. There is only one truth here, that there are 1.75 million people, a hodgepodge of Arabs and Turks, intentionally or maybe unwittingly, masquerading as a 'people,' and made into a 'people' by the PLO and many in the world community who relished attacking the Jews in yet another novel way."

Roger David Carasso

Palestinian Population Worldwide

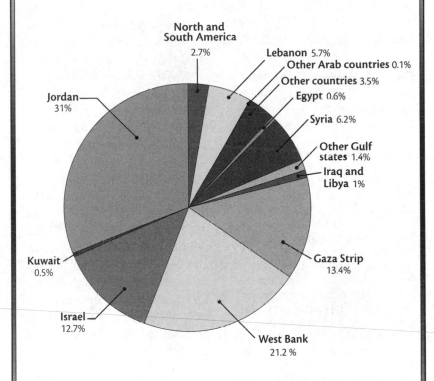

North and South America 2.7%
Lebanon 5.7%
Other Arab countries 0.1%
Other countries 3.5%
Egypt 0.6%
Syria 6.2%
Other Gulf states 1.4%
Iraq and Libya 1%
Jordan 31%
Gaza Strip 13.4%
Kuwait 0.5%
Israel 12.7%
West Bank 21.2 %

The total Palestinian population worldwide, as claimed by the Palestinian Authority, is approximately 7.8 million people.

14

WHAT ARE THE PLO AND THE PALESTINIAN AUTHORITY?

In 1963 the Arab League created the Palestine Liberation Organization (PLO) and the Palestine Liberation Army with the support of Egyptian President Nasser and under the direction of Ahmad al-Shukairy (a former Saudi delegate to the United Nations) to wage a terror campaign against Israel. The PLO was officially founded the next year by the first Arab summit and, until 1967, continued as an umbrella organization for various Islamic and communist factions under the control of the Arab states (especially Egypt). The PLO was created to give the Palestinian refugees in Lebanon a voice, bring the Palestine issue back into the international political arena, demonstrate to the Arab world an armed struggle in Palestine, and to incite the Arab world to war against Israel. Its stated purpose, as its National Charter (or Covenant) declares, is "to liberate Palestine" through "the destruction of Israel" because "the partitioning of Palestine in 1947 and the establishment of Israel are fundamentally null and void...." At the time, Palestine was defined by the Arab states as the territory occupied by Israel since 1948. This "occupied territory" did not include the West Bank, the Gaza Strip, or the Golan Heights, which were then "occupied" respectively by Jordan, Egypt, and Syria. Therefore, the "occupied territory" to be "liberated" was the land in which the State of Israel had been established. The PLO's "Palestinian Army," a contingent of

Fast Figure

Yasser Arafat

Arafat has been chairman of the PLO since 1969 and "president" of the Palestinian Authority since 1994. Born in Egypt (1929) as Muhammad Rauf el-Codbi el-Husseini, he was the nephew of Haj Amin al-Husseini, the mufti who pursued the Final Solution of the Jewish people in Palestine with the Nazis. Though not a Palestinian, he championed the Palestinian cause and became the leader of the movement's armed struggle against Israel. As the leader of *al-Fatah* (Arabic: "conquest by means of *jihad*"), a terrorist group within the PLO, he eventually took control over the entire organization and has been in power ever since. A politically perceptive yet ruthless dictator, he entered peace negotiations with Israel as part of the Oslo Accord. However, he never renounced his terrorist tactics and opened the twenty-first century with the greatest wave of terrorism ever in Israel's history. These acts removed him from the status of a peace partner with Israel, and his failure to bring independence to the Palestinians has lessened his status as a national leader.

Fast Feature

The Palestinian Authority

The legitimate governing entity of the Palestinian people in the West Bank and Gaza Strip. It is led by President Yasser Arafat, who runs it as a dictatorship. The religious terrorist groups Islamic Jihad and Hamas are rivals of the Palestinian Authority (PA) because they believe that the PA has betrayed the Palestinian cause by engaging in a peace process with the Israelis. The PA has been given weapons by Israel in order to police its own people within the occupied territories. These police are supposed to stop terrorist attacks by Palestinians, though they have done very little to help Israel. It is still unknown whether the PA police are either unable or simply unwilling to stop the terror. Currently, Israelis believe the PA to be a haven for terrorism and no longer look to Arafat and the PA as peace partners.

guerilla terrorists, then began launching attacks in Israel against Israeli civilians. Each year these attacks increased in number, rising to 41 separate raids the year before the Six-Day War.

Before 1967 the PLO was controlled by the Arab states, but after the Six-Day War it was taken over by Palestinian nationalists, who made it an autonomous organization. In 1969 Yasser Arafat, the founder of Fatah (1958), the ruling party within the PLO, became chairman of the PLO. He included as "occupied territory" of Palestine all areas of the pre-1967 war lines, although most of this territory was claimed by the Arab countries, which had lost this land to Israel. Over the next two decades, in an attempt to gain dominance in the Arab countries bordering Israel, Arafat moved the PLO headquarters from Jordan after Black September (1970) to Lebanon (after its Civil War), to Tunis and, with the Oslo Process, to Gaza and Ramallah (after 1993).

From its inception until the Oslo Accords in 1993, the PLO was generally recognized as a terrorist organization. In 1987 the PLO launched an international propaganda campaign aimed at gaining recognition and support for its cause in the form of a popular uprising (the first Intifada), releasing its Palestinian Declaration of Independence on November 15, 1988. On September 13, 1993, Yasser Arafat signed the Declaration of Principles on Interim Self-Governing Arrangements, which resulted from the Oslo Peace Process (which was intended to help solve the Israeli-Palestinian conflict), and the PLO became the Palestinian National Authority (PA) and was removed from the U.S. State Department's list of terrorist organizations. The Palestinian Authority from this point worked toward the aims of establishing an independent Palestinian state beginning in the Gaza Strip and the West Bank and later extending to the whole of Palestine, in agreement with its founding Charter (which has never been changed). When the five-year transitional period under the Oslo Process ended in 1998 with no success in diplomatic negotiations or in the intervention of the United States (1998–1999), the Palestinian Authority launched a second Intifada in September 2000 with the purpose of again calling international attention to its cause and provoking intervention by the Arab states and the western powers.

Fast Quote

The State of Palestine

"The State of Palestine is an Arab state, an integral and indivisible part of the Arab nation, at one with that nation in heritage and civilization, with it also in its aspiration for liberation, progress, democracy and unity. The State of Palestine affirms its obligation to abide by the Charter of the League of Arab States, whereby the coordination of the Arab states with each other shall be strengthened. It calls upon Arab compatriots to consolidate and enhance the reality of state, to mobilize potential, and to intensify efforts whose goal is to end Israeli occupation."

*Palestine Declaration of Independence
(November 15, 1988)*

15

HOW IS THE PALESTINIAN AUTHORITY FUNDED?

The Palestinian Authority, which seeks an independent, democratic, national existence, has consistently operated at a deficit and today claims its complete economic infrastructure has been destroyed. Its refugee population exists in poverty and often-desperate conditions. The reason for this, according to the Palestinian Authority, is Israeli occupation and border closings, which have destroyed roads, offices, businesses, and prevented workers from traveling to jobs within Israel.

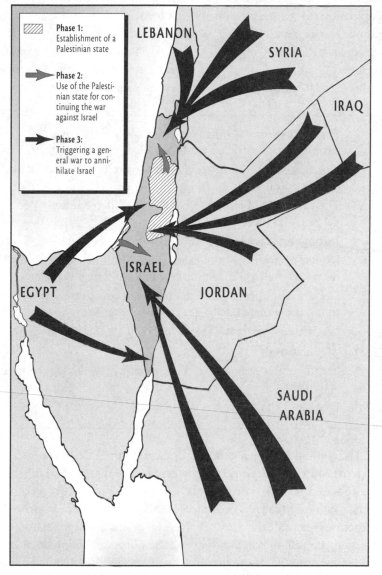

The "Phased Plan"

as adopted by the Palestine National Council in Cairo on June 8, 1974

Phase 1:
Establishment of a Palestinian state

Phase 2:
Use of the Palestinian state for continuing the war against Israel

Phase 3:
Triggering a general war to annihilate Israel

LEBANON

SYRIA

IRAQ

ISRAEL

EGYPT

JORDAN

SAUDI ARABIA

"Once it is established, the Palestinian National Authority will strive to achieve a union of the confrontation countries, with the aim of completing the liberation of all Palestinian territory, and as a step along the road to comprehensive Arab unity."

Although wartime maintenance puts an extra strain on the budget, the Authority's funding comes primarily from outside sources and is not affected by these conditions. Therefore, it should be able to care for its population (for which purpose international charities and relief organizations donate funds) as well as wage its resistance (Intifada) to Israel based on its income, especially if it expects to become a recognized country. What, then, are the sources of revenue for the Palestinian Authority? Historically, there have been ten sources of income:

1. Financial support from non-Arab countries (Soviet Union, Latin America, Africa, Third-World countries)
2. Official contributions from Arab League member states and Islamic countries
3. The Palestinian Liberation tax fund (a 5 percent tax on every Palestinian's income)
4. Income from legitimate and illegitimate investments
5. Donations from wealthy Palestinians and international organizations such as the United Nations and European Union
6. "Extortion of protection" charges from companies and states to not use terrorist activities against them
7. Charitable organizations
8. Illegal arms deals
9. Fraud, money laundering, counterfeiting, and other criminal activities
10. Drug trafficking

The amount of money officially donated to the Palestinian Authority from the Arab Muslim world has increased more than 80 percent since it incorporated religion into its political rhetoric and added *jihad* to its agenda with its Intifadas. The United States has given a total of $1.1 billion to date in direct aid, and Europe's total donations are $2.52 billion. Arab states donate $55 million monthly, and the European Union donates €10 million monthly, while organizations such as UNRWA (United Nations Relief and Work Agency) donate more than $1 million. According to data from Info-Prod, an economic research center, the Palestinian Authority received a minimum of $4,938,868,000 by the end of August 2002.

The Palestinian Authority also has investments, earning over $5 million daily from SAMED (Palestinian Martyrs' Sons Enterprises) and has at least to £5 billion in numbered bank accounts in Zurich, Geneva, and New York as well as other sums in Europe, Asia, and North Africa. It owns shares on international stock exchanges and property in prime locations in Paris, London, Geneva, and New York. It also receives $300 million annually in revenues from monopolies in the Palestinian Authority, not including the $60 million from Arafat's gambling casino in Jericho (until shut down). And this represents only a percentage of other revenue sources!

However, as the chart on the previous page reveals, there are hidden sources of income as well—illegal fundraising endeavors such as arms smuggling, money laundering, counterfeiting, shakedowns (extortion, bribery, kidnapping for ransom), car theft, and drug trafficking have been used by the Palestinian Authority to amass a fortune estimated by the British National Criminal Intelligence Services (in 1993–94) at $10 billion. Drug trafficking was instituted by the PLO under Yasser Arafat in 1983, and Sallah Dabbagh, then-PLO treasury chief, stated this tool as vitally necessary for the organization: "...the entire future of the PLO operation for liberation may hinge on our exporting more drugs throughout the world."[15]

The Palestinian Authority spends at least €10 million monthly (the amount it receives from the EU) to sponsor terrorism (such as terrorist leaders and cell groups who carry out suicide missions) and fund hate propaganda (in Palestinian schools and textbooks and for lobbyists and media in the United States and elsewhere). In addition, UNRWA refugee camps are being used for terrorist training, bomb manufacturing, and illegal arms storage. Strangely, the UN bans any kind of military training in their UNRWA camps *except* in the Middle East. Replying to this double standard, a UNRWA spokesman in one of the Lebanese Refugee Camps, where training for homicide bombing occurs, lamely stated in a Fox television interview on March 12, 2003, that "these activities take place with the children after school and the UNRWA has no control over them." Yasser Arafat has personal holdings of $1.3 billion (including $500 million of PLO funds he controls). The Kuwaiti newspaper *Al-Watan* also reported that on June 7, 2002 Arafat deposited $5.1 million into a personal account—money that was siphoned from funds that were donated to aid the Palestinians.[16] Based on documents discovered at the Orient House (after it was closed by the

Israelis), the late Faisal Husseini, who had administrative control of Jerusalem affairs for the Palestinian Authority, was found to have funneled $1.8 million into his private accounts in Switzerland and Austria. Similar violations can be documented in relation to other PA leaders. However, the Palestinian Authority refuses to be monitored or meet any demands for accountability by those who donate economic aid. These facts and figures led Rachel Ehrenfeld of the American Center for Democracy to conclude in a report, "The Palestinian Authority, led since its inception by Yasser Arafat, has been engaged in massive-scale corruption and terrorism. Yet, all this time, the international community has turned a blind eye and continued its support."[17]

Fast Quote

The PA and Financial Accountability

"I completely refuse any controls by anybody on Palestinian Autonomy, except the Palestinians themselves. We didn't finish military occupation to get economic occupation."

Yasser Arafat

16

HOW HAS THE PALESTINIAN AUTHORITY PRESENTED ITS INTIFADA TO THE PRESS?

Since the inception of the first Intifada, Yasser Arafat sought to capture media attention because he knew the power of the press could be used to mold international opinion—and policy—in favor of the Palestinians. If he could successfully characterize the Palestinian people as indigenous nationals who were forced out of their "historic homeland" and depict "the Palestinian problem" as "occupation" and its enemies as "aggressors" who used "excessive force" against defenseless women and children armed only with "sticks and stones," or as "martyrs" driven by "desperation" to "sacrifice" their children or their young lives for "freedom," he could win in the propaganda war. Moreover, if he could suppress contrary images of Palestinians as terrorists, savagely murdering their own people who are suspected of collaboration with Israel, cheering the attack on America on September 11, and of homicide bombers packed with explosives, nails, and infectious materials, for the purpose of indiscriminately blowing apart innocent Israeli civilians, he would achieve the leverage he desired in the political playing field.

In keeping with his plan to play to the media, and knowing that most Westerners are ignorant of the history of the Middle East, an essential ingredient in Arafat's propaganda has been the creation and dissemination of a revisionist "Palestinian history." As we noted earlier, Roger David Carasso has observed, "The Arabs learned their disinformation tactic from the Nazis: if you repeat the lie long enough, and loud enough, people will actually believe you."[18] Every statement made by Palestinian spokesmen to the media is from the revisionist perspective and is an attempt to propagandize the West.

A second goal of the Palestinian Authority has been to use the press to gain international recognition as an independent Arab nation despite the fact that it has never officially existed as such. Among the nationalistic actions performed by the Palestinian Authority are the flying of a Palestinian flag, the election of Yasser Arafat as "president" and his wearing a military uniform, the adoption of a constitution and declaration of independence, the proclamation of Jerusalem as the "capital" of Palestine,

Fast Fact

The Double Standard

Israel is often held to a different standard than the rest of the world. Government corruption in Israel or a mistake by Israel Defense Forces (IDF) officers attracts far more attention than similar violations by the Palestinian Authority or in the Arab world. When a Palestinian is killed by an Israeli (even in self-defense or as part of military action), it receives a greater condemnation than when an Israeli is murdered in cold blood or blown apart by a homicide bomb blast. When Jordan killed thousands of Palestinians and drove them homeless from their country to Lebanon or when Kuwait deported hundreds of Palestinians after the Persian Gulf War, there was no outcry. However, when Israel deports individual Palestinian terrorists who are connected to acts of terror, human rights groups protest "Israeli aggression." Another example of the double standard is the United States's requirement for Israel to negotiate with terrorists, while U.S. policy in the War on Terrorism states that it will not negotiate with terrorists, have a summit with them, or peacefully coexist with them.

and the reception of foreign diplomats at the PA headquarters, and previously in Jerusalem at the Orient House. The press has covered such events, thus helping establish the perception that the Palestinian Authority is a legitimate national entity rather than a political one.

What the media has never reported is that except for the kingdom of Jordan, a Palestinian national entity has never existed at any time. UN population figures record that 1,600,000 Palestinians reside in Jordan (about one-third of the total population). Jordanian sources believe that at least 50 percent of the country is Palestinian. Historically, from 1948–1967, Jordan

Fast Feature

The Media in the Middle East

The Arab world is sometimes referred to as the "Arc of Silence" because of the strict controls on the media in the Middle East. The Arab media presents the stories and pictures the dictators want the world to see and hear. The Western media has difficulty obtaining accurate information from Arab sources, and Western journalists take risks when they report from the region. Speeches and information released in English may be very different from those originally delivered in Arabic. Since most journalists do not speak Arabic or have an in-depth understanding of the social and political history of the region, they are at a disadvantage in interpreting their sources. Moreover, those who do not present an "Arab perspective" are subject to being followed, escorted away from politically sensitive events, intimidation, interrogation, and even blackmail. For example, after the Associated Press (AP) filmed Palestinians celebrating the September 11, 2001 attack on America, the Palestinian Authority told the AP that it could not guarantee the safety of their cameraman if the footage was aired. The AP never released the footage, but pictures of "the celebrations" were shown by other news agencies, but not after September 11. By contrast, in Israel, reporters have complete journalistic freedom because Israel is a modern democracy, although censorship applies where military security may be compromised. An understanding of the problems in reporting from the Arab world should caution listeners to not accept everything reported by the media as entirely objective and factual. Alternate reporting agencies should also be considered to obtain a balanced view on controversial issues surrounding the Middle East conflict.

occupied the West Bank and its "Palestinian" population was Jordanian. Even after Jordan was defeated by the Israelis in the Six-Day War and lost this territory, it continued to declare that the West Bank was "occupied Jordan" and insisted that it be returned by the Israelis under UN Resolution 242. Then in 1987, when the Palestinians began their Intifada, a decision was made the next year by the Arab League (of which Jordan is a part) to recognize the PLO as the official representatives of the Palestinian people and to negotiate the status of the West Bank and Gaza Strip as part of an independent Palestinian state. Even so, when Israel entered into a peace agreement with Jordan in 1994, Jordan alone was recognized as the protector of the Islamic holy sites on the Temple Mount, which was actualized in 1995 by the installation of a Jordanian mufti in Jerusalem and a restoration of the Dome of the Rock. But before the restoration project was completed, Yasser Arafat installed his own Palestinian mufti, who ordered Palestinians to ignore the dictates of the Jordanian mufti. Not until 1998 did King Hussein of Jordan announced his support for the Palestinian cause to establish a Palestinian state in the West Bank. This rivalry over Jerusalem was not widely broadcast by the mainline media. Today, the Palestinian Authority has its administrative headquarters in Gaza City and Ramallah, and the Palestinian mufti, Ikrima Sabri, has complete control of the *Harem*, site of the Muslim holy places in Jerusalem, despite the lack of any official agreement with Israel to usurp its sovereignty over Jerusalem as Israel's capital (a status that the Palestinian Authority does not recognize). Again, this violation of status quo on the Temple Mount (*Harem*) has been unreported or underreported by the mainline media.

Fast Figure

King Hussein

When King Abdullah of Jordan was assassinated in 1951, his grandson, Hussein, succeeded him. Hussein was one of the most pro-Western Arab monarchs in the Middle East as well as one of the best. Even though over half of the Jordanian population was Palestinian, he skillfully ruled the country and continually overcame both the sensitive issues related to the Palestinians and numerous assassination attempts. He died from cancer in 1999 and was succeeded by his son, Abdullah II.

Fast Quote

Arafat's Terrorism

"The overwhelming number of attacks against Israeli civilians were not perpetrated by Hizballah or Hamas but by Arafat's own Fatah Tanzim militia members."

Joseph Farah,
From Arab America,
February 22, 2002

Arafat's Terrorism

Yasser Arafat's deception via the media is evident as he continues to denounce to the press the terrorism of groups such as Hamas and Hizballah, while his own *Fatah* and Al-Aqsa Martyr's Brigade carry out homicide bombings on Israelis. This fact was established (and reported by the press) on April 2, 2002 when the Israel Defense Forces discovered in Yasser Arafat's compound in Ramallah an invoice from the PLO's chief financial officer requesting money for homicide bombers. Fortunately, some in the media are savvy to Arafat's deception. Arab American Joseph Farah, the founder of WorldNet Daily, states correctly concerning Arafat:

> In Arabic, Arafat praises the terrorists as "martyrs"…His hand-picked mufti in Jerusalem continues to call for the complete destruction of Israel in his Friday sermons. If you want to know the real Arafat, the unrepentant murderer of innocents, the tin-pot tyrant who sends impressionable young Arab children to their deaths, the schemer who says one thing and does another, the man who has fooled the West and Israel for too long… watch him call for unending jihad and total victory over Israel…watch his spokesmen deny the reality of the Holo-caust…watch his organization training Arab children as young as four years old in commando-style warfare and the indoctrination of the young in martyrdom—using subsidies from U.S. taxpayers.[19]

Arafat and other Palestinian leaders will continue to use the media to win popular and international support for their cause while hiding the unsavory side of their movement, which is filled with despotism, corruption, organized crime, and connected with radical Islam and worldwide terrorism, including connections with al-Qaeda.

17

WHO ARE THE PALESTINIAN REFUGEES?

Many people groups in modern history have experienced a refugee crisis. The Jewish people experienced such a crisis because of the Nazi persecution in eastern Europe and the forced exile of Jews from Arab countries after World War II. Today, the world's focus has been trained on the problem of the Palestinian refugees because of the Middle East conflict. By historical definition, the Palestinian refugees are those Arabs of Palestine who, as a result of the wars of 1948 and 1967, lost their homes and were reduced to refugee status. According to a census taken before and after the 1948 war, no more than 649,100 Arabs could have become refugees, although a report by the UN mediator on Palestine arrived at an even lower figure of 472,000. In 1967, an estimated 325,000 Jordanians living in the West Bank moved to the east bank of Jordan, which they considered another part of their country. These refugees today live in "refugee camps" (which in most cases are towns or cities) in the West Bank and Gaza Strip and in Jordan, Lebanon, and Syria. The present Palestinian population in the West Bank is 2,090,000 people with 1,180,000 in Gaza, for a total population of 3,270,000.[20] Despite the dreadful conditions often reported for these refugees, there is an 80 percent literacy rate and the average life expectancy is 72.3 years. The Palestinian Authority, along with the Arab world, identify all of the Arabs who remained in the West Bank and Gaza—all of those who left their homes and now live in other countries, along with all of their descendants—as Palestinian refugees. This number, according to the Palestinian Authority, is estimated to be about 7.8 million people. (See chart "Palestinian Population Worldwide," page 63.)

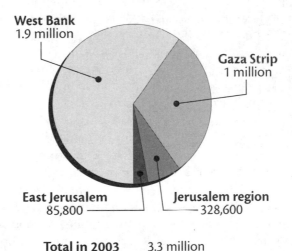

Where the Palestinians Are

West Bank
1.9 million

Gaza Strip
1 million

East Jerusalem
85,800

Jerusalem region
328,600

Total in 2003   3.3 million

18

WHO CAUSED THE REFUGEE PROBLEM?

One of the goals of the PLO has been to resolve the Palestinian refugee problem that resulted from the loss of Arab property in the 1948 war. Article 9 of the Palestine National Charter says, "The Palestinian Arab people assert their absolute determination and firm resolution to continue their armed struggle and to work for an armed popular revolution for the liberation of their country and their return to it." Since that time, Palestinian spokesmen have created and fostered the international opinion that Israel alone was responsible for both the initial cause and the continued status of the Palestinian refugees. While some Arabs in Palestine in 1948 were removed from their homes by Israeli troops or left out of fear of the Israeli army, most of the departing Arabs, approximately 400,000 of them (or 68 percent), never saw an Israeli soldier. To understand the cause of the Arab evacuation and the resulting refugee problem, we need to consult Arab sources of the time. For instance, the Jaffa newspaper *Ash Sha'ab*, on January 30, 1948, reported the Arab exodus from Palestine and criticized it as a betrayal of the Arab objective: "The first of our fifth column consists of those who abandon their houses and businesses and go to live elsewhere....At the first signs of trouble they take to their heels to escape sharing the burden of struggle."

Fast Quote

Whose Fault?

"The fact that there are these refugees is the direct consequence of the act of the Arab states in opposing partition and the Jewish state. The Arab states agree upon this policy unanimously and they must share in the solution of the problem."

Emile Ghoury, secretary of the Palestine Arab Higher Council, Beirut Telegraph, September 6, 1948

These hasty retreats were also reported in another Jaffa newspaper, *As Sarih* (March 30, 1948), which excoriated Arab villagers near Tel Aviv for "bringing down disgrace on us all by abandoning the villages."

What these Arab papers were criticizing at the time was the initial departure of 30,000 wealthy Palestinians immediately after the announcement of the UN partition resolution in 1947. They left in anticipation of the war and set up shop in neighboring Arab countries, planning to wait until the conflict ended and then return home. Less affluent Arabs from cities with a mixed Arab and Jewish population

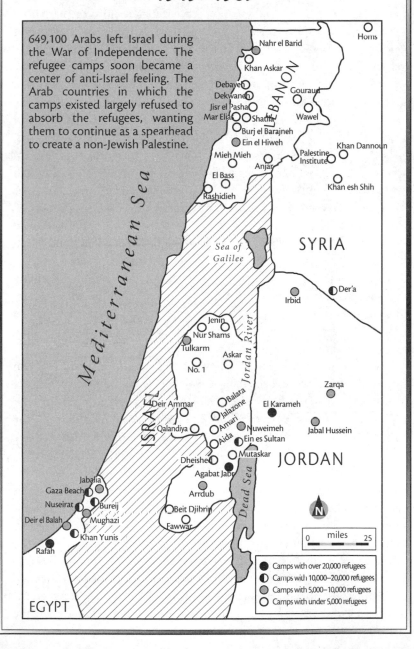

Arab Refugee Camps
1949–1967

649,100 Arabs left Israel during the War of Independence. The refugee camps soon became a center of anti-Israel feeling. The Arab countries in which the camps existed largely refused to absorb the refugees, wanting them to continue as a spearhead to create a non-Jewish Palestine.

Horns

Nahr el Barid

Khan Askar

Debaye
Dekwaneh
Jisr el Pasha
Mar Elias
Shatila
Burj el Barajneh
Ein el Hiweh

Gouraud

Wawel

Khan Dannoun

Palestine
Institute

Mieh Mieh

Anjar

El Bass

Khan esh Shih

Rashidieh

LEBANON

Mediterranean Sea

Sea of
Galilee

SYRIA

Der'a
Irbid

Jenin
Nur Shams
Tulkarm
Askar
No. 1

Jordan River

Zarqa

Deir Ammar
Balata
Jalazone
Amari
Qalandiya
Aida

El Karameh

Jabal Hussein

Nuweimeh
Ein es Sultan
Mutaskar
Dheisheh

JORDAN

ISRAEL

Agabat Jabr

Jabalia
Gaza Beach
Nuseirat
Bureij
Deir el Balah
Mughazi
Khan Yunis
Rafah

Arrdub

Beit Djibrin
Fawwar

Dead Sea

N

0   miles   25

● Camps with over 20,000 refugees
◑ Camps with 10,000–20,000 refugees
◉ Camps with 5,000–10,000 refugees
○ Camps with under 5,000 refugees

EGYPT

followed the money and jobs that went with the wealthy Arabs and moved to all-Arab towns to stay with relatives or friends.

Thousands of additional Arabs left Palestine in 1948 because they were heeding *Arab* leaders' warnings to evacuate before the arrival of the advancing Arab armies. According to the Jordanian newspaper *Falastin* (February 19, 1949), "The Arab states, which encouraged the Palestine Arabs to leave their homes temporarily in order to be out of the way of the Arab invasion armies, have failed to keep their promise to help these refugees." Even 14 years later, and one year before the founding of the PLO, Arab sources continued to state this fact. For example, the Cairo daily *Akhbar el Yom* (October 12, 1963) declared, "The 15th May 1948, arrived....On that day the mufti of Jerusalem appealed to the Arabs of Palestine to leave the country, because the Arab armies were about to enter and fight in their stead." However, appeals were not always sufficient to cause Arab families to leave their properties, so more forceful measures were taken by the Arabs, as the Jordanian newspaper *Al Urdun* (April 9, 1953) reported: "For the flight and fall of the other villages it is our leaders who are responsible because of their dissemination of rumors exaggerating Jewish crimes and describing them as atrocities in order to inflame the Arabs....By spreading rumors of Jewish atrocities, killings of women and children, etc., they instilled fear and terror in the hearts of the Arabs in Palestine, until they fled, leaving their homes and properties to the enemy."

As noted previously, some Arabs certainly were expelled by Jewish troops, as would be expected in a war. However, in most cases, the Jewish forces acted in order to *avoid* being accused of confiscation. For instance, when Jewish forces seized Tiberias on April 19, 1948, and the entire Arab population of 6,000 was evacuated under British military supervision, the Jewish Community Council issued a statement of clarification: "We did not dispossess them; they themselves chose this course....Let no citizen touch their property." Likewise, in both Tiberias and Haifa, the Haganah issued orders that none of the Arabs' possessions should be touched, and warned that anyone violating these orders would be severely punished.

A second refugee population was created in 1967 by the Six-Day War. Ignoring warnings to stay out of the war, King Hussein of Jordan joined the other Arab states that had attacked Israel and launched his own attack on Jerusalem. The United Nations estimated that during the fighting, about 350,000 Palestinians left Palestine for the first time, and another 175,000 fled for a second time, most of these coming from the West Bank, which was under Jordanian control. About 200,000 moved to Jordan, 115,000 to Syria, and approximately 35,000 left Sinai for Egypt. During the six years following the war, more than 54,000 returned.

As in the 1948 war, rumors spread by Arab leaders caused the Palestinian exodus in 1967. A Palestinian refugee who served as an administrator in the Jericho UN Relief and Works Agency camp said that many Arabs had left because Arab politicians had told all the young people they would be killed. People had also heard on the radio that the war would last a long time and others heard rumors that under Israeli rule they would not be able to receive money from foreign relatives. In addition, the Israeli army relocated a small number of Arab families for what was termed "strategic and security reasons." In these ways, the war in 1967 further increased the refugee problem created by the war in 1948.

19

WHY HAVE THE PALESTINIANS CONTINUED TO BE REFUGEES?

The history of the refugee peoples around the world after World War II reveals that every group, except the Palestinians, was successfully absorbed into their own people's lands. Ironically, some 820,000 Jewish refugees were forced to leave Arab countries and went to Israel in the years following Israel's independence. This was a number, incidentally, *greater* than that of the Arabs who left Palestine for Arab lands in 1948 and 1967. Most of these Jews could take nothing more than the shirts on their backs. Yet 586,000 were resettled in the tiny territory allotted to Israel at great expense, and without any offer of compensation from the Arab governments who confiscated their possessions. Since then, millions more Jews from around the world, and most notably entire communities of Jews in Russia and Ethiopia, have been absorbed into an Israel of only 9,000 square miles. Why could not the Palestinian Arabs be absorbed by the neighboring Arab states? These are underpopulated nations which control a vast territory of some 5,000,000 square miles.

Jewish Refugees from Arab States

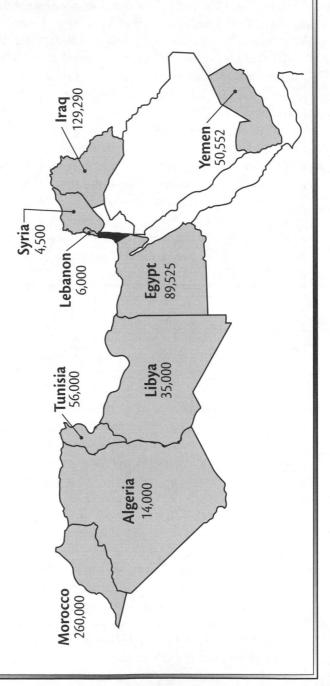

Arab states showing number of Jews who sought refuge in Israel between 1948 and 1972

Israel between 1948 and 1967

Morocco 260,000

Algeria 14,000

Tunisia 56,000

Libya 35,000

Egypt 89,525

Lebanon 6,000

Syria 4,500

Iraq 129,290

Yemen 50,552

One explanation is that the Palestinian refugees have been and still are *unwanted* by these Arab states. This was first witnessed in January 1948 when the Arab exodus was at its height. The Palestine Arab Higher Committee asked the Arab countries near Palestine to seal off their borders to prevent refugees from entering those Arab countries. This position did not change with the 1967 war, and to date, no Arab state but Jordan has attempted to absorb Palestinian refugees. Jordan's reason for doing so, however, has been more political than humanitarian. As one writer explained, "Jordan accepted the refugees as citizens as a matter of self-interest. Jordan wanted to integrate them as Jordanians so they would not have to form a Palestinian government on the West Bank which would have threatened Jordan's rule there."[21]

From the refugees' viewpoint, those moving to the east bank were escaping the impoverished conditions in the West Bank—conditions that had resulted from Jordanian rule. At the time, they did not consider themselves as Palestinian refugees but as Jordanians who were moving from one part of their country to another. Yet when Jordan relinquished its claim to the West Bank in 1988, its practice toward refugees in Palestine became the same as that of the other Arab countries. When the Palestinian Authority renewed its Intifada in 2000, some 150,000 Palestinians in the West Bank sought to move to Jordan to escape the conflict. This time, however, the Jordanian government closed its borders to all but those with Jordanian passports. Lebanon, too, took in some refugees after 1948, but complaints about the matter were voiced in the Beirut Muslim weekly *Kul-Shay* (August 19, 1951): "Who brought the Palestinians to Lebanon as refugees, suffering now from the malign of newspapers and communal leaders, who have neither honor nor conscience? Who brought them over in dire straits and penniless, after they lost their honor? The Arab states, and Lebanon amongst them, did it."

Another factor to consider is the enormous wealth controlled by the Arab and Muslim world of the Middle East. If the Arab members of the Organization of Oil Exporting Countries (OPEC) were to share a small percentage of their considerable oil revenues (estimated at $113 billion), the Palestinians' economic plight could easily be reversed. In fact, if Palestinian leader Yasser Arafat, who is a billionaire, would share some of his private fortune, he could single-handedly relieve his people's suffering! (For more on the income of Arafat and the Palestinian Authority, see pp. 66–70.) Moreover, all Muslims are required to

Israel and the Arab Middle East

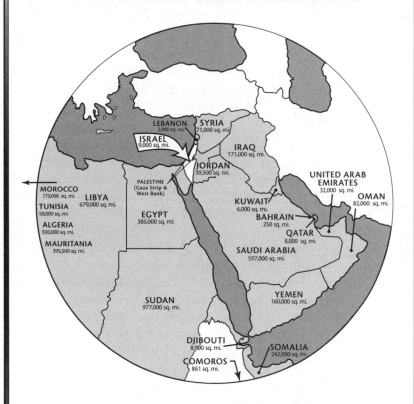

The Arab League comprises 22 separate Islamic states spanning an area of more than 5,000,000 square miles. Israel, by contrast, consists of only one state of 9,000 square miles.

pay a tax for the support of the poor, known as *zakah* (the third pillar of Islam), and the pious give additional alms to the poor (*fitrah*) at the end of the Muslim holy month of Ramadan. Imagine what could be accomplished if only a fraction of this money were directed to help the Palestinian Muslims. Yet today, the Palestinian infrastructure is in shambles, Palestinian refugee camps are filled with squalor, and the Palestinian people are horribly impoverished.

20

HOW IS AID TO THE PALESTINIAN REFUGEES FUNDED?

Since 1948, Palestinian refugees have received economic assistance through the United Nations Relief Works Agency (UNRWA), which was given an annual budget of $50 million. Initially, the United States contributed $25 million and Israel some $3 million, while the total Arab pledges were around $600,000. For the first two decades of the program the United States contributed more than two-thirds of the funds, with Israel donating more funds than most Arab states. In fact, until 1994, Israel gave more than all Arab countries except Saudi Arabia, Morocco, and Kuwait. Since 1994, with the establishment of the Palestinian Authority and Israel's transfer of territories to the Palestinian Authority, Israel has reduced the amount of its contributions. And the United States continues to be the largest single contributor to UNRWA. It donated more than $80 million in 1999 (28 percent of the organization's receipts that year) as opposed to Saudi Arabia ($5.8 million), Kuwait ($2.6 million), the United Arab Emirates ($1 million), and Egypt ($10,000). However, since these funds come under the control of the Palestinian Authority and they permit no independent auditing, it is unknown how much of the money actually reaches the refugees. It is known that the UNRWA refugee camps have been used as terrorist bases and for illegal weapons production, and that UNWRA representative Saheil Alhinadi, in a speech, praised the terrorist suicide attacks.[22]

Facts like these raise concerns over the allocation and distribution of funds for purposes other than the intended relief of Palestinian refugees. Stories of corruption among the Palestinian leadership are common, and it's disconcerting to know that money is given to Palestinian families whose children kill themselves and others as homicide bombers. Yasser Arafat gives $10,000 to each family and Iraqi dictator Saddam Hussein gives $25,000. Recently, a telethon in Saudi Arabia raised $100,000,000 for the same purpose.

Fast Quote

Taking Care of Their Own

"The transfer of trillions of dollars (and pounds, yen, and euros) to oil-producing nations should have elevated the lives of everyone on the receiving end. It hasn't, because the political and religious dictators, in order to maintain their privileged positions, keep their people in intellectual, theological and economic poverty."

Cal Thomas,
Fox News commentator

As a whole, the Arab nations currently contribute less than 5 percent of the UNRWA budget. One would wonder why millions of people in the Islamic world continue to be devoted to regimes that have not only utterly failed to improve their lives, but also display little value for those same lives!

Why does the Arab world do so little to assist the Palestinian refugees as well as the Palestinian people? The reason, says Joseph Farah, an Arab American, is that "the suffering of millions of Arabs [Palestinians] is perpetuated only for political purposes by the Arab states. They are merely pawns in the war to destroy Israel."[23]

21

IS THE PALESTINIAN REFUGEE CRISIS THE STATE OF ISRAEL'S RESPONSIBILITY?

As a result of the Six-Day War, many Palestinians in the conquered territories were displaced; that is, they had to leave their homes and move to another place in the *same* country. These "displaced persons" were the subject of Security Council Resolution 237 of June 4, 1967, which called upon the government of Israel "to facilitate the return of those inhabitants [of the areas where military operations have taken place] who have fled the areas since the outbreak of hostilities." This resolution does not speak of a "right" of return, yet Israel has agreed to their return in various agreements that have formed the Israeli position in peace negotiations. In one Israeli document entitled "Principles Guiding Israel's Policy in the Aftermath of the June 1967 War," Prime Minister Levy Eshkol stated only a month after the conflict that "Israel will cooperate fully in the solution of the refugees problem...within the framework of an international and regional plan."[24] In 1949 and 1967 Israel offered families that had been separated during the war to return and repatriate 100,000 (in 1949). It also unfroze the refugees' bank accounts in Israeli banks and paid compensation for abandoned lands. Israel has continued to offer compromises to the Palestinian Authority, but all have been rejected. Israel's position is that while it did not create the refugee problem, it is willing to do its part to help resolve it, even though it is the responsibility of the Arab world to absorb Arab refugees.

This is the same Arab world, incidentally, that deported hundreds of thousands of Jews without hope of repatriation or reparation and whom Israel alone absorbed. This point is well made by Arab American Joseph Farah, who said, "There were some 100 million refugees around the world following World War II. The Palestinian Arab group is the only one in the world not absorbed or integrated into their own people's lands. Since then, millions of Jewish refugees from around the world have been absorbed in the tiny nation of Israel. It makes no sense to expect that same tiny Jewish state to solve a refugee crisis that it did not create."[25] Unlike the Palestinians, who have received compensation from Israel, Jewish refugees have never been compensated by the Arab states, nor were any UN organizations ever established to help the Jewish refugees.

22

WHY DOESN'T ISRAEL WANT
ALL THE REFUGEES TO RETURN?

Jewish leaders in fact tried to prevent a refugee problem by urging the Arabs to remain in Palestine and become citizens of Israel at the time of the UN vote for partition. The Assembly of Palestine Jewry issued the following appeal to the Arab community on October 2, 1947: "We will do everything in our power to maintain peace, and establish a cooperation gainful to both [Jews and Arabs]. It is now, here and now, from Jerusalem itself, that a call must go out to the Arab nations to join forces with Jewry and the destined Jewish State and work shoulder to shoulder for our common good, for the peace and progress of sovereign equals." In addition, David Ben-Gurion sent Golda Meir to Haifa to try to persuade the Arabs to stay, but she was unable to convince them because they feared they would be judged traitors to the Arab cause. Israel repeatedly has offered Israeli citizenship with all of its benefits (including a free education and the opportunity to hold public office) to those Palestinians who would be willing to live within the State of Israel.

During the Oslo Peace Process, Israel continued to negotiate with the Palestinian Authority on this matter, offering a right of return to a limited number of Palestinians who met the refugee criteria. However, the Palestinian Authority and the UNRWA have developed a new definition of a refugee as "a person whose normal residence was Palestine for a minimum of *two years* immediately preceding the outbreak of the conflict in 1948 and who, as a result of that conflict, lost both his home and his means of livelihood...." This definition extends refugee status to *all* Palestinian descendants living as residents in other countries (not simply in refugee camps) the right of return. By this definition, as many as five million foreign Palestinians are now counted as "refugees." With less than six million Jews in the present State of Israel, it is easy to see why Israelis are apprehensive about accepting this extended definition and granting open immigration rights to all who believe themselves to be Palestinian. It would be demographic suicide for so small a country as well as physical suicide, since the Palestinians could easily overrun the Jews if they were to follow the call of the surrounding Arab countries to invade Israel.

Fast Quote

Palestinian Right of Return

"This [Palestinian right of return] is a euphemism for the elimination of Israel, and no government will accept it. There is a thin line between a calculated risk and yielding to terror."

Ehud Barak,
former Israeli prime minister

This threat to Israel was made even more certain by some words Yasser Arafat spoke a few years ago. In a statement made to a closed meeting of Arab ambassadors in Stockholm, where Arafat had gone to receive a peace prize on January 30, 1996, Arafat explained the real goal for his demand for a right of return: "Within five years we will have six to seven million Arabs living on the West Bank and Jerusalem. All Palestinian Arabs will be welcomed by us. If the Jews can import all kinds of Ethiopians, Russians, Uzbekians, and Ukrainians as Jews, we can import all kinds of Arabs. We plan to eliminate the State of Israel and establish a Palestinian state. We will make life unbearable for Jews by psychological warfare and population explosion. Jews will not want to live among

Arabs....They will give up their dwellings and leave for the United States. We Palestinians will take over everything, including all of Jerusalem."[26]

Arafat's statement was nothing new. A similar viewpoint was reported at the time of the original Arab exodus: "It is well known and understood that the Arabs, in demanding the return of the refugees to Palestine, mean their return as masters of the Homeland and not as slaves. With a greater clarity, they mean the liquidation of the State of Israel."[27] Given such rhetoric and the continued Intifada against Israel, UN Security Council Resolution 194 recognized that Israel could not be expected to repatriate a hostile population that might endanger its security and become a fifth column. While Israel continues to offer the right of return to a portion of the refugee population, it has reserved the right to limit this number due to security and demographic concerns.

Fast Feature

Complications with the Palestinian Right of Return

Each side has a rationale for and against this issue. Here are some key points:

Israeli viewpoint:
- Demand: Willing to help solve the problem; not willing to absorb millions of Palestinians.
- Concern: The potential danger of allowing millions of vengeful Palestinians into the Jewish state who could later join with coalition Arab states in a future attack on Israel.
- Complication: Not willing to endure the political destruction of the "Jewish" character of Israel.
- Proposals: Permit limited Palestinian return only to areas outside of Israel proper, segregate the Jewish and Palestinian populations by a perimeter wall, and demilitarize the area under Palestinian autonomy.

Palestinian viewpoint:
- Demand: Refugees must be allowed to return to their former homes or be given compensation for choosing not to return.

Continued on page 88

Fast Feature

Continued from page 87

- Concern: Israel is not honoring the U.N. Security Council Resolutions 194 and 242, which grant Palestinians right of repatriation and war reparations.

- Complication: Undesired compromise on right of return creates possibility of backlash against Palestinian leadership and further escalation of the conflict.

- Proposals: Complete return of all Palestinian refugees, no segregation that would cut off access to Palestinian livelihood in Israeli areas, sovereignty as an independent state with full military status.

WAR IN THE MODERN MIDDLE EAST

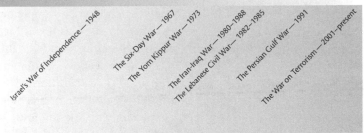

Fast Focus

World War II
▼

Israel's War of Independence—1948

The Six-Day War—1967

The Yom Kippur War—1973

The Iran-Iraq War—1980–1988

The Lebanese Civil War—1982–1985

The Persian Gulf War—1991

The War on Terrorism—2001–present

23

HOW MANY WARS HAVE BEEN FOUGHT IN THE MODERN MIDDLE EAST?

Including the U.S.-led war against Iraq which began March 19, 2003, 13 wars have been fought in the modern Middle East: six between Israel and various Arab nations, one between Israel and the Palestinians, two between factions within the Arab nations (Jordanians and Palestinians in Black September and the Lebanese Civil War), two between Arab nations (Iran-Iraq and Iraq-Kuwait), two between Arab terrorist regimes and the U.S. Alliance (Gulf War and the War on Terrorism), and then Operation Iraqi Freedom. The Israeli-Palestinian War, though announced on both sides as such, has not yet escalated to the level of a confrontation that forces a resolution, and the War on Terrorism has thus far included a war against the forces of the Taliban regime in Afghanistan. Let us consider each of these wars briefly with respect to their history and effect on the region.

The War of Independence (1947–48)

When the UN decision to partition Palestine and create separate Arab and Jewish states was announced on November 29, 1947, it was immediately met with opposition by the British Mandatory Government in Palestine, the Arab Higher Committee in Palestine, and the greater Arab League. The Arabs in Palestine launched violent riots, and the Jews responded with attacks on both Arab and British targets. The lack of a military provision in UN Resolution 181 as well as international politics prevented the major powers in the United Nations from intervening to quell the conflict and implement the Partition Plan, so as hopes for a successful partition ended, the war began. The war was initiated when some 1,000 Arabs attacked Jews in northern Palestine. In this first phase of the war, which lasted until April 1, 1948, the Arabs had the advantage. The British Mandatory Government prevented Jewish immigrants from coming to Israel (these immigrants were needed for the war) through a naval blockade and forbid the Jews in Palestine from training soldiers or forming an armed militia to defend themselves. Meanwhile, the British treaty with Transjordan (whose King Abdullah believed it was his duty to save Palestine from the Jews) obligated the British to supply the Arabs with arms to fight the Jews.

The tide turned for the Jews after April 1, which began the second phase of the war. In an effort to relieve the stranglehold of Arab forces on Jerusalem and free convoys from sniper fire en route to Jerusalem, the Jewish

Fast Fact

The Legend of Deir Yassin

During the War of Independence in 1948, the Arabs took control of Jerusalem and held many strategic vantage points along the road from Tel Aviv to Jerusalem. One of these was the village of Deir Yassin. The Irgun attacked this village in April of 1948 and found themselves in heated battle. They left an escape route open for the Arab citizens who did not wish to fight. Many of the Arabs who feigned surrender later fired upon the Irgunists. After this, the Jews no longer discriminated between fleeing civilians and armed soldiers. In fact, among the dead, there were many Arab men disguised as women. So why do Arabs consider this battle a massacre? The casualty figures change depending on who you ask. The *New York Times* reported 200 Arabs dead and 40 captured. A more recent study states that 107 Arabs were killed. The Arabs say this was a massacre partially because the militant Irgun were the attackers. But the Arabs also thought that by calling this a massacre, they would inspire more Arabs to fight against the Jewish state. But the opposite happened, and there was a mass exodus of fearful Arabs from Eastern Palestine.

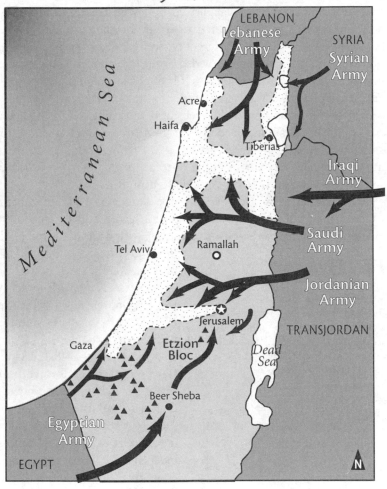

The Arab Invasion
May 15, 1948

LEBANON
Lebanese Army

SYRIA
Syrian Army

Acre

Haifa

Tiberias

Mediterranean Sea

Iraqi Army

Saudi Army

Tel Aviv

Ramallah

Jordanian Army

Jerusalem

TRANSJORDAN

Etzion Bloc

Dead Sea

Gaza

Beer Sheba

Egyptian Army

EGYPT

N

Held by Israel on eve of Arab invasion

Arab-controlled areas on eve of Arab invasion

● Jewish city

○ Arab city

▲ Isolated Jewish settlement

underground military forces, the Irgun and Haganah, attacked Arab strongholds at Deir Yassin and Kastel. Although the attack on Deir Yassin has been labeled a "massacre" in which it is claimed an innocent village of women and children were slaughtered by Jewish troops, history shows that the residents of Deir Yassin opened fire on the Irgun and that the battle lasted several hours. Moreover, some 200 of the residents left unharmed by an escape route provided by the Irgun and were later trucked to a safe village by Jewish soldiers.[1] Only after the remaining Arabs in the village had pretended to surrender and then attacked the Jewish troops did some Jews fire indiscriminately. Even then, according to Dr. Mitchell G. Bard of the AICE, among the bodies of the 107 dead were Arab men disguised as women.[2] The Arab League used the report of this "massacre" to incite Arab countries to join in the war against the Jews, but it had the reverse effect and provoked an Arab flight from Palestine.

Four days after the Deir Yassin report was published, a number of Arabs carried out a true massacre when a Jewish convoy en route to Hadassah Hospital was ambushed and 77 Jewish doctors (including the hospital director), nurses, and patients were gunned down. Two weeks later, 148 Jewish settlers at Kfar Etzion were killed by the Arab Legion (many were killed *after* they had surrendered).

Fast Figure

David Ben-Gurion

The leading figure in Zionist/Israeli politics for almost half a century. He played a major part in the evolution of the kibbutz and the Haganah. Ben-Gurion, the leader of both the World Zionist Organization and Jewish Agency for many years, declared the birth of the State of Israel in May of 1948 and served as prime minister on and off until 1963, but remained politically active until the 1970s. Many Israelis revere Ben-Gurion in the same way Americans revere George Washington.

On May 14, 1948 the Israeli state was born as former Irgun leader David Ben-Gurion, now the first prime minister, implemented the UN Partition Plan (which had never been rescinded) and declared independence. The next day, armies from five Arab nations (Transjordan, Egypt, Syria, Iraq, and Lebanon) invaded Israel in a "war of extermination," which Azzam Pasha, secretary-general of the Arab League, called "a momentous massacre, which will be spoken of like the Mongolian massacres and the Crusades."[3] Initially, things looked bleak for the new Jewish state. On May 29, the Jewish Quarter of Jerusalem's Old City, which had been under siege for five months, surrendered, ending almost 2,000 years of continuous Jewish residence in the Old City and Jewish access to the Western Wall. The Jewish residents of the New City were able to hold out with the intervention of Jewish forces trained by American commander Mickey Marcus, and eventually the newly formed Israel Defense Forces defeated all the Arab armies (except the Jordanian Arab Legion) and stopped the Arab offensive.

As an outcome of this war, which Israelis call the War of Independence, the State of Israel was established. The Arabs suffered the shame of defeat and ended up with less land than they would have had if they had accepted the Partition Plan. As a result, they refer to this war as *Al-Nakba* ("the Great Catastrophe"). In 1949 the Arab nations (except Iraq) signed an armistice with Israel; however, none of them recognized Israel's independence nor negotiated for peaceful relations. Instead, they pledged to remain in a state of war.

The Suez War/Sinai Campaign (1956)

After the 1949 Armistice Agreement was signed by the Arab states that had attacked Israel in 1948, Egyptian president Gamel Abdel Nasser (who had supported the Nazis during World War II) continued to act belligerently toward Israel. Nasser refused to allow Israeli ships and Israeli-bound ships access to the Suez Canal and Gulf of Aqaba.

This closure was an act of aggression and a clear violation of the armistice. In 1951 the UN Security Council, in support of Israeli protests, ordered Egypt to open the canal to Israeli shipping, but Egypt continued its blockade. In 1955 Nasser launched terrorist squads (*fedayeen*) to attack Jewish towns just across Israel's borders. Between 1949–1956, these Arab attacks resulted in some 1,300 Israeli civilian casualties.

Nasser's intent in these hostile actions was made clear when he announced to the Arab world, "Egypt has decided to dispatch her heroes, the disciples of Pharaoh and the sons of Islam, and they will cleanse the land of Palestine.... There will be no peace on Israel's border because we demand vengeance, and vengeance is Israel's

Fast Figure

Gamel Abdel Nasser

An officer of the Egyptian Army, who, along with other officers, staged a coup in 1952 and became president soon after. A powerful and charismatic leader, he was most famous for his Pan-Arab vision, in which the Arab world was to unite under his direction and destroy Israel in the process. Despite defeats in both 1956 and 1967, he remained the hero of the Arab world and the leader by whom all other Arab leaders are measured.

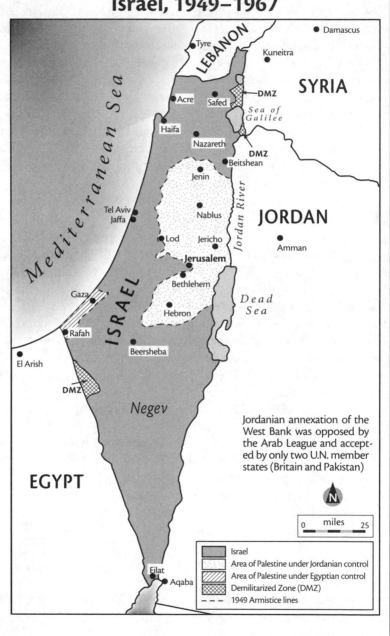

Israel, 1949–1967

Damascus

Tyre

LEBANON

Kuneitra

SYRIA

Acre
Safed
DMZ

Sea of Galilee

Haifa

Nazareth
DMZ
Beitshean

Jenin

Tel Aviv
Jaffa

Nablus

Jordan River

JORDAN

Lod
Jericho

Amman

Jerusalem

Bethlehem

Dead Sea

Gaza

Hebron

Rafah

El Arish

Beersheba

DMZ

Negev

ISRAEL

Mediterranean Sea

EGYPT

Jordanian annexation of the West Bank was opposed by the Arab League and accepted by only two U.N. member states (Britain and Pakistan)

N

0   miles   25

Eilat
Aqaba

Israel
Area of Palestine under Jordanian control
Area of Palestine under Egyptian control
Demilitarized Zone (DMZ)
1949 Armistice lines

death."[4] This was another violation of the armistice, which had prohibited the initiation of hostilities by paramilitary forces. Further evidence of Egypt's intentions to destroy Israel surfaced in 1955 when the Egyptians began importing massive quantities of Russian military equipment from the Soviet Bloc, which altered the balance of armament in the Middle East and started a new arms race. The imminent threat to Israel was intensified with Egypt's signing of an alliance with Jordan and Syria, its conversion of the Sinai Peninsula into a military base, and finally, in July 1956, with the blockade of the Straits of Tiran, which cut off the Red Sea route to Israel's southernmost port of Eilat. This severed Israel's only supply route with Asia and access to its primary source for oil, Iran.

These provocations prompted Israel to mobilize her army, and, with the support of Britain and France, mount an attack on Egypt through the Sinai Desert on October 29, 1956. This campaign, which became known as "Operation Kadesh," was so successful that by the end of the eighth day, Israel had killed or wounded 3,000 Egyptian soldiers and taken 6,000 prisoners (Israel lost 171 soldiers with several hundred wounded), captured an Egyptian destroyer (off Haifa) and immense quantities of military equipment, taken the Gaza Strip, much of the Sinai, Gaza, Sharm el-Sheikh (located on the tip of the Sinai Peninsula between the Gulf of Suez and the Gulf of Aqaba near the site of the blockade), and was poised to invade the Egyptian capital of Cairo. As a result, the United Nations stationed its Emergency Force (UNEF) along the Egyptian-Israeli border and the Egyptians reopened the shipping lanes, allowing Israel to carry on trade with Asian and African countries and import oil from the Persian Gulf. Israel then withdrew its troops in stages (November 1956–March 1957), and ended up gaining international respect for its impressive victory.

Fast Quote

Arab Intentions

"The Arab people will not be embarrassed to declare: We shall not be satisfied except by the final obliteration of Israel from the map of the Middle East."

Muhammad Salah al-Din,
Egyptian foreign minister (1954)

The Six-Day War (1967)

The humiliating defeat suffered by Egypt in 1956 was shared by the Arab League in particular and the Islamic world in general. The Arabs wanted revenge, and a strategy for attack was planned. That the Arabs considered this the only acceptable course was voiced by Egyptian president Nasser in response to Israeli prime minister Golda Meir's continued plea for peace in an address to the UN General Assembly (October 10, 1960). Neither Egypt nor any other Arab country would ever recognize, much less negotiate with, Israel!

Three years later the PLO, with its "Phased Plan," was formed with Nasser's support as a means to implement the Arab world's planned revenge. As the PLO waged terror attacks against Israeli civilians from across Egyptian and Jordanian borders during 1964–67, the Syrians, provoked by Israel's increased use of water from the Jordan River, began an artillery bombardment of Israeli farms, kibbutzim, and towns in the Galilee from the Syrian-controlled Golan Heights during 1965–66. On April 7, 1967, Israel retaliated against the intensive Syrian shelling, shooting down six Syrian fighter jets. Despite Israel's assurances of no further attacks, Syrian leaders believed an attack was imminent and called upon Egypt for help. On May 15, Egypt responded by moving large numbers of troops into the Sinai Desert for "total war which will result in the extermination of Zionist existence."[5] As Syria prepared, in its words, "to initiate the act of liberation...to explode the Zionist presence in the Arab homeland...to enter into a battle of annihilation,"[6] Nasser demanded the withdrawal of the multi-national UNEF troops out of the demilitarized zone (where they had been deployed since 1956). Nasser also reimposed a blockade of the Straits of Tiran and entered a military alliance with Jordan and Iraq.

Faced with the threat of an all-inclusive Arab war bolstered by calls for *jihad* (holy war) and the problem of keeping its entire army mobilized for an attack, Israel had no choice but to strike Egypt preemptively on June 5. Less than two hours after takeoff, Israeli fighter jet pilots had destroyed 300 Egyptian planes still on the ground and followed with a counterattack on Jordanian and Syrian Air Forces and the closest Iraqi airfield. By the end

Fast Quote

Arab Aim

"We aim at the destruction of the State of Israel. The immediate aim: perfection of Arab military might. The national aim: the eradication of Israel."

Egyptian president Nasser (1965)

Fast Quote

Arab Goal

"The existence of Israel is an error which must be rectified. This is our opportunity to wipe out the ignominy, which has been with us since 1948. Our goal is clear—to wipe Israel off the map."

Iraqi president Abdur Rahman Aref (June 4, 1967)

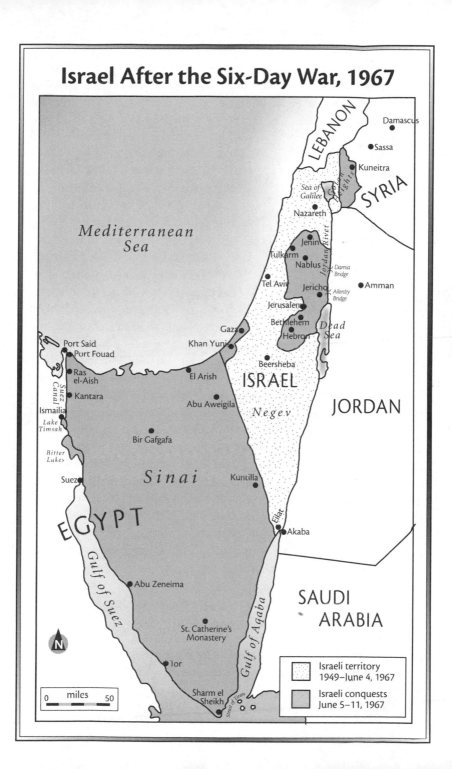

Israel After the Six-Day War, 1967

Damascus

Sassa

LEBANON

Kuneitra

SYRIA

Sea of Galilee

Golan Heights

Nazareth

Mediterranean Sea

Jenin

Tulkarm

Nablus

Jordan River

Damia Bridge

Tel Aviv

Jericho

Allenby Bridge

Amman

Jerusalem

Bethlehem

Gaza

Hebron

Dead Sea

Khan Yunis

Port Said

Port Fouad

Beersheba

Ras el-Aish

El Arish

ISRAEL

Suez Canal

Kantara

Abu Aweigila

Negev

JORDAN

Ismailia

Lake Timsah

Bir Gafgafa

Bitter Lukes

Sinai

Kuntilla

Suez

EGYPT

Eilat

Akaba

Gulf of Suez

Abu Zeneima

Gulf of Aqaba

SAUDI ARABIA

St. Catherine's Monastery

N

Tor

Sharm el Sheikh

Strait of Tiran

0   miles   50

Israeli territory 1949–June 4, 1967

Israeli conquests June 5–11, 1967

of the first day of fighting, Israeli planes had destroyed almost all of the Egyptian, Syrian, and Jordanian Air Forces. This surprise air offensive was designed to enable the Israeli ground forces to move across the Sinai and reopen the Straits of Tiran to Israeli shipping. Israeli troops virtually wiped out the Egyptian army and pushed that army all the way to the east bank of the Suez Canal (despite the orders of General Moshe Dayan to keep ten kilometers' distance), forcing the remaining Egyptian forces to withdraw.

Fast Fact

Outnumbered and Outgunned
In the Six-Day War, Israel faced the forces of eight Arab countries (Egypt, Syria, Jordan, Iraq, Lebanon, Saudi Arabia, Algeria, and Kuwait) and was surrounded on all sides by a total Arab strength of 547,000 troops, more than 2,800 tanks, and 957 warplanes. Israel had less than half the number of troops and less than a third of the number of tanks and aircraft.

King Hussein of Jordan had initially been reluctant to join the Syro-Egyptian military alliance, but intense domestic pressure, coupled with Nasser's call for *jihad* (incumbent on all Muslims) and the confident assurances of victory from the Arab states, forced him to follow suit. Hussein was warned by the Israelis to stay out of the war and Israel pledged to not attack Jordan, but Hussein rejected this offer based on Nasser's declaration that Egyptian forces were pressing toward the defeat of the Zionist entity. However, the king had been deceived, for even as Nasser was giving his guarantee, the Egyptian Air Force (the largest in the Middle East) lay utterly in ruins and Egyptian forces were retreating in disarray as Israel took the Sinai, the Suez Canal, and the Gaza Strip. Resorting to the Arab convention of saving face, Nasser did not tell Hussein the gravity of the situation, and so Jordan entered the fray. This resulted in immediate counteraction by the Israelis that, within two days, had cost Jordan all of East Jerusalem and its holy sites and most of the West Bank, making King Hussein the greatest loser in the Syro-Egyptian alliance.

Israel's final assault was made against Syrian troops entrenched in heavily fortified positions on the Golan Heights. Despite the enormous tactical advantage of the Syrians, the Israelis captured the Golan Heights after a 20-hour uphill battle and would have pressed on to Damascus had it not been for the consequent crisis of an American-Soviet engagement over the Israeli invasion. Israel's swift and stunning conquests led all the Arab countries to accept a cease-fire. The Arab world was shocked and utterly humiliated by the outcome of this war, which had lasted only six days: 18,000 Arab casualties (11,000 Egyptian, 6,000 Jordanian, and 1,000 Syrian), 5,600 Egyptians taken prisoner, 400 combat planes destroyed, and 500 tanks destroyed or captured (about 70 percent of the three armies' heavy armament).

By contrast, the Israelis had suffered 776 casualties with 2,586 wounded, and had become the dominant military power in the Middle East, capturing an immense amount of territory that had been occupied by Egypt, Syria, and Jordan: 28,000 square miles in the Sinai, Gaza Strip, the West Bank, and Golan Heights, which more than tripled Israel's previous land holdings (8,500 square miles). Above all, Israel had regained the Temple Mount, the center of Jewish prayers, enabling Jewish people for the first time in almost 2,000 years to reunify an independent Jerusalem. However, this triumph also set Israel up for more future conflicts. Israel now ruled over more than three-quarters of a million Palestinians, most opposed to the Jewish state, and maintained sovereignty over the third holiest site in Islam. In addition, when Jordan launched its attack on June 5, more than 325,000 West Bank Palestinians fled to Jordan to avoid the bloodbath promised by Arab propaganda, and another 116,000 later left the Golan Heights for Syria, adding many more people to the already-existing refugee population. This was a situation the defeated Arab states would use in the future to escalate the conflict to international proportions.

Fast Figure

Moshe Dayan

Israeli hero and military leader from the War of Independence to the Yom Kippur War. A native Palestinian Jew, he joined the Haganah at age 14 and later served with the British when they took control of Lebanon from Vichy French forces, where he would lose an eye but gain the eye patch that would forever distinguish him among Israeli heroes. Dayan became Israel's minister of defense just before the Six-Day War, but after not being prepared to go to war during the Yom Kippur War of 1973, he resigned out of shame. He got back into politics in 1977 by becoming foreign minister and playing a large role in the Camp David Accords of 1979, which restored his reputation. No one has symbolized Israel's stubbornness and will to survive more than Dayan.

The War of Attrition (1968–70)

The defeat of the Egyptian forces in the Six-Day War led Egyptian president Nasser to resign his office, but an Egyptian demonstration in his support convinced him to remain. Although Nasser had agreed to a cease-fire he had not agreed to give up the war, and there was no better way to prove his people's confidence in him as a leader than to continue the conflict against Israel. Nasser believed that Israel was vulnerable to a sustained attack through terrorism because most of its army was made up of reservists. He conjectured that if he initiated a lengthy war, Israel's economy would fail and the constant casualties would demoralize the nation. So, just three weeks after the end of the Six-Day War, Egypt began a bombardment of Israeli troops stationed near the Suez Canal, and three months later, sank an Israeli destroyer, killing 47. Egypt also struggled with Israeli troops over points in the Sinai Peninsula that had not yet been taken by Israel.

While the Egyptians continued the shelling of Israeli positions in the Suez, Yasser Arafat and his *Fatah* movement began terrorist raids from Jordan. Despite Israel's initial killing of some 60 Palestinian guerillas and capturing 300, the *Fatah* and other groups continued their attacks, climaxing in the battle of al-Karameh, in which the Jordanian army joined forces with the Palestinians and inflicted considerable losses on Israel. This bloody "War of Attrition" lasted two years until 1970, but persisted on a smaller scale through terrorist attacks (as Nasser had planned) up until the next bigger war in 1973. This low-intensity warfare ended up proving so effective that the PLO adopted it for their Intifadas over the next two decades.

Black September (1970)

After 1967, the *fedayeen* (the Arab guerilla army) had grown into a large and well-funded military establishment. The Palestinian guerilla groups that were part of the *fedayeen* took over control of the Palestinian refugee camps in the West Bank and launched attacks on Israel. Initially Jordan had supported these efforts in the War of Attrition and aided the Palestinians at al-Karameh. However, when political and military concerns forced these guerilla organizations to move into Jordan, King Hussein decried this as a violation of Jordanian sovereignty and as an attempt to create a PLO state within Jordan. In addition, the more radical groups in the PLO exempted themselves from Jordanian control and called publicly for the overthrow of King Hussein's Hashemite dynasty. By November 1968 this resulted in violent clashes between the PLO guerillas and the Jordanian Army. Despite an attempt to negotiate a peace and avoid a civil war in Jordan, violations of agreements by the PLO and further attempts by the Jordanian Army to control the guerillas led to furious clashes in Amman (Jordan's capital and largest population center), with a death toll in the hundreds.

An Arab summit conference was set up to help mediate the conflict, and preserved the Hashemite rule while giving greater political power to the PLO. As a result, Palestinians gained substantial influence in Jordan's government, with nine of the 17 ministers being Palestinian (many in support of the guerillas), and numbers of Jordanian youths joined the PLO's guerilla army. When King Hussein agreed to an American proposal to renew an international mediation to make peace with Israel, the PLO, now headed by Yasser Arafat, denounced the move. Then on September 6, 1970, a faction of the PLO (the Popular Front for the Liberation of Palestine) hijacked TWA and KLM airliners, landed them at the Amman airport, and threatened to blow them up if Jordanian troops approached the planes. Ten days later, guerillas attempted to assassinate King Hussein. This brought an imposition of martial law and a full-scale military offensive against PLO groups in Amman and the Palestinian refugee camps. This offensive, called by the Palestinians "Black September," caused some 3,000 Palestinian casualties (according to Red Cross estimates), although Yasser Arafat (whose *Fatah* organization later operated under the name "Black September"), claimed 20,000 were killed.

Fast Fact

Improved Relations

As a result of Israel's willingness to intervene in support of Jordan (although for its own self-interests) during the Jordanian-Palestinian conflict, improved relations existed between the two countries and helped forge a peace treaty in 1994. Except for a small military contingent sent to Syria for border defense during the Yom Kippur War and being allied with Saddam Hussein (who attacked Israel in the Gulf War), Jordan has never since been involved in a military offensive against Israel.

Next, Syrian forces in support of the PLO disguised themselves as Palestinian guerillas and invaded Jordan from the north. The Jordanian Army routed this assault and inflicted heavy losses, although it was the joint threat of Israeli and American intervention that forced the Syrian troops to finally withdraw. Although the PLO continued acts of terrorism against the Jordanian regime, such as assassinating the Jordanian prime minister in Cairo, by the summer of 1971 King Hussein had completely destroyed the PLO power base, restored his sovereignty, and had driven the PLO leadership and thousands of Palestinians into Lebanon.

The Yom Kippur/October War (1973)

While Israelis enjoyed the newfound peace and security brought to them by their victory in 1967, the Arab League continued to plan their revenge. This plan involved at least nine Arab countries and four non-Middle Eastern (but Muslim) nations simultaneously invading Israel with a surprise attack in the same way Israel had preemptively attacked Egypt, Syria, and Jordan on the first day of the Six-Day War. The surprise came at 2:00 P.M. on October 6, 1973, which was Yom Kippur day (the "Day of Atonement"), the holiest day on the Jewish calendar. The attack was totally unexpected because it also came during the Islamic holy month of

Fast Figure

Golda Meir

A Russian Jew who was raised and educated in the United States, Meir was active in Zionist/Israeli politics beginning in the 1930s. She was a signer of the Proclamation of Independence in 1948, was elected to the first Israeli knesset (parliament), and helped serve in various cabinet positions in the Israeli government until 1969, when she became Israel's first female prime minister. Although Israel won the Yom Kippur War of 1973, she shared the blame for not being ready for war and resigned in 1974.

Ramadan, during which Muslims are required to fast. With most of Israel's reservist army at home with their families, Egypt crossed the Suez with 600,000 troops, 2,000 tanks, and 550 warplanes to face a paltry 500 Israeli soldiers with only three tanks. On the Golan Heights, 1,400 Syrian tanks attacked 180 Israeli tanks. This contingent was joined by 18,000 Iraqi troops, 230 Iraqi tanks, and 15 Iraqi aircraft, 80 Jordanian tanks, 150 Algerian tanks, a bomber and armored brigade, 1,500 Moroccan troops, 3,000 Saudi soldiers, 2,000 Tunisian soldiers, 3,500 Sudanese troops, 2,500 Moroccan forces, and technology, men, or armaments from Lebanon, Kuwait, and the PLO—all backed by $3.5 billion in Soviet military aid by air and sea.

The early days of the war proved to be disastrous for Israel. The country's desperate condition is best remembered in a famous exchange between U.S. president Nixon and Israeli prime minister Golda Meir. Nixon delayed sending needed military support because of an Arab oil embargo imposed on the United States (and any other countries allied with Israel) and told Golda Meir to trust international guarantees. To this she replied, "Mr. President, by the time *you* get here, *we* won't be here!"

On October 12, the United States sent $2.2 billion in aid, including vital airlifts of armaments (some 566 flights), and the tide of the war turned in the Israelis' favor. On that same day, to the north, Israeli soldiers had defeated Syrian troops on the Golan and were marching toward Damascus, while in the south, by October 18, Israeli forces had retaken the Suez and were moving toward Cairo. This turn in the war caused the Soviets, who had backed the Arabs, to threaten direct intervention in the fight. This threat was balanced by the United States putting its military on alert. On October 22, the UN Security Council adopted Resolution 338, which called for all parties in the war to cease firing and terminate all military activity, for the situation had the potential of growing into a conventional and nuclear confrontation between the superpowers. U.S. pressure on Israel brought Israeli compliance with the cease-fire and prevented the invasion of Damascus and Cairo. The Soviet troops were never sent, and with this latest cease-fire, the region counted their dead: Israel had lost 2,688 lives, Egypt lost 7,700, and Syria lost 3,500. The Arab world was again humiliated.

Fast Fact

The Oil Embargo

During the Yom Kippur War, the Arab nations found the perfect way to attack Israel in a nonviolent manner—by withholding oil from Israel's allies, particularly the United States. The embargo caused a severe gasoline shortage and raised prices almost 400 percent during the 1970s. The embargo was eventually lifted; however, the effects were felt by the American economy for years to come. The most significant result of the embargo is that it forced the United States to always have to consider its foreign policy in the Middle East so as not to provoke the Arab nations toward future embargoes.

The Lebanese Civil War (1975–76)

After being driven from Jordan in 1970, the PLO moved their base of operations to the south of Lebanon and eventually, along with other Palestinian organizations, usurped control of the country. The introduction of this new element produced a split of Lebanon's political community into a conservative camp (dominated by the Maronite Christian Phalange) and a radical camp (dominated by Sunni-Muslim factions) as well as arousing interreligious and interethnic tensions. Eventually this division led to a cycle of violence that erupted in a civil war on April 13, 1975, provoked by a violent attack by Christian Phalangists on Palestinian terrorists in Beirut. The Muslim-dominated radical camp became allied with the radical PLO Palestinian organizations (including the Palestinian mainstream faction

Fatah) against the Christian Phalangists. The Phalangists adopted a policy of ethnic cleansing and sought to capture Palestinian refugee camps in East Beirut and eliminate or expel their residents.

During the 20 months of fighting, nearby Syria seized the opportunity to invade Lebanon and sent thousands of troops to gain control of much of the country. By the time Syria established its control, Lebanon had been partitioned into three regions with the PLO dominant in the south and West Beirut, the Christian Phalange dominant in the north and East Beirut, and the Syrians dominating the central and northern zones. Despite Christian Phalangist attempts to drive out both the Syrians and the PLO, Lebanon remained a satellite of Syria and the PLO strengthened its militia and hold on the southern border with Israel, thus posing a new terrorist threat to the Jewish state.

Fast Fact

The Phalange

Founded in 1936, the Phalange was the largest Maronite Christian party in Lebanon and was dedicated to preserving the communal structure of the country. It later became a political party representing the Maronite Christians and was the military mainstay of the conservative camp.

The Iran-Iraq War (1980–88)

In recent decades, Iran and Iraq have frequently quarreled over certain border and shipping disputes. Quarreling has always come naturally to

Fast Feature

Silence About Syrian Occupation

Although the Arab world and international community have demanded Israel's withdrawal from territories it won in defensive wars and which is essential for its defense, no similar protest or demand has been made concerning Syria's invasion of Lebanon in 1976 and continued occupation of the country. It is surprising that groups that protest Israeli occupation and call so vehemently for the Palestinians to gain an independence they have never had should be so silent about Syria's occupation of Lebanon and the fact that the Lebanese *lost* their independence (which went back to 1920), and of the PLO's role in causing the loss.

these countries, because while both are religiously Muslim, Iran is comprised of Shiite Muslims and Iraq is made up of Sunni Muslims, and these two sects have been rivals for centuries. Furthermore, at the time the nine-year war began, Iran was controlled by the fundamentalist Muslim cleric Ayatollah Khomeini and Iraq was under the secular dictatorship of Saddam Hussein. Khomeini's goal was to spread the Islamic revolution, which, to him, made it necessary to overthrow Saddam's anti-Islamic regime. However, Saddam also had designs on dominating the region and establishing himself as the leader of the Arab world. His main competition was neighboring Iran.

The Iran-Iraq war began in June 1980 and went through a series of highs and lows for both countries. Iraq invaded Iran in September 1980, but was driven out by June 1982. The two sides targeted each other's oil tankers in

Fast Figure

Ayatollah Khomeini

An Islamic cleric whose extreme interpretation of Islam became popular in Iran in the late 1970s. Though never a political leader, he was the supreme power in Iran from 1979 until his death in 1989. Khomeini was disgusted with the decadence of Western culture and the Islam of the Arab nations. He desired to set up an Islamic republic firmly rooted in fundamentalist Islam. Khomeini did just that throughout the 1980s and became a feared enemy of the Western nations and secular Arab states. Though he did not mastermind the Iranian hostage situation, he did nothing to alleviate it. (See Question 38 for more information.)

the Persian Gulf on and off between 1984 and 1988. By August of 1988, both countries' economies had been crippled and no clear winner was in sight. The advantage, however, went to Saddam Hussein, whose ability to use chemical weapons on a large scale against Iran forced a UN-mediated cease-fire.

All of the Arab states (except Syria and Libya) had supported Iraq in the war against Iran, as did France and the Soviet Union. Israel supported Iran because it saw Iraq as a greater threat and because it needed to maintain good relations in order to immigrate Iranian Jews to Israel. U.S. policy wavered in support of both countries. Khomeini, with his radical Islam, was a greater threat to the region and ultimately to U.S. oil interests and the security of Israel. And Saddam, while less of a threat, was supported by the Soviet Union and posed a greater threat in the future. The United States generally supported Iraq, but in 1985 gave arms to Iran as part of a secret attempt to win the release of American hostages held by terrorists in Lebanon. Ideally, the United States hoped both countries would decimate

Israeli Vulnerability to Air Attacks

Map showing proximity of Israel's enemies to the State with respect to military engagement.

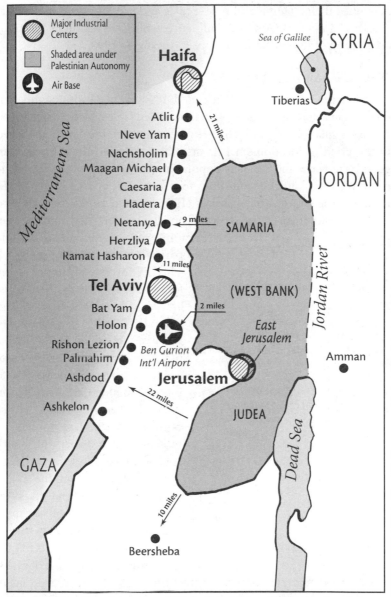

Israeli Vulnerability to Air Attacks

Legend:
- Major Industrial Centers
- Shaded area under Palestinian Autonomy
- Air Base

SYRIA

Sea of Galilee

Haifa

Tiberias

JORDAN

Atlit
Neve Yam
Nachsholim
Maagan Michael
Caesaria
Hadera
Netanya — 9 miles — SAMARIA
Herzliya
Ramat Hasharon — 11 miles

Mediterranean Sea

21 miles

Tel Aviv

(WEST BANK)

Bat Yam
Holon — 2 miles
Rishon Lezion
Palmahim — *Ben Gurion Int'l Airport*
Ashdod
Jerusalem

East Jerusalem

Jordan River

Amman

Ashkelon — 22 miles

JUDEA

GAZA

Dead Sea

10 miles

Beersheba

Close-up map showing vulnerability of major Israeli cities to attack from Palestinian Authority in West Bank and access for other enemy nations.

their military might and drain their economies to the point of becoming lesser threats in the region. After the war, however, Iranian revolutionaries continued their attempts to topple secular and pro-Western Gulf monarchies and undermine American influence, while Iraq rebuilt its forces for an invasion of Kuwait, which took place in August 1990.

The Lebanon War (1982–85)

When the Lebanese Civil War ended, the PLO had captured much of the southern portion of Lebanon that bordered Israel. Some 18,000 Palestinian guerillas (6,000 of which were foreign mercenaries) became lodged in a myriad of locations in Lebanon. Not only did these Palestinian guerillas terrorize the Lebanese population, but because of their strategic position, they launched multiple terrorist attacks against Israel. In response, the Israel Defense Forces (IDF) entered Lebanon in 1978 to drive the Palestinian guerillas away from the border. Afterward the IDF withdrew and allowed UN troops to monitor the border and prevent terrorists from returning to Israel. The UN forces were unsuccessful, for by 1982 more than 270 terrorist attacks in Israel had killed 29 and wounded 300. When a Palestinian terrorist faction led by Abu Nidal made an assassination attempt against the Israeli ambassador to England in June 1982, Ariel Sharon (who had become Israel's defense minister in 1981) responded by moving 80,000 soldiers into south Lebanon to support the Christian Phalangists, root out the Palestinian terrorists, and end attacks on Israel. The Syrians, who occupied and controlled the country, immediately sent reinforcements to help their forces engage the Israelis.

Fast Figure

Hafez al-Assad

After years of coups and overthrows, Syria found itself as a ship without a sail. After Black September, the Syrian minister of defense, Hafez al-Assad, gained the opportunity to seize power. Assad was as ruthless as he was popular—he gained the support of the Syrian people through a variety of popular political moves while destroying any dissension. Assad was firmly against peace with Israel, so instead of following Anwar Sadat's lead, he organized terrorist activities against Israel, particularly after gaining control of Lebanon. Though he passed away in 2000, Assad's legacy continues, with terrorist attacks from Syria showing no signs of ceasing.

However, a stunning air force victory by the Israelis forced Syrian president Hafez al-Assad to withdraw his country's troops and stay out of the battle. The IDF then captured Beirut, accepted a cease-fire, and permitted members of the PLO to retreat from Beirut with their personal weapons. Israel remained in the country to allow the Christian Phalange to regain control of the government and remove Syrian dominance. Despite the cease-fire and initial stabilization (along with a U.S. peace initiative rejected by both sides), the Lebanese president-elect Bashir Germayel was assassinated by terrorists on September 14, 1982. Consequently, the IDF entered West Beirut to deal with the Palestinian terrorists.

During this operation, the Israelis allowed Christian Phalangist militia into the two refugee camps of Sabra and Shatila, where over 200 Palestinian terrorists were believed to be residing.

Fast Fact

The Shatila and Burj-el Barajneh Massacres

Three years after the Sabra and Shatila massacre, in May 1985, the Shatila and Burj-el Barajneh Palestinian refugee camps were attacked by Muslim militia who killed 635 and wounded 2,500. For the next two years, fighting raged between Syrian-backed Shiite Amal militia and the PLO. More than 2,000 casualties resulted from these battles, including the deaths of many civilians. However, unlike the massacre of 1982, from which Israel received international censure, there was no such international outcry against the PLO, the Syrians, or the Muslim militia.

This was done as part of a plan to transfer authority to the Phalange. Once in charge, the Phalangists entered and destroyed the camps, violently avenging past atrocities the PLO had afflicted on Phalangist citizens. When the Phalangists were finally ordered out of the camp, hundreds of men (including Palestinians, Syrians, Lebanese, Iranians, Algerians, and Pakistanis) were found dead (estimates range from 460–800), including 35 women and children. The world was horrified, and although the Phalangists had committed the massacre, the blame was placed on the IDF, and especially on Ariel Sharon and Israel's chief of staff, General Raful Eitan. Nevertheless, the PLO was driven out of Lebanon, with Yasser Arafat and his *Fatah* group moving to Tunis, while other groups fled to Syria and Jordan.

Following this incident, a multinational peacekeeping force (including U.S. Marines) was stationed in Beirut. The IDF began withdrawing, and Lebanese militia re-entered the vacated positions to establish control. The Druze and Muslims in Lebanon soon targeted the Marine detachment guarding the Beirut airport, bringing greater U.S. backing to support their forces. In a successful move to drive the United States from Lebanon, these groups bombed the Marine barracks, killing 241. Not only did the United States withdraw, but in 1985 the Israelis decided to do the same, although

Fast Fact

Who Cares?
When the IDF pulled back, Druze forces moved into Christian villages and massacred 1,000 civilians and drove 50,000 more from their homes. In October 1990, Syrian troops massacred 700 Christian Phalangists to secure their dominance in Lebanon. Unlike the international outcry over the Palestinian refugee crisis, little has been said of these acts or of the Muslim atrocities and persecutions of the Maronite Christian community in Lebanon.

a 1,000-man force remained deployed to aid the Christian South Lebanese Army. In the end, Israel had lost 1,216 soldiers and its economy had been left in shambles. In the years that followed, the Israeli presence in Lebanon continued to be a costly venture. Terrorist organizations such as Hizballah launched Katyusha rocket attacks on northern Israel and a mounting death toll of Israeli soldiers and civilians eventually provoked Israeli prime minister Ehud Barak to withdraw the remaining troops on May 24, 2000. As a result, Hizballah continues, under Syrian and Iranian support, to wage terrorist attacks on Israel.

The Persian Gulf War (1991)

In the Iran-Iraq War, Kuwait supported Saddam Hussein, giving Iraq billions of dollars in loans and grants. Hussein repaid Kuwait by invading the country with 30,000 troops on August 2, 1990, one month after he pledged to Americans and Egyptians that he would not use force against Kuwait. Within one day, Hussein controlled Kuwait and assembled his forces for an invasion of Saudi Arabia. With the capture of Kuwait, Iraq controlled 20 percent of the world's oil reserves. If he had gone on to take the oil fields in the Saudi kingdom, he would have controlled 45 percent, or nearly half the world's oil. Saddam delayed the invasion and the United Nations imposed a trade embargo on Iraq while a U.S. naval blockade stopped shipments of Iraqi oil.

In response to Saddam's attack, a coalition of three dozen nations, including the United States and its allies and Arab and European states, was formed. The Arab/Islamic states in the coalition included Kuwait, Saudi Arabia, the United Arab Emirates, Egypt, Syria, Turkey, Qatar, Oman, Pakistan, Morocco, Bahrain, Afghanistan, Niger, Senegal, and Bangladesh. Because of its large pro-Iraqi Palestinian population and shared border with Iraq, Jordan was the single Arab state to side with Saddam, although Libya also opposed the Arab League resolution calling for Iraq's withdrawal from Kuwait. Throughout the conflict, Yasser Arafat and his PLO also supported Saddam, calling the invasion of Kuwait the first step toward the "liberation of Palestine" and Saddam "the defender of the Arab nation of Muslims...."

When Saddam rejected the coalition's demands and instead announced he was annexing Kuwait, the United States launched Operation Desert Shield, stationing troops in Saudi Arabia to restrain an Iraqi invasion and help defend the Saudis. By October, a sufficient allied force had been massed on the Saudi-Iraqi border to make an offensive. Saddam realized he would need to do something to counter these forces. His plan was to get the Arab states to leave the Western-led coalition and side with him by making an attack on Israel. Because Arab leaders were already sensitive to Western influence and opposed to Israel, a war that included Israel on the side of the West would force the Arab states to shift their allegiance.

On October 8, Saddam saw his opportunity in an Orthodox Jewish group called The Temple Mount Faithful, which had planned to symbolically lay a cornerstone for the Third Temple at the entrance to the Temple Mount. Israeli police had assured Muslim authorities that the group would not be allowed to enter the site, but rumors persisted among the Arabs that the group was coming to pray on the Temple Mount (in violation of Islamic law). On the morning of October 8, during the opening of the Feast of Tabernacles celebrations, when more than 20,000 Jews were assembled at the Western Wall, 3,000 Palestinian Arabs began to pelt the crowd with stones as loudspeakers on the Temple Mount called Muslims to come and kill the Jews who were trying to take their holy places. The Israeli police responded to the riot with tear gas and rubber bullets, eventually resorting to live rounds. When the fighting was over, some 17 Arabs were dead and the United Nations condemned Israel for the incident. Hussein stepped into the fray to call for *jihad* against Israel to help liberate the Palestinians and restore Arab honor, with himself in the lead. As soon as the United States moved against Iraq, Saddam began a bombardment of Tel Aviv with long-range Scud missiles. But for the restraint of Israel, brought in part by the intense pressure and assurances of the United States, Israel would have retaliated against Saddam, the Arab coalition would have split, and the entire region might have become engulfed in the conflict. As it turned out, 39 missiles hit Israel over a period of six weeks, damaging 3,300 apartments and businesses and killing 74 people (although only two died from the missile hits themselves).

During this period, Operation Desert Shield became Operation Desert Storm and 670,000 coalition troops (with 75 percent of the soldiers being from the United States) joined the effort to force Saddam from Kuwait. Beginning on January 17, 1991, Iraq was attacked by F-117 stealth bombers, wiping out Saddam's communication centers, control capabilities, and anti-aircraft batteries. Bombing by B-52s followed as ground troops led by the U.S. Marines advanced on the retreating Iraqi forces. On February 27 the coalition forces liberated Kuwait City, and on the next day, military operations ceased. On April 6, Iraq agreed to a cease-fire and accepted the responsibility of making reparations to Kuwait and destroying its own stockpiles of biological and chemical weapons and its nonconventional weapons production facilities.

Saddam, however, remained in power, the Iraqi army was still strong, and Iraq's nonconventional weapons facilities continued to exist. It was hoped Saddam's defeat would provoke a domestic rebellion to replace Saddam, but when Shiite Muslims in the south and the Kurds in the north attempted to rebel, Saddam ruthlessly slaughtered 5,000 of them with his Republican Guards and chemical weapons, proving it would be only a matter of time before Saddam would again become a threat to the region and the West.

The War on Terror (2001–present)

After the United States experienced a catastrophic terrorist attack on its shores on September 11, 2001, President George Bush, Jr. declared a "War on Terror" against terrorists and terrorist organizations and the states or countries that harbor them. Vice President Dick Cheney stated the U.S. policy with respect to this new war: "We cannot deal with terror. It will not end in a treaty. There will be no peaceful coexistence, no negotiations, no summit, no joint communiqué with the terrorists." The U.S.-led coalition against terror began its war with an attack on the Taliban regime in Afghanistan and the destruction of the al-Qaeda infrastructure, although Osama bin Laden, who had orchestrated the September 11 attack, escaped with some of his top aides. The United States next turned its attention on what it called "the axis of evil" made up of Iraq, Iran, and North Korea, with Iraq as its first target. While the United States focused on Iraq, North Korea revealed its nuclear readiness and has threatened nuclear war if the United States attempts to challenge North Korea's sovereignty. And in January 2003, the United States established the Department of Homeland Security to investigate domestic terrorist activity and safeguard Americans from future terrorist attacks.

Although Israel has declared that it has been fighting a war on terrorism for almost a century, and has labeled Yasser Arafat as a terrorist and his *Fatah* and al-Aqsa Martyr's Brigade as terrorist organizations, it has been unable to get the United States to accept this or to return Yasser Arafat to its official list of terrorists. Indeed, even countries such as Syria, which promotes terror and harbors and abets Hamas and Hizballah (organizations which the United States identifies as terrorist) have not been included. Moreover, the U.S. policy of no peaceful co-existence or negotiations with terrorists is not applied to Israel's dealing with the Palestinian Authority, even though *Fatah* and the Al-Aqsa Martyr's Brigade claim direct responsibility for many of the homicide bombings. This makes the United States guilty of a double standard, particularly because the United States continues to condemn Israel for military responses when its civilians have been attacked. Such condemnation has been referred to as "the moral equivalency doctrine," in which Israel and the Palestinians are supposedly judged equally for their actions and responses. However, we cannot equate morally Israel's measured responses, yet which specifically target terrorists and not civilians, with the Palestinian Authority's deliberate yet indiscriminate suicide attacks against civilians in places such as private homes, synagogues, restaurants, night clubs, and weddings.

War with Iraq (1991–2003)

After the Persian Gulf War, the United Nations established "no-fly" zones over the northern and southern portions of Iraq to prevent Iraqi planes from making attacks on Iraqi Kurds to the north and Iraq's Shi'a population to the south. Iraq has frequently violated the "no-fly" zone regulations, resulting in numerous confrontations between Iraqi and Allied forces. Other incidences have also occurred. In 1993, Saddam moved missiles into southern Iraq and the United States attacked the missile sites and a nuclear facility in Baghdad. In the same year, then-president Bill Clinton sent a cruise missile against Saddam's intelligence headquarters in retribution for an assassination attempt on former president George Bush, Sr. In 1997 Saddam expelled the United Nations Special Commission (UNSCOM), which had been appointed to inspect his weapons stockpiles and remnants of his nuclear program. In

December 1998, the United States and Britain launched Operation Desert Fox, a three-day air raid to destroy Iraqi weapons facilities and the Republican Guard. However, the raid failed to reach its objective.

In 2002, UN inspectors were allowed to return to Iraq, but with access restricted from places where weapons were believed to be hidden. Israeli intelligence announced that it had evidence that Iraq had hidden prohibited weapons in Syria, which, in turn, had been smuggling banned Iraqi oil to the Mediterranean.[7]

By early 2003, the United States and Great Britain had deployed their forces in the Persian Gulf and were waiting for "marching orders" to topple Saddam's regime and restore freedom to Iraqi society. At the same time, Palestinians demonstrated in Gaza and the West Bank in favor of Saddam, shouting, "Beloved Saddam, strike Tel Aviv!" In concert, Yasser Arafat had stated in 1997 that "a Palestinian victory over Israel and Iraqi victory over the U.S. are mutually dependent."[8] The Palestinian Authority hoped that an Iraqi victory would result in the United States pulling out of the Middle East and leaving Israel without its support. Israel's military, on the other hand, led by a re-elected Ariel Sharon, hoped that a U.S. strike and expected Iraqi attack on Israel would allow Sharon to exile Arafat and begin a final offensive against Palestinian terrorism in Israel— and Lebanon and Syria as well (see Section IX).

On March 19, 2003, the United States and United Kingdom, leading a coalition of some 45 nations, initiated "Operation Iraqi Freedom," and coalition forces based in Kuwait began the drive toward Baghdad. By May 1, U.S. president George Bush declared an official end to major engagement in Iraq, although alliance forces continued to face pockets of resistance and ambushes for many months afterward. Principal figures in the Iraqi regime were captured, but the location of certain other figures (believed to still be in the country) eluded troops. Difficulty, too, was faced in setting up a provisional government elected by the people. Since people had no experience with democracy, a city-by-city education was necessary to prevent them from re-electing a dictatorship or an Islamic theocracy. With Saddam and his threat to Israel removed, the stage was set for the next "battle" in the Middle East—that of renewing the negotiations between the Israelis and the Palestinians through a two-state proposal called "The Road Map to Peace."

THE BATTLE FOR JERUSALEM

Fast Focus

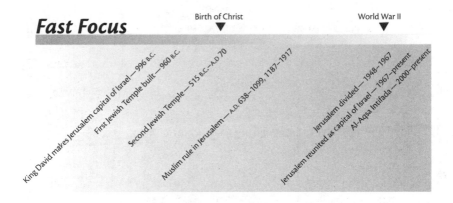

Birth of Christ ▼

World War II ▼

King David makes Jerusalem capital of Israel—996 B.C.

First Jewish Temple built—960 B.C.

Second Jewish Temple—515 B.C.–A.D. 70

Muslim rule in Jerusalem—A.D. 638–1099, 1187–1917

Jerusalem divided—1948–1967

Jerusalem reunited as capital of Israel—1967–present

Al-Aqsa Intifada—2000–present

24

WHAT IS THE SIGNIFICANCE OF JERUSALEM TO THE JEWS?

Jerusalem has been revered for 3,000 years by the Jewish people as a holy city above all other cities on earth. The Jewish Babylonian Talmud boasts that "of the ten measures of beauty that came down to the world, Jerusalem took nine" (*Kidushin* 49b), and that "whoever has not seen Jerusalem in its splendor has never seen a beautiful city" (*Succah* 51b). To Jews, Jerusalem is the apple of God's eye (Zechariah 2:8), the place above all others chosen for His habitation (Psalm 132:13-14). It is the Throne of the Lord (Jeremiah 3:17), the mountain of the house of the Lord (Isaiah 2:2), the Holy Mountain, the City of Truth (Zechariah 8:3)—Zion, the eternal and indivisible capital of the nation of Israel. Those born in Jerusalem are said to be counted by God with a special distinction (Psalm 87:5-6).

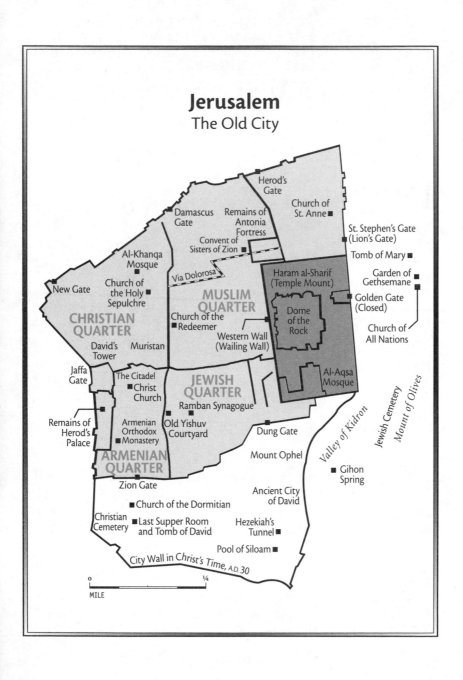

Jerusalem
The Old City

Herod's Gate

Church of St. Anne

Damascus Gate

Remains of Antonia Fortress

Convent of Sisters of Zion

St. Stephen's Gate (Lion's Gate)

Tomb of Mary

Al-Khanqa Mosque

New Gate

Church of the Holy Sepulchre

Via Dolorosa

Haram al-Sharif (Temple Mount)

Garden of Gethsemane

Golden Gate (Closed)

MUSLIM QUARTER

CHRISTIAN QUARTER

Church of the Redeemer

Dome of the Rock

Church of All Nations

Western Wall (Wailing Wall)

David's Tower

Muristan

Jaffa Gate

The Citadel
Christ Church

JEWISH QUARTER

Al-Aqsa Mosque

Ramban Synagogue

Remains of Herod's Palace

Armenian Orthodox Monastery

Old Yishuv Courtyard

Dung Gate

Valley of Kidron

Jewish Cemetery

Mount of Olives

ARMENIAN QUARTER

Mount Ophel

Gihon Spring

Zion Gate

Church of the Dormitian

Ancient City of David

Christian Cemetery

Last Supper Room and Tomb of David

Hezekiah's Tunnel

Pool of Siloam

City Wall in Christ's Time, A.D. 30

0   ¼

MILE

Jerusalem is even said to have a central geographical position assigned by God Himself: "This is Jerusalem; I have set her at the center of the nations, with lands around her" (Ezekiel 5:5). The Babylonian Talmud declared that Jerusalem's centrality extended beyond its Middle Eastern location to all of the world: "Israel lies at the center of the earth, and Jerusalem lies at the center of the Land of Israel" (*Tanhuma* 106). This belief was embellished on the maps of medieval cartographers, where Jerusalem itself appears as the hub from which all the other continents proceed like spokes on a wheel. It was to Jerusalem and Mount Moriah that Abraham, the father of the Jewish people, came bearing his son as an intended offering (Genesis 22:2-14). It was to Jerusalem that King David brought the Ark of the Covenant (2 Samuel 6:12-17), and where David's son Solomon built the First Temple, to which the presence of God descended (1 Kings 8:10-13).

Fast Quote

Zion

"The Land of Israel without Jerusalem is merely Palestine. Down through the generations the Jews have been saying not 'Next year in the Land of Israel' but 'Next year in Jerusalem.'...One can create Tel Aviv out of Jaffa but one cannot create a second Jerusalem. Zion lies within the walls, not outside them."

Menachem Mendel Ussishkin (1947)

It will be to Jerusalem that the Messiah will one day come to wage war against all the nations (Zechariah 14:2-4). When He comes, He will rule from Zion (Psalm 109:2) and establish the city as the rallying point for the worship of the world (Isaiah 2:2-3). Only in Jerusalem can the Jewish mandate to be a "light of the nations" (Isaiah 49:6) be fulfilled. Thus, a Jewish midrash states: "Jerusalem is destined to become a beacon lighting the way for the nations" (*Yalkut Shimoni*, midrash on Isaiah 49:9).

The Jewish Bible proclaimed at the time of the dedication of the First Temple in Jerusalem, "Now My eyes will be open and My ears attentive to the prayer offered in this place. For now I have chosen this house that My name may be there forever, and My eyes and My heart will be there perpetually" (2 Chronicles 7:15-16; see also 1 Kings 8:29). Based on this passage, religious Jews, wherever they may be on earth, pray three times a day facing in the direction of Jerusalem. In like manner, the psalmist records the vow made by the Jews who were exiled from the city when taken into captivity: "If I forget you, O Jerusalem, may my right hand forget her skill. May my tongue cleave to the roof of my mouth, if I do not remember you, if I do not exalt Jerusalem above my chief joy" (Psalm 137:5-6). The Jewish people have retained this affection for Jerusalem for the past two millennia.

The unification of Jerusalem by Jews in 1967 has been viewed by Jews around the world as the fulfillment of God's ancient promises to the fathers. Prime Minister Ariel Sharon expressed this when he opened an address to members of the U.S. Congress, saying, "I bring you greetings from Jerusalem, the eternal capital of the Jewish people for the past 3,000 years and of the State of Israel for the past 52 years and forever. Jerusalem belongs to all the Jewish people—we in Israel are only custodians of the city....Jerusalem will remain united under the sovereignty of Israel forever!"[1] For the Jew, situated again in the place where his final destiny will be fulfilled, only a Jewish Jerusalem

Fast Quote

United Jerusalem

"Now we are in Jerusalem, never to be divided, never to be split again, never to pull out from the most ancient and sacred place in Jewish history. Jerusalem is a commitment to our history. Jerusalem is also a commitment to our future."

Ehud Olmert,
Mayor of Jerusalem

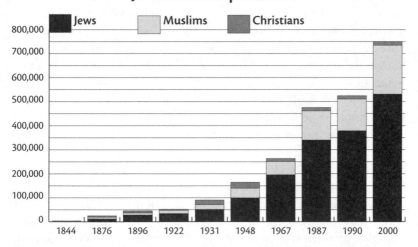

Jerusalem's Population

■ Jews   ☐ Muslims   ■ Christians

Years: 1844, 1876, 1896, 1922, 1931, 1948, 1967, 1987, 1990, 2000

A Jewish Majority in Jerusalem

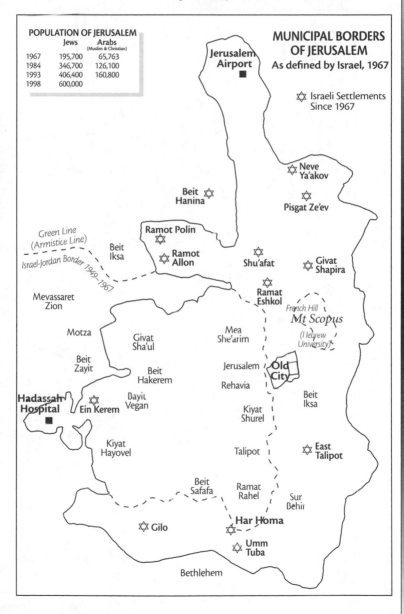

POPULATION OF JERUSALEM		
	Jews	Arabs
		(Muslim & Christian)
1967	195,700	65,763
1984	346,700	126,100
1993	406,400	160,800
1998	600,000	

MUNICIPAL BORDERS OF JERUSALEM
As defined by Israel, 1967

✡ Israeli Settlements Since 1967

Jerusalem Airport ■

Neve Ya'akov ✡

Beit Hanina ✡

Pisgat Ze'ev ✡

Green Line (Armistice Line)

Israel-Jordan Border 1949–1967

Ramot Polin ✡

Beit Iksa

Ramot Allon ✡

Shu'afat ✡

Givat Shapira ✡

Mevassaret Zion

Ramat Eshkol ✡

French Hill

Mt Scopus (Hebrew University)

Motza

Givat Sha'ul

Mea She'arim

Beit Zayit

Beit Hakerem

Jerusalem

Old City

Hadassah Hospital ■

Ein Kerem ✡

Dayit Vegan

Rehavia

Beit Iksa

Kiyat Shurel

Kiyat Hayovel

Talipot

East Talipot ✡

Beit Safafa

Ramat Rahel

Sur Behir

Gilo ✡

Har Homa ✡

Umm Tuba ✡

Bethlehem

Jewish Jerusalem (Since 1967)

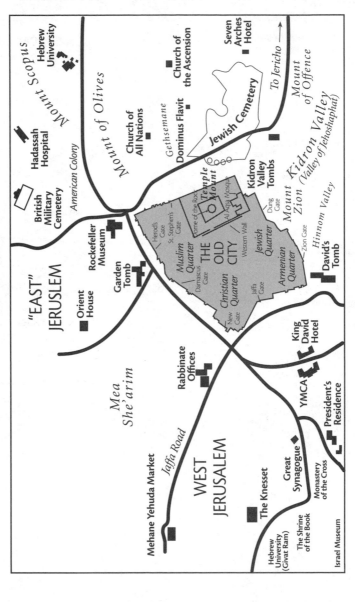

"EAST" JERUSLEM

WEST JERUSALEM

THE OLD CITY

Muslim Quarter

Christian Quarter

Jewish Quarter

Armenian Quarter

Temple Mount

Dome of the Rock

Al Aqsa Mosque

Western Wall

Herods Gate

St. Stephen's Gate

Damascus Gate

Jaffa Gate

New Gate

Zion Gate

Dung Gate

Mount of Olives

Mount Scopus

Hebrew University

Hadassah Hospital

British Military Cemetery

American Colony

Rockefeller Museum

Garden Tomb

Orient House

Church of All Nations

Church of the Ascension

Seven Arches Hotel

Gethsemane

Dominus Flavit

Jewish Cemetery

To Jericho →

Kidron Valley (Valley of Jehoshaphat)

Mount of Offence

Kidron Valley Tombs

Mount Zion

Hinnom Valley

David's Tomb

King David Hotel

YMCA

President's Residence

Rabbinate Offices

Mea She'arim

Jaffa Road

Mehane Yehuda Market

The Knesset

Great Synagogue

Monastery of the Cross

Hebrew University (Givat Ram)

The Shrine of the Book

Israel Museum

holds the promised prospect for peace. In keeping with this belief there is inscribed around the city the verse from the Psalms that reads, "Pray for the peace of Jerusalem" (Psalm 122:6).

25

What is the Significance of Jerusalem to the Arabs?

Jerusalem's primary importance to Arabs is rooted in the Qur'anic account of the Night Journey of Islam's founder Muhammad. According to the first verse of *Sura* 17 in the Qur'an, Muhammad was sleeping near the Ka'aba stone in Mecca when the angel Gabriel brought to him a winged horse with a human head, named *al-Buraq* ("the bright one"). This creature carried him from *al-Masjid al-Haram* (the mosque in Mecca) to *al-Masjid al-Aqsa* ("the Outer" or "Farther Mosque"), and from there to heaven ("Ascent to Paradise"). Though many have interpreted this as a dream, the official position in Islam is that it was a literal journey taken while the Prophet was awake. In like manner, while the "Farther Mosque" has been interpreted to be heaven or the mosque in Medina, the traditional interpretation places it in Jerusalem. Apart from this contested reference, Jerusalem is not mentioned by name in the Qur'an. Jerusalem is regarded as Islam's third-holiest shrine, but some Arab states, such as Iraq, Iran, Turkey, and Syria, also claim to have Islam's third-holiest shrine on their soil.[2] Despite these contested claims, all Muslims regard Jerusalem as *al-Quds* ("the Holy"), which cannot be ruled by non-Muslims. Any such allowance would amount to a betrayal of Islam.

Fast Quote

Arab View of Jerusalem
"Anyone who relinquishes a single inch of Jerusalem is neither an Arab nor a Muslim."
Yasser Arafat

Historically, in political terms, Arabs have not demonstrated their reverence for Jerusalem. Under Muslim rule, Jerusalem was never made a political capital of a state or even a province. The Umayyad caliph Suleiman (A.D. 715–717) ordered that Damascus remain the capital of his empire and built Ramla as the administrative center of the district to which Jerusalem belonged. When Jerusalem was under Jordanian rule (1949–1967), the city was neglected and purposefully left impoverished. The then-governor of Jerusalem, Abdullah al-Tall, stated that Jordan's

King Abdullah was deliberately downgrading Jerusalem. Jordan's main government offices were placed in Amman as was the Religious Court of Appeals, and even the Supreme Muslim Council was abolished. Jordan's attitude toward Jerusalem during this time was reflected in the complaint by the Jerusalem-based British counsel to its foreign office in London: "…we are not prepared to allow them to treat the Old City of Jerusalem as though it were nothing more than a provincial townlet in Jordan, without history or importance."[3] Likewise, Palestinians in East Jerusalem whined, "Look at the palaces, which are being built in Amman and not in Jerusalem, erected after 1948 on Palestinian shoulders. They [should have been] built in Jerusalem but were removed from there so it would stay like a village!"[4]

In recent years, Palestinian Arabs have made the battle for Jerusalem the most important issue in their conflict with Israel. Having gained dominance over the Muslim holy places in eastern Jerusalem, the Palestinian Authority demands the city be recognized as the capital of their expected Palestinian state. The Al-Aqsa Intifada, which began September 2000, seeks to provoke international intervention to force Israel to withdraw from East Jerusalem in compliance with UN Resolution 242. For this reason, the Palestinian Authority has focused its terrorist efforts on Jerusalem. In 2002, when Yasser Arafat was under siege by the Israeli army in Ramallah, he called for a million martyrs to march to Jerusalem and exhibit resistance to Israel. Just as riots and acts of terrorism in Jerusalem in the past forced the British to restrict Israel by issuing the White Papers, so the Palestinians today have forced the European Union and the United States, through Saudi and Jordanian pressure, to press Israel toward a resolution on Jerusalem with the Palestinians.

Fast Quote

War for Jerusalem

"We are announcing a war against the sons of apes and pigs [the Jews] which will not end until the flag of Islam is raised in Jerusalem."

Hamas leaflet (September 1, 1993)

26

WHAT IS THE CONFLICT OVER THE TEMPLE MOUNT?

The Jewish Temple Mount or Arab *Haram* has become the centerpiece of the political conflict over Jerusalem. It is a holy site over which is threatened a holy war. At the Camp David II Summit, the decisions regarding Jerusalem's holy sites were key in determining the outcome of the negotiations. Yasser Arafat rejected any compromise with the Israelis that recognized, even symbolically, the Jewish Temple Mount. This impasse led to the failure of Camp David II and led to the second Palestinian Intifada, which blamed both the inability to resolve the status of Jerusalem and the Israeli violation of Islamic sanctity on the *Harem* for the renewal of the conflict. In this light, Islamic clerics and spokesmen for the Palestinian Authority have repeatedly asserted that the Israeli government's ambition has always been to destroy the Muslim mosques and rebuild the Temple.

Fast Quote

No Temple Mount!

"Jerusalem is not a Jewish city, despite the biblical myth implanted in some minds....There is no tangible evidence of Jewish existence from the so-called 'Temple Mount Era.'... The location of the Temple Mount is in question...it might be in Jericho or somewhere else."

Walid Awad, Palestinian Authority Ministry of Information official

However, since 1967, the Israeli government has actually *defended* Muslim religious laws at their holy places, which forbids Jewish access for religious purposes (such as prayer) at the site.

Maintaining this status quo has been such an imperative for the Israelis that they have regularly closed the Temple Mount to Jews and banned and arrested Jewish Temple activists. Despite these facts, Adnan Husseni, the director of the Islamic Waqf, which has jurisdiction over the Islamic holy places on the Temple Mount, believes so-called "Jewish extremist groups"—such as the Temple Mount Faithful—are agents of the Israeli government: "We see no difference between these...groups and the government. We consider the government and these...groups as one body. The government leaves these persons working....What the Jews want there is a pure Jewish country. If they want to fight us, they will have to fight Islam....They [the Temple Mount Faithful] want to convert the *Haram* into another place. The stone [cornerstone] symbolizes that they have started to build the Third Temple."[5] Likewise, Yasser Arafat's top aide, Nabil Abu Rudeina, said the Israeli government bore full responsibility for the "provocations of radical Jews." "They are playing with fire and will only plunge the region into a religious war. It is a pure provocation and a blatant challenge to Arabs, the Muslim world and the international community."[6]

The Temple Mount Today
(showing Muslim mosque construction)

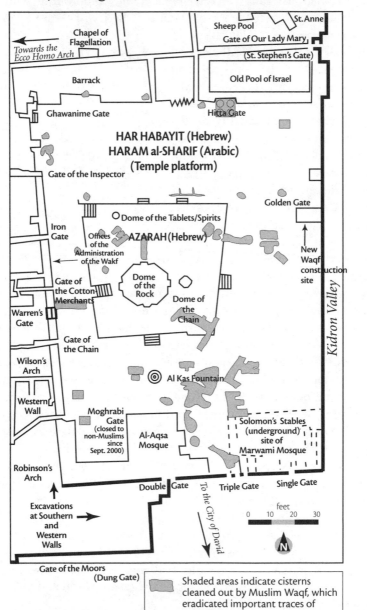

Towards the Ecco Homo Arch

Chapel of Flagellation

Sheep Pool — St. Anne

Gate of Our Lady Mary

(St. Stephen's Gate)

Barrack

Old Pool of Israel

Ghawanime Gate

Hitta Gate

HAR HABAYIT (Hebrew)
HARAM al-SHARIF (Arabic)
(Temple platform)

Gate of the Inspector

Golden Gate

Iron Gate

Dome of the Tablets/Spirits

AZARAH (Hebrew)

Offices of the Administration of the Wakf

New Waqf construction site

Gate of the Cotton Merchants

Dome of the Rock

Dome of the Chain

Warren's Gate

Gate of the Chain

Wilson's Arch

Al Kas Fountain

Western Wall

Moghrabi Gate (closed to non-Muslims since Sept. 2000)

Al-Aqsa Mosque

Solomon's Stables (underground) site of Marwami Mosque

Robinson's Arch

Double Gate

Triple Gate

Single Gate

Excavations at Southern and Western Walls

To the City of David

Kidron Valley

feet
0   10   20   30

N

Gate of the Moors
(Dung Gate)

Shaded areas indicate cisterns cleaned out by Muslim Waqf, which eradicated important traces of Jewish history.

Adding to the incitement of Palestinians on this issue has been a revisionist history of Jerusalem and the Temple Mount created by the Palestinian mufti and the Ministry of Information. This revisionist history asserts there is no evidence of a Jewish history in Jerusalem and that no Jewish Temple ever existed in the city. This revisionist history fills the textbooks used in Palestinian schools and broadcasts on Palestinian television and radio.

After the riots on the Temple Mount in connection with the beginning of the Al-Aqsa Intifada, the Islamic Waqf banned all Jews (including the Israeli police who enforced Muslim rights at the site) from the site. This, in turn, resulted in a complete closure of the Temple Mount to all non-Muslims, since the Israelis could no longer ensure the protection of visitors. In addition, from 1996 onward, the Islamic Waqf has been transforming the *Haram*, destroying ancient Jewish structures related to the Temple and building new mosques and related buildings at the site. This is believed to be part of a master plan by Yasser Arafat to eradicate any trace of Jewish history at the site and convert the whole of the *Haram* into a mosque complex rivaling those in Saudi Arabia. Since Ariel Sharon's re-election in January 2003, in which Israeli security was the major issue, Sharon has pledged to defend Jerusalem and re-open the Temple Mount as a demonstration of Israeli sovereignty. According to the Palestinian Authority and the Palestinian mufti Ikrima Sabri, this will be a provocation that will lead to a war with 1.3 billion Muslims worldwide.

In 2002, a bulge appeared in the southern wall of the Temple

Fast Quote

No Jewish Jerusalem!

"No stone of the Western Wall has any connection to Hebrew history.... There is not the smallest indication of the existence of a Jewish temple on this place in the past. In the whole city, there is not even a single stone indicating Jewish history.... The Temple Mount was never there.... There is not one bit of proof to establish that. We do not recognize that the Jews have any right to the wall or to one inch of the sanctuary.... Jews are greedy to control our mosque.... If they ever try to, it will be the end of Israel."

Ikrima Sabri,
Palestinian mufti of Jerusalem

Fast Figure

Ikrima Sabri

Appointed to be the mufti of Jerusalem by Yasser Arafat in the mid-1990s, Ikrima Sabri is a belligerent Islamic cleric who opposes a Jewish state on Islamic grounds. His primary rhetoric and preaching involves the renunciation of any Jewish claim to Jerusalem and the Temple Mount.

Mount that increased in size over the next year. Israeli archaeologists have determined that the bulge was caused by the Waqf's construction of the underground mosque adjacent to the inside of the wall and have warned that the wall's collapse is imminent. Waqf officials made a vain attempt to repair the damage yet forbade Israeli experts from assisting. Should the wall collapse, undoubtedly the Palestinian Authority will blame the collapse on Israel and proclaim to the Arab world that it was due to Jewish efforts to destroy Islamic holy sites and rebuild the Temple. Realizing that such a disaster could provoke an all-out war in the region, international journalists have dubbed the structure the "Armageddon Wall."

27

WHY HAS JERUSALEM BECOME THE GREATEST OBSTACLE TO PEACE?

A joint Israeli-Palestinian declaration proposed on July 25, 2001 stated in part, "The way forward lies in international legitimacy and the implementation of UNSCR 242 and 338 leading to a two-state solution based on the 1967 borders, Israel and Palestine living side-by-side, with their respective capitals in Jerusalem." However, neither Resolutions 242 nor 338 mention Jerusalem. This was not an oversight on the part of those who drafted the resolutions, since Jerusalem was at the center of dispute. As U.S. ambassador Arthur Goldberg, who helped draft Resolution 242, stated, it "in no way refers to Jerusalem, and this omission was deliberate....Jerusalem was a discrete matter, not linked to the West Bank."[7]

Despite this understanding, the way toward peace has not moved forward, but violently backward. Jerusalem has been the single greatest obstacle to the Israeli-Palestinian peace process, just as it was in the past to plans for a Jewish-Arab partition. The difficulty of resolving the stalemate can be seen in the hard-line positions maintained by both sides. Yasser Arafat

Fast Quote

Islamic Jerusalem

"Jerusalem is the property of the Muslim nation....Nobody can ever decide the fate of Jerusalem. We shall re-take it with the help of Allah out of the hands of those of whom the Qur'an said: 'It was written of them that they shall be demeaned and made wretched.'...We are getting ready for them, O brethren!"

Former Egyptian president Anwar Sadat

declared, "Whoever does not accept the fact that Jerusalem will be the capital of a Palestinian state, and *only* that state, can go drink from the Dead Sea."[8] Likewise, Muhammad Hussein, sheikh of the Al-Aqsa Mosque, warned in his broadcast on the official Palestinian Authority radio station Voice of Palestine: "Whomever has occupied part of Palestine or Jerusalem faces *jihad* [holy war] until Judgment Day!"[9] Responding to such statements, Israeli prime minister Binyamin Netanyahu swore, "I will never allow Jerusalem to be divided again. Never! Never! We will keep Jerusalem united and…we will never surrender those ramparts."[10] Because these opposing and intransigent positions cannot be resolved through negotiation, Jerusalem will remain the greatest obstacle to peace so long as the demand to redivide the city continues.

Fast Feature

Arab Politics and the Sanctity of Jerusalem

The Muslim scholar Aref el Aref has stated that the only text needed for a study of the history and present structures of the Temple Mount are the [Muslim] buildings themselves and the Arab inscriptions that both adorn and explain them. However, Jewish historian Shelomo Dov Goitein notes that "most of the traditions about Jerusalem and its sanctuary were local and largely of foreign origin and had no foundation in old Muhammedian stock."[11] Indeed, Professor M.J. Kister demonstrated in 1969 that the tradition whereby Jerusalem has been fixed as the third holiest city by Islam is a later development of an original tradition that spoke of Mecca as the only holy Islamic sanctuary. In fact, for four centuries most Islamic scholars doubted the degree of sanctity attached to Jerusalem as evidenced by the noted Arab geographer Yakkut, who wrote in 1225 that Jerusalem was "holy to Jews and Christians," whereas Mecca was sacred to Muslims. One explanation for the accrued sanctity of Jerusalem to Muslims has been the influence of Arab politics. Some scholars contend that Abd al-Malik, the first caliph after the Muslim conquest of A.D. 638, boosted the sanctity of Jerusalem in order to compete with Damascus, the new and expanding capital of the Islamic empire, as well as with a rival caliph in Mecca, ibn Zubayr. According to the ninth-century historian Ya'qubi, Abd al-Malik built the Dome of the Rock to attempt to divert the crowds of Muslims making the Hajj—the Muslim pilgrimage to Mecca—to Jerusalem.[12]

Continued on page 128

Fast Feature

Continued from page 127

Other scholars maintain that the true motive was religious competition with the pre-existing Jewish traditions and Christian churches that adorned the city. Miriam Ayalon, professor of Islamic Art and Archaeology at the Hebrew University, has stated, "The first and foremost of these considerations is undoubtedly the religious associations of ideas and events with the city prevailing among both Jews and Christians. Indeed, the fact that Jerusalem was already important to the two monotheistic faiths from earlier times, and the fact that Islam considered itself as the last of the revelations...made it legitimate for Islam to absorb and identify with former beliefs obtaining there. Jerusalem could not be ignored.... Moreover, the very fact that some of the preexisting Byzantine buildings remained in Jerusalem and could provoke admiration, or eventually jealousy, required a Muslim response."[13]

The tenth-century historian of Jerusalem, al-Muqaddasi, appears to confirm this assessment: "Caliph 'Abd al-Malik, noting the greatness of the Dome of the Holy Sepulchre and its magnificence, was moved lest it should dazzle the minds of Muslims and so erected the Rock, the Dome....During the building of it they had for a rival and as a comparison the great Church of the Holy Sepulchre...and they built this to be even more magnificent than the other."[14] This act of supercessionism (or theological replacement) explains why the Dome of the Rock was erected 60 years after the Muslim conquest of Jerusalem. Islam lacked an established culture and monumental architecture to rival that of centuries-old Byzantine Christianity. This was especially true in Jerusalem, where from the time of Constantine magnificent churches, basilicas, and monasteries had been erected to the glory of Christ.

In the 1920s, Jerusalem Mufti Haj Amin el-Husseini used Jerusalem and the holy places to provoke riots and foster Arab nationalism. After 1948, and especially after 1967, supercessionism again became an important political tool. From 1948 to 1967 Jordan controlled the eastern area of the city. It destroyed everything Jewish in the Jewish Quarter and exercised exclusive control over Jewish holy places such as the Wailing Wall. Since 1967, Arab political demands have increasingly denied all historical Jewish claims to the city and denied the past existence of a Jewish Temple.

THE PURSUIT FOR PEACE
IN THE MODERN MIDDLE EAST

Fast Focus

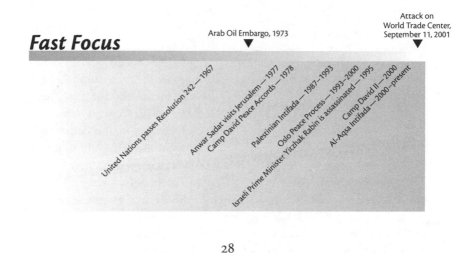

Arab Oil Embargo, 1973 ▼

Attack on
World Trade Center,
September 11, 2001 ▼

United Nations passes Resolution 242 — 1967

Anwar Sadat visits Jerusalem — 1977
Camp David Peace Accords — 1978

Palestinian Intifada — 1987–1993
Oslo Peace Process — 1993–2000
Israeli Prime Minister Yizzhak Rabin is assassinated — 1995
Camp David II — 2000
Al-Aqsa Intifada — 2000–present

28

WHAT WAS THE SIGNIFICANCE
OF THE CAMP DAVID PEACE ACCORDS?

After several wars in which Egypt lost most of its air force, a large portion of its army, and its status in the Arab world, an Egyptian leader agreed to make peace with Israel (which, after each war, had offered peace negotiations to Egypt). The event occurred on September 17, 1979 at Camp David between Egyptian president Anwar Sadat and Israeli prime minister Menachem Begin as the result of the peace initiative and direct moderation of U.S. president Jimmy Carter. The Israel-Egypt Peace Treaty itself was signed on the White House lawn on March 26, 1979.

Prior to this, Begin and his defense minister, Moshe Dayan, had sought to make a deal with Egypt by exchanging land for peace. Israel had captured the vast Sinai desert in 1967 and had continued to hold it as a

Fast Figure

Anwar Sadat

Shortly after Black September in 1970, Egyptian president Nasser died of a heart attack. He was replaced by his vice president, Anwar Sadat. Sadat did away with Nasser's Pan-Arab vision and keyed in on restoring Egyptian pride lost during the Six-Day War. After the Yom Kippur War, Sadat felt that some of that lost honor had been restored and was therefore more open to making peace with Israel. He did just that at Camp David in 1979. However, he was assassinated in 1981 by Islamic radicals. He is seen throughout the Western world as a peacemaker, but in the Arab world, he is considered little more than a traitor.

vital defensive buffer and as the largest source of oil for Israel, supplying half the country's energy needs. However, for the prospect of peace, Israel was willing to trade part of the Sinai, but retain control of Israel's settlements and military bases in the area. Sadat, in response, on November 19, 1977, made a historic trip to Jerusalem to address the Israeli Knesset. Despite the psychological breakthrough that was accomplished by the fact Sadat was the first Arab leader to talk peace with Israel—in its own capital—Sadat's insistence on a total withdrawal of Israel from all territory captured in the Six-Day War remained unchanged.

The next month, Begin went to Egypt to meet with Sadat and work out an agreement, but with no success. At this point Carter entered the picture, forming a friendship with Sadat and supporting the Egyptian position of total withdrawal from the "occupied territories" (although allowing for security concerns). Carter believed that Israel's settlement policy was an obstacle to the peace process, and in an attempt to compromise, Israel agreed to freeze settlement expansion. This did not appease either Carter or Sadat, who continued to press for total withdrawal as well as Palestinian self-determination in the Gaza Strip and West Bank.

In the end, Sadat agreed to limit the territorial concessions to the Sinai, and Begin agreed to withdraw the Israeli presence from all of the Sinai including the settlements, military bases, and oil fields. Begin also had to agree to recognize the rights of the Palestinians, with Sadat as their representative in consultation with Jordan and Palestinian representatives. This agreement resulted in the Camp David Accords, which stated that Israel would withdraw from the Sinai (within three years) in exchange for normalized relations with Egypt and, within a five-year transition period, the Palestinians in the Gaza Strip and West Bank would be given autonomy and discussions would begin to determine

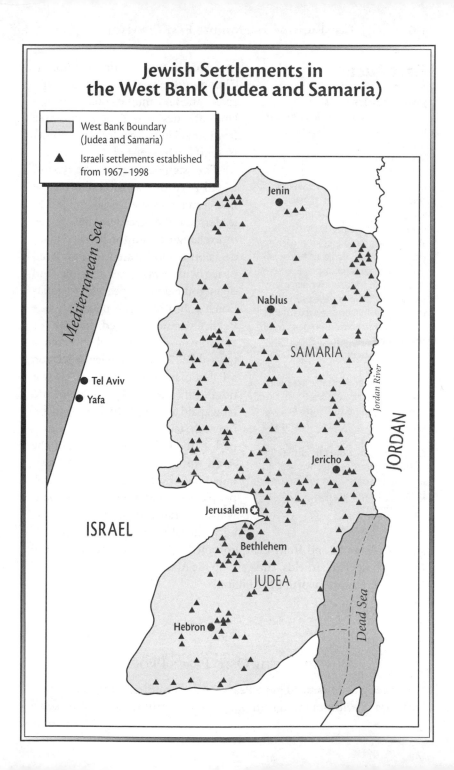

Jewish Settlements in the West Bank (Judea and Samaria)

West Bank Boundary
(Judea and Samaria)

▲ Israeli settlements established
from 1967–1998

Mediterranean Sea

Jenin

Nablus

SAMARIA

Tel Aviv

Yafa

Jordan River

JORDAN

Jericho

Jerusalem

ISRAEL

Bethlehem

JUDEA

Hebron

Dead Sea

Fast Fact

Jewish Settlements

One of the most politically sensitive issues in the Middle East today is that of the Jewish settlements in the West Bank and Gaza Strip. These settlements are not like the original kibbutzim of the early twentieth century; they are modern neighborhoods with all the amenities of any other modern suburb or city. But should they be there? Considering that the West Bank is historical Judea and Samaria, a place where Jews have lived for millennia, many would say that Jews have every right to be there. In fact, the settlements comprise only about two percent of the West Bank and are primarily suburbs of places such as Jerusalem and Hebron. Others claim the settlements are an obstacle to peace and that the more isolated settlements should be disbanded. However, without a peace arrangement from the Palestinians, the Israelis refuse to change the current status of the settlements. This will remain an issue of contention for the time being, but compromise is foreseeable in the future.

the final status of the territories. Clinching the deal was $5 billion in economic and military aid from the United States as well as a guarantee from the United States to support Israel if Egypt violated the treaty.

The significance of the Camp David Accords was the milestone of first contact between Arab and Israeli leaders and the precedent that was set of exchanging land for peace. Sadat's decision demonstrated that an Arab peace with Israel was possible and opened the door to peaceful negotiations with other Arab nations, while Begin's decision opened the way for Palestinian autonomy and set a course toward Palestinian independence and a Palestinian state (although this was not Begin's intention). Both Egypt and Israel paid a price for their agreement; the Arab states ostracized Egypt, which had formerly been the leader of the Arab world, and Sadat was assassinated in Cairo for betraying the Arab people. Israel lost 1,000 miles of roadways, factories, hotels, health spas, and agricultural villages, relinquished its shipping lanes to and from Eilat, uprooted 7,000 settlers, relocated 170 military bases and airfields, and gave up the Alma oil field, with estimated untapped resources worth $100 billion.

29

WHAT WAS THE OSLO PEACE PROCESS?

Although the Israel-Egypt Peace Treaty eventually proved to be a "cold peace" without the agreed normalized relations, it was still a peace.

Despite the plan for Palestinian autonomy brokered by Sadat, the PLO, which had designated itself the only legitimate representatives of the Palestinian people, felt left out of the action. At that time the PLO, under Yasser Arafat, had been operating as a terrorist organization out of Jordan, Syria, Lebanon, and Tunisia, and wanted to regain recognition and control. To this end Yasser Arafat began a violent uprising (Intifada) in 1987 in the Gaza Strip that spread throughout the Jewish areas of Judea and Samaria (West Bank). The Americans and Soviets, having by this time made strides in peaceful relations of their own, began pressuring Israel to negotiate with the PLO to resolve the conflict.

Fast Figure

Yitzhak Rabin

The first native-born Israeli prime minister, Rabin is an Israeli hero for many reasons. The first is his distinguished military career, which included the masterminding of the Six-Day War along with Moshe Dayan. The second is his political career in which he was prime minister in two different decades, the late 1970s and mid-1990s. Rabin's contributions to the peace process include his agreement with the Palestinians and treaty with Jordan in the mid-1990s. As a result of the Oslo Accords, Rabin and Yasser Arafat shared the 1994 Nobel Peace Prize. Rabin's willingness to concede to the Palestinians land that was part of biblical Israel angered Orthodox Jews, leading to his assassination in 1995.

The Israeli government could not sanction a public meeting with a terrorist such as Arafat, so secret meetings took place between Israeli and Palestinian leaders in Oslo, Norway. Public negotiations were initiated in Madrid, Spain, but were soon deadlocked over the issue of Jerusalem. The Arabs demanded a resolution on the status of the city, but it was impossible for such an agreement to be reached at that time with a recognized terrorist (Yasser Arafat).

Eventually, the secret meetings prevailed and included a provision in the agreement for a deadline that committed both sides to resolving Jerusalem's status after their fifth-year anniversary as "peace partners." This inaugurated the "Oslo Peace Process," which was to oversee the implementation of the Oslo Accords and the final-status negotiations on Jerusalem.

Under the Oslo Accords, Israel and the PLO were to officially recognize each other and autonomy was to be granted progressively to the Palestinians, first in Gaza and Jericho, and then in the rest of the territories through continued negotiations. Following the land-for-peace pattern set by the Camp David Accords, Israel would also withdraw in stages from the territories. The PLO, which became the Palestinian National Authority (PNA) or the Palestinian Authority (PA), was to recognize Israel's right to exist (not simply *that* it exists), renounce terrorism, and revoke the provision in its charter that called for the destruction of Israel. Israel was to accept the PLO as a "peace partner" without a trial period to test its sincerity, and in spite of the risk to Israeli security, to permit the Palestinian Authority to have rifles and train armed forces for the purpose of policing their territories and controlling terrorism within their borders. The formal agreement, known as the "Declaration of Principles," was signed on the White House lawn on September 13, 1993.

30

WHAT CAUSED THE BREAKDOWN OF THE PEACE PROCESS?

From the beginning of the Oslo Peace Process, there have been people on both sides who believed it was a treasonous agreement and attempted to force its end by acts of terror. The first of these attempts was on the Israeli side. Israeli settler Baruch Goldstein murdered 29 Palestinians who were praying in the Ibrahim Mosque within the Tomb of the Patriarchs in Hebron on February 25, 1994. On the Palestinian side, terrorist activity has continued in spite of the agreement. More importantly, Arafat's failure to follow through on any of the terms of the Declaration of Principles and continued acts of terrorism and threats of *jihad* ("holy war"), including threats from himself, made many Israelis distrust the agreement. On the one hand, if Arafat could not control the terrorists, which was part of his agreement, then why was the agreement

Fast Figure

Shimon Peres

Yitzhak Rabin's political rival within the Labor party, but likeminded negotiator for peace, Shimon Peres is an elder statesman of Israel. He has served Israel since before its independence as a commander of the Haganah, and later the head of the Israeli navy. He has been a figurehead in Israeli politics since the 1950s and served as prime minister in 1984–85, and again after Rabin's death in 1995. Known as a dove among doves, peace has always been his top priority. This has brought him into conflict with conservatives, who feel that security is more important than peace.

made with him? On the other hand, if he could control them, but wasn't doing so, then he was not a true peace partner.

The tension between parties was growing, so on September 28, 1995, a new interim agreement, known as Oslo III, was signed. Under this accord, Israel was to expand the area of Palestinian autonomy and withdraw from six West Bank areas, including Bethlehem, Jenin, Nablus, Qalqilya, and Tulkarm. For many Orthodox Jews, this agreement to give up biblical land to the enemy was against the Torah and branded Israeli prime minister Rabin a traitor to the Jewish people. Consequently, Jewish activist Yigal Amir assassinated Rabin on November 4, 1995. Labor party leader Shimon Peres succeeded Rabin, but he was considered left-wing and thought by conservative Israelis to be more conciliatory than Rabin on the Palestinian issue. Peres attempted an unsuccessful negotiation with Syrian prime minister Hafez Assad, and was replaced in elections by right-wing Likud party leader Binyamin Netanyahu, whose campaign was based on opposition to the Oslo Accords.

Once Netanyahu assumed office along with the obligations of the territorial concessions, he had to implement the withdrawal of the Israel Defense Force from Hebron, second only to Jerusalem in sanctity for the Jewish people. This act created a rift in Netanyahu's coalition and, as Palestinian violence escalated, he became equally unpopular in agreeing to an additional 13 percent in territorial concessions at the Wye River Plantation Summit. As a result, support for

Fast Fact

Politics in Israel

Israeli politics are a lot different from American politics due to security issues being the top priority in the country. There are two main parties, Labor and Likud. The Labor party is a liberal party leaning toward socialist policies. Leaders within this party are also commonly thought to be doves, or more open to land-for-peace negotiations. The Labor party held power in Israel from the founding of the state until 1977, when Menachem Begin was elected as prime minister and the Likud party came to power. Likud is a conservative party leaning toward nationalist and free-market policies. Leaders within this party are generally known to be more hawkish, or less willing to make territorial compromises and unwilling to negotiate for peace during times of violence. It is important to note that the first Israeli peace treaty with an Arab state came not with a Labor government in power, but with Menachem Begin, a Likud. Another difference between Israeli and American politics is that when neither party can gain control of the Knesset, Labor and Likud will join forces in what is known as a National Unity Government. Israel is the only true democracy in the Middle East.

Fast Figure

Binyamin Netanyahu

A native Israeli who was educated at the Massachusetts Institute of Technology in the United States, Netanyahu is one of the world's foremost experts on terrorism. Elected as prime minister in 1996 due to the continuation of violence during the peace process, he clamped down on terrorists in the late 1990s. He is currently Israel's most recognized face in America due to his stint as Israel's ambassador to the United Nations and his frequent appearances in churches and conferences around the United States. Known as a security hawk, he mellowed some during his two years as prime minister, but has recently gotten back into politics and become more hawkish than ever as foreign minister under Ariel Sharon.

Fast Figure

Ehud Barak

Israel's most decorated soldier and war hero, he was considered the true successor to Yitzhak Rabin's legacy. Elected as prime minister in 1999, Barak and his Labor government tried their best to present the ultimate peace plan to the Palestinians at Camp David in 2000. Yasser Arafat and the Palestinians did not find the plan to be satisfactory, however, and both parties returned to the Middle East frustrated and angry. Soon after, the Al-Aqsa Intifada began and the peace process that began in the early 1990s was in disrepair. Barak, defeated and dejected, was replaced by Ariel Sharon as prime minister in 2001.

Netanyahu's government collapsed and he was replaced in the next election by military general Ehud Barak. Israelis hoped that Barak, as a military commander, would be able to contain the Palestinian terrorism and work toward a peaceful solution that maximized Israel's security.

Barak inherited from Netanyahu the task of dealing with the end of the Oslo interim period and the unresolved issue of the status of Jerusalem. Surprising the conservative majority that elected him, Barak had come to accept the inevitability of a Palestinian state and at the Camp David II Summit offered to Arafat greater concessions than any previous Israeli leader—up to 98 percent of the territories and half of Jerusalem, retaining only symbolic sovereignty over the underground remains on the Temple Mount.

Equally surprising was Arafat's rejection of Barak's offer and abrupt departure from the summit. Arafat demanded complete sovereignty over East Jerusalem and an automatic right of return for up to five million Palestinian refugees—an impossible concession for Barak to accept as well as a slap in the face after the exceptional concessions already offered. Both Barak and President Clinton (who was denied a legacy of peacemaking by Arafat's intransigence) concurred that Arafat had derailed the Oslo Peace Process.

Arafat believed that the only way to force the greater concessions he desired was to return to the Intifada conditions that had forced Israel to begin the Oslo Accords. So, on September 2000, he announced the beginning of his Al-Aqsa Intifada, which centered on the battle for Jerusalem and targeted Likud leader General Ariel Sharon, who had caused the PLO's departure from Lebanon. Instead, the Palestinian Authority's resumption of terrorism convinced the Israeli electorate to make Sharon the next prime minister in hopes that he would deal decisively with Arafat. As Palestinian terrorist activity increased, Sharon again officially declared Arafat a terrorist, removing him from the status of peace partner. Thus, the second Intifada effectively ended any chance of a continuation of the Oslo Peace Process.

Fast Quote

Cheated Us All

"Once Oslo's assumptions collapsed, it cast a disturbing shadow in retrospect on what has happened since 1996. Maybe Arafat cheated all of us....It was an end to what Arafat had done for years—namely, talk in English about his readiness to make peace and in Arabic about eliminating Israel in stages....My feeling is that we won't have a peace agreement with Arafat."

Former Israeli prime minister Ehud Barak

31

WHAT IS THE CONTROVERSY OVER UN RESOLUTION 242?

The Palestinian Authority has claimed that Israel has violated the demands to withdraw from all lands occupied in 1967 as required by UN Resolution 242, while Israel has claimed to have fulfilled these demands and accuses the PA of itself violating the provisions of the resolution. What, then, is the meaning and significance of Resolution 242?

The resolution, unanimously adopted by the UN Security Council on November 22, 1967, establishes the principles that were to guide the negotiations for "a peaceful and accepted settlement" (an Arab-Israeli peace agreement). It required the establishment of "a just and lasting peace in the Middle East" and called for the following: 1) The "withdrawal of Israeli armed forces from territories occupied in the recent conflict (1967)," and 2) the "termination of all claims or states of belligerency" and recognition that "every State in the area has the right to live in peace within secure and recognized boundaries free from threats or acts of force." The final language of the resolution was the result of negotiations between the two parties so that it would not later be interpreted differently by each party.

However, that is exactly what has happened. The Arabs read the phrase "withdrawal from territories occupied in the recent conflict" to mean *all* territories. However, according to Arthur Goldberg, the American ambassador who led the U.S. delegation to the United Nations in 1967, "The notable omissions—which were not accidental—in regard to withdrawal are the words, 'the' or 'all' and 'the June 5, 1967' lines.... the resolution speaks of withdrawal from occupied territories without defining the extent of withdrawal."[1] The Arab states pressed for the word *all* to be included, but this was rejected. Even so, they asserted that they would read the resolution as *if* it included the word *all*. For this reason the British ambassador who drafted the approved resolution, Lord Caradon, declared after the vote, "It is only the resolution that will bind us, and we regard its wording as clear."

Moreover, while the resolution argues for the "inadmissibility of the acquisition of territory by war," it has in mind an *offensive war* in which territory is occupied by invasion, not a *defensive war* in which territory is occupied as a result of aggression by another party. If that were not the case, the resolution would provide an incentive for aggression. If one country attacks another and the defender repels the attack and acquires territory in the process, the former interpretation would require the defender to return the land it took. Thus, aggressors would have little to lose because they would be insured against the main consequence of defeat. While it's true that Israel launched a pre-emptive strike in 1967, it was a *defensive* response to a clear buildup of enemy forces on its borders and public announcements in the aggressor countries calling for an invasion to destroy Israel. Given that scenario, Israel's survival depended on preemptive action.

It is also important to observe that the resolution does not specify how much territory Israel is required to give up. Also, that the withdrawal mentioned in the resolution did not mean a withdrawal from the pre-1967 lines was understood. When asked to explain the British position, Lord Caradon said, "It would have been wrong to demand that Israel return to its positions of June 4, 1967, because those positions were undesirable and artificial." Since Israel has already withdrawn from 91 percent of the territories as a result of giving up the Sinai, withdrawing from portions of the Gaza Strip and the West Bank under the Oslo Accords, it has already partially, if not wholly, fulfilled its obligation under Resolution 242. Israel has also made peace agreements with Egypt and Jordan, so the only remaining territorial disputes are with Lebanon and Syria. Whether or not the resolution requires Israel to withdraw from the Golan Heights as "additional compliance" with the withdrawal clause has yet to be settled.

The withdrawal clause is also linked to the second unambiguous clause, which calls for "termination of all claims or states of belligerency" and the recognition that "every State in the area" has the "right to live in peace within secure and recognized boundaries free from threats or acts of force." U.S. ambassador Goldberg explained that this phrase was included because the parties were expected to make "territorial adjustments in their peace settlement encompassing less than a complete withdrawal of Israeli forces from occupied territories, inasmuch as Israel's prior frontiers had proved to be notably insecure." Therefore, while the resolution does not demand that Israeli withdrawal be a prerequisite for Arab action, it does demand that the Arab states cease their hostilities toward Israel, a requirement that has never been fulfilled. Most Arab states continue to maintain a state of war with Israel, and even Arab states that have no territorial disputes with Israel (such as Saudi Arabia, Iraq, and Libya) have refused to grant Israel diplomatic recognition and have conditioned their relations in the Saudi Peace Proposal on an Israeli withdrawal to the pre-1967 borders.

Of greater significance is the fact that Palestinians are not mentioned anywhere in Resolution 242. They are only alluded to in the second clause of the second article, which calls for "a just settlement of the refugee problem." However, there is no provision whatsoever requiring that Palestinians be given any political rights or territory. Even then, the term "refugees" was left generic on purpose to acknowledge the fact that Jewish people had become refugees as a result of Arab conflict. Almost as many Jews fled Arab countries as Palestinians left Israel. Despite the absence of any reference to the Palestinians, the PLO accepted Resolution 242 (and 338) as the basis for negotiations with Israel when it signed the Declaration of Principles in September 1993. Since then, the different interpretations of the significant clauses in the resolution have been an ongoing source of conflict.

32

WHAT IS THE SAUDI PEACE PLAN?

In 2002, Crown Prince Abdullah of Saudi Arabia proposed a new peace plan that promised "normal relations" with Israel. As the House of Saud had never previously initiated such a proposal, the idea received more than usual reception among members of the Arab League, which approved it. The United States, noting that "normal relations" was a distinct departure from the previous promise to simply "end belligerency," also saw its acceptance as a means to further relations and build an Arab coalition for the United States's War on Terrorism. Unlike UN Resolution 242, which had carefully avoided requiring Israel to withdraw from defined lines or defining the extent of such withdrawal, the Saudi Peace Plan is exceptionally inclusive, going beyond the Arab interpretation of the controversial withdrawal clause in Resolution 242. It requires Israel to "fully withdraw from Arab-occupied territories including the Syrian Golan, to the June 4, 1967, line and from the territories that are still occupied in South Lebanon." Whereas UN Resolution 242 vaguely alluded to the Palestinians in the "refugee clause," the Saudi plan has several explicit provisions regarding Palestinian demands. Two of the most important require Israel to 1) reach a just solution for the Palestinian refugee problem, to be agreed upon in conference with the United Nations General Assembly Resolution 194 (right of return and reparation), and 2) accept the establishment of an independent and sovereign Palestinian state on the Palestinian territories occupied since June 4, 1967 in the West Bank and the Gaza Strip, with East Jerusalem as its capital.

To Israelis, the Saudi Peace Plan is a rather curious development. Why would the Saudis want "normal relations" with Israel? They are not at war with Israel and have no claim to territories in Israel. They have no

Fast Quote

Pre–Six-Day War Lines

"Most of all I wanted the world to know what would have happened to us had we withdrawn before the war [of 1973] to pre-Six-Day War lines of 1967—the very lines, incidentally, that had not prevented the Six-Day War itself from breaking out, although no one seems to remember that. I have never doubted for an instant that the true aim of the Arab states has always been, and still is, that even if we had gone back far beyond the 1967 lines to some miniature enclave, they would still have tried to eradicate it and us."

Golda Meir

reason to not have "normal relations" with Israel. Moreover, Egypt and Jordan were supposed to already have "normal relations" since they signed peace treaties with Israel, and a number of Arab nations (Qatar, Oman, and Morocco) were in the process of normalizing relations with Israel. All of these Arab nations had made peace or were making strides toward peace without requiring Israel to withdraw to pre-1967 lines or agree to the establishment of a Palestinian state. Although Israel believed, as do many political analysts, that Abdullah put forth the peace plan to deter U.S. investigations of Saudi support for terrorism, the country still stated that it was willing to negotiate since this was a plan accepted by the entire Arab League (not simply the Palestinian Authority) and offered the prospect of peace with the whole Arab world.

Fast Feature

The Road Map to Peace in the Middle East

On April 30, 2003 the U.S. administration unveiled a new plan for peace in the Middle East, known simply as "The Road Map," and outlined the steps believed necessary for resolving the Israeli-Palestinian conflict. On June 4, a summit was held in Aqaba, Jordan, to hear pledges from the represented Israeli and Palestinian leadership to the Road Map as well as promises of support from an international quartet comprising the United States, United Nations, European Union, and Russia. Here are the requirements and expectations of the Road Map:

What does the Road Map aim to accomplish?

- A "final and comprehensive settlement" of the Israeli-Arab conflict by 2005
- An "independent, democratic and viable Palestinian state living side by side in peace and security with Israel"
- An end to Israeli occupation of the West Bank, Gaza, and East Jerusalem with adjustments to the final borders of both countries

How will we know each side is complying with the plan?

- The "quartet" (U.S., UN, EU, and Russia) will meet regularly to discuss and evaluate compliance with the Road Map

Continued on page 142

Fast Feature

Continued from page 141

What are the timetables and details of the Road Map?

Phase 1: *Timetable:* To be immediately accomplished

- The Palestinian Authority must:
  - Undergo a visible and productive process of reform
  - Issue an official statement declaring Israel's right to exist in peace and call for an immediate and unconditional end to hostilities
  - Undertake visible and productive efforts to arrest, disrupt and restrain individuals and groups conducting and planning attacks on Israelis
  - Dismantle the terrorist network and capabilities
  - End all incitement against Israel
- The Israel government must:
  - Issue an official statement affirming its commitment to an independent and sovereign State of Palestine and call for an end to violence against Palestinians
  - Freeze all settlement construction and dismantle settlements built after March 2001
  - Progressively withdraw from Palestinian autonomous zones reoccupied during the Palestinian uprising
  - End the demolition of the homes of Palestinian terrorists as a practice of war

Phase 2: *Timetable:* To be accomplished as early as the end of 2003

- The ratification of a Palestinian constitution
- A major international conference held to begin the official process of establishing a Palestinian state
- The U.S., UN, EU, and Russia begin promoting international recognition of the Palestinian state and its membership in the UN

Phase 3: *Timetable:* To be accomplished in 2004 and 2005:

- A second major international conference finalizing permanent status solutions for Jerusalem, refugees (right of return), borders, Jewish settlements, and peace between Israel and the Arab nations

THE PALESTINIAN UPRISINGS

Fast Focus

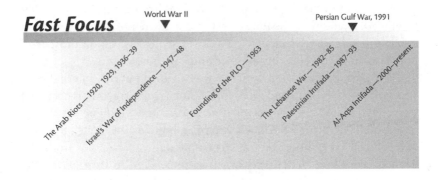

33

WHAT CAUSED THE FIRST PALESTINIAN UPRISING?

In 1987 Yasser Arafat and his PLO, headquartered in Tunisia, were operating a long distance from the Palestinian people and were anxious to find a means of returning to the region and bringing the Palestinian cause into international focus. On December 7, an incident in Gaza gave Arafat his opportunity. On that day, four residents of the Jabalya Palestinian refugee camp were killed by an Israeli in an auto accident. The previous day an Israeli had been stabbed in a shopping center, and rumors had been spread that the auto accident was in fact a revenge killing. This led to rioting in Jabalya, in which a Palestinian teen was shot and killed by Israeli soldiers when he threw a Molotov cocktail at their patrol.

Arafat used these events to foment an uprising (Arabic *Intifada*= "shaking off") among the Palestinians in the Gaza Strip, which soon spread to the West Bank and Jerusalem. By the end of the week the local unrest had become a full-scale popular revolt in which six Palestinians had been killed and 30 wounded and the U.S. consulate in East Jerusalem had been bombed. The PLO directed this uprising, escalating it by spreading propaganda against Israel, issuing directives for forced business closings, and selecting targets for attack. By 1991 the insurrection had grown into a war of attrition with terrorist acts against Israeli civilians, including more than 3,600 Molotov cocktail attacks, 600 armed assaults, and 100 hand grenade attacks. More than a dozen civilians had been killed and 1,400 injured, and 11 soldiers had been killed and 1,700 wounded. In addition, the PLO directed the murder of Palestinians who "collaborated" with Israel, placing a death sentence even on those who sold land to or had close business dealings with Israelis.

The next phase of the Intifada was to bring about international recognition of the PLO and force concessions from Israel. This occurred as Arafat declared his renouncing of terrorism and willingness to recognize Israel. This achieved Arafat's aim of convincing the United States to give official recognition to the PLO and remove the PLO from the United States's list of terrorist organizations. This, in turn, paved the way for secret negotiations in Oslo that would lead to the peace process in 1993 and bring an end to the first uprising.

34

WHAT CAUSED THE SECOND PALESTINIAN UPRISING?

Despite the presence of a peace process from 1993–2000, Palestinian unrest and acts of terror under the Palestinian Authority did not decrease, but rather, increased. In addition, Palestinian terrorist organizations such as Islamic Jihad and Hamas, working with the permission of, if not the collusion of, Yasser Arafat, had launched more than 100 suicide attacks. When the Oslo Peace Process came to an impasse at the Camp David II summit, Arafat, who had repeatedly threatened a resumption of the Intifada, decided to make good on his threat.

During a scheduled inspection of the Temple Mount to report on the Islamic Waqf's construction activity, Sharon stated to Israeli reporters, "The Temple Mount is in our hands and will remain in our hands. It is the holiest site in Judaism and it is the right of every Jew to visit the

Temple Mount." As a result of these statements, violence erupted and a group of 1,000 demonstrators tried to get through to attack the Israelis and threw stones at the police, wounding 30 policemen and four Palestinians. More disturbing were the broadcasts on Palestinian radio and television some few hours later that accused Sharon and the Israeli delegation of "defiling" the mosques. On the Voice of Palestine radio program, Yasser Arafat declared the Sharon visit to be "a serious step against the Muslim holy places," and called all Arabs and Muslims throughout the world to unite and "move immediately to stop these aggressions and Israeli practices against holy Jerusalem."

The next day, during the Friday sermon in the Al-Aqsa Mosque, the mufti focused on the "desecration" by the Israeli government and called for *jihad* "to eliminate the Jews from Palestine." As expected, whipped into action by the mufti's message, the congregation numbering in the hundreds rushed onto the Temple Mount to apply the sermon. Some wrestled with police guarding the Mughrabi Gate, which leads to the Jewish Western Wall, while others hurled stones from above down upon the Jews who were praying at the Wall. Within a week the violence spread throughout the country, with a rising death toll reported minute by minute by CNN. By week's end another Jewish holy site, Joseph's Tomb in Nablus (the biblical city of Shechem), had been attacked and torched by a Palestinian mob, and little Mohammed al-Dura had been killed—an event that was given widespread television coverage.

This new uprising was immediately dubbed the Al-Aqsa Intifada on the belief that Sharon desecrated an Islamic holy place and that, as a result, these sites need protection from the Israeli government. While the media, adopting the Palestinian perspective, reported the event as "the incitement" of the Palestinians by "the provocative visit" of Ariel Sharon to the Temple Mount, Sharon's visit as a representative of the Israeli government was perfectly legal and no intrusion of Muslim holy places occurred. It's also important to note that three months of Palestinian anti-Israel violence had *preceded* Sharon's visit. In fact, at a PLO rally in Ein Hilwe refugee camp in South Lebanon on March 2, 2001, Palestinian Authority communications minister Imad Faluji said that the then-five-month old Intifada was not a spontaneous reaction to Sharon's visit, but had been planned after the failure of the peace talks earlier in July.[1] The actual start of the second uprising dates to September 27 (two days *before* Sharon's visit) at the Netzarim junction where violence was initiated by the Palestinians. There, rocks and fire-bombs were thrown at Israeli positions and an Israeli soldier was killed by a roadside bomb. Such acts continued even to the very day of Sharon's visit. On that day, an Israeli police officer was murdered by a Palestinian policeman who had served with him on joint patrol. The "incident" of the Sharon visit, which was not an incident in itself, was used by the Palestinians as an excuse to unleash the next stage of aggression against Israel, a local war of attrition that's part of a phased plan that they hope will lead to a regional war with the Arab states for the "liberation of Palestine."

Thus, Al-Aqsa Intifada was simply a pretext to escalate the premeditated campaign of violence that had never actually abated during the Oslo Peace Process—all in an attempt to gain international sympathy and support for the Palestine people and provoke international intervention. During the first two years of this second Intifada, more than 700 Israelis and 1,700 Palestinians have been killed. This cycle of violence between the Israelis and Palestinians, resulting from sustained terrorism by the latter and reprisals by the former, has become the unresolved center of the Middle East conflict and the unwanted focus of the U.S.-led War on Terrorism.

35

WHY HAVE THERE BEEN PALESTINIAN UPRISINGS?

The method of using armed uprisings alternated with temporary cease-fires or peace treaties follows the tactic of Islamic conquest advocated in the Qur'an for Muslims dealing with nations that are too strong to be overcome by military force. This method was modeled by Muhammad himself in his relations with the Quraysh tribe of Mecca. In that scenario, Muhammad called for a 10-year cessation of hostilities until his military became strong enough to conquer the enemy. Then, it was required that the warfare continue until victory. This tactic was first employed in Palestine by Jerusalem mufti Haj Amin al-Husseini in the Arab insurrection under British Mandate in the 1920s. It was used by the Palestinian guerillas in their war of attrition against Israel and in attempts to take over Jordan and Lebanon. Yasser Arafat himself explained his use of this tactic in justification for his taking part in the Oslo Peace Process. In a speech made in a mosque in Johannesburg,

South Africa on May 10, 1994, Arafat compared his actions in the signing of the Declaration of Principles with Israel with Muhammad's conquest of the Quraysh tribe, inviting his audience to join him "to continue our way to Jerusalem" as "*mujaheddin* [warriors of *jihad*]."[2]

This use of uprisings is but a part of the "phased program" originally adopted at the twelfth session of the Palestinian National Council (PNC) on June 8, 1974 and reconfirmed in 1988. Yasser Arafat also reaffirmed the goals of this program to 19 Arab ministers assembled in Cairo on September 19, 1993, just days after the signing of the Declaration of Principles: "Our first goal is the liberation of all occupied territories…and the establishment of a Palestinian state whose capital is Jerusalem. The agreement we arrived at is not a complete solution…it is only the basis for an interim solution and the forerunner to a final settlement, which must be based on complete withdrawal from all occupied Palestinian lands, especially holy Jerusalem."[3] The goals of the "phased program" are: 1) The establishment of a Palestinian state; 2) the use of the Palestinian state for continuing the war against Israel; and 3) triggering a general war to annihilate Israel.

> **Fast Quote**
>
> **The Phased Plan**
> "We seek to establish a state which we can use in order to liberate the other part of the Palestinian soil."
>
> *George Habash, leader of the Popular Front for the Liberation of Palestine*

The statement made at the original Palestinian National Council summarizes and clarifies these objectives: "Once it is established, the Palestinian National Authority will strive to achieve a union of the confrontation countries, with the aim of completing the liberation of all Palestinian territory, and as a step along the road to comprehensive Arab unity." The "confrontation countries" are the Arab states that exist in a state of belligerency with Israel and that launched attacks on Israel in previous wars. The "liberation of all Palestinian territory" refers not only to the West Bank and Gaza Strip, but the whole of Palestine from the Jordan River to the Mediterranean Sea, an area that includes the State of Israel. The phrase "comprehensive Arab unity" refers to the concept of restoring a single Islamic state in the Middle East without a non-Muslim element—namely, Israel.

> **Fast Quote**
>
> **Goal of Palestinian State**
> "Now we accept the formation of the Palestinian state in part of Palestine, in the Gaza Strip and West Bank. We will start from that part and we will liberate Palestine, inch by inch."
>
> *Salah Khalaf Abu Iyad, Arafat's principal deputy (1991)*

36

What is happening during the second Palestinian uprising?

When Arafat began the second Intifada, he believed that the Israeli government, having been pressured by the international community to keep the peace process going, would not have the will to fight. He thought it would soon buckle and return to the negotiating table (as Shimon Peres initially attempted to do) and he could increase his demands beyond Ehud Barak's exceptional offers at the Camp David II summit. This assessment was made by defense analyst Ze'ev Schiff: "Among the Arabs there is an increasing feeling that they have hit on the formula for bringing Israel to its knees." How? "Ongoing, low-level war that combines massive terrorism, guerrilla warfare and the international media.…This strategy will expose Israel's Achilles' heel: an extreme sensitivity to loss of life and the kidnapping of its soldiers."[4]

To achieve this goal, the Palestinian Authority revived its military action groups, such as the Fatah Hawks, the Kassam Brigades, and the Red Eagle. These groups, along with the Palestinian army, the Tanzim, and Arafat's personal guard, Force 17, launched a new campaign of terrorism against Israel. However, what Arafat did not take into consideration was the Israeli public's unified shift to the right and election of hard-liner Ariel Sharon. Palestinian intelligence had predicted that Israel would be split into two camps over the new Intifada and even wage a civil war. The opposite occurred, with most of the country coming together around a leader who

Fast Figure

Ariel Sharon

Known as "the Bulldozer," Sharon is hated by the Palestinians for his role in the Lebanon War and is blamed for inciting the Al-Aqsa Intifada. He served in the Israeli government for many years, primarily in the military wing, and was elected prime minister in 2001 and 2003 in response to increasing Palestinian violence after the failure of the Oslo II Summit. Sharon stayed true to his campaign promise to not negotiate while terror attacks continued, and launched repeated reprisals against Palestinian militants after their attacks on Israeli civilians, a move that often frustrated U.S. attempts for a cease-fire. However, with the threat of Saddam Hussein to Israeli security removed and U.S. pressure to accept the terms of the Road Map, Sharon modified his hardline stance at the Aqaba Summit and pledged to "end occupation" and support the establishment of a Palestinian state. This move surprised both Israeli hawks and doves alike.

could guarantee their security—of all people, a leader whom the Palestinians considered a warmonger and a butcher!

Sharon's initial strategy was to hold the line on the Jewish settlements and Jerusalem and make no further concessions. After the attack on America, Sharon believed the United States would consider Israel an ally in its war on terrorism and even help Israel defeat Palestinian terrorism. Sharon openly refused to accept Arafat as a peace partner and called for his exile from the country.

However, the United States was unable to support Sharon's strategy. That's because President George W. Bush was determined to downplay the United States's support of Israel as a cause of the September 11, 2001 terrorist attack on America, to separate religion from terrorism, and to build a coalition of Arab states. To do all this, Bush found it necessary for the United States to keep an "acceptable" distance from Israel. Bush, however, still censured Arafat and condemned the terrorist acts of the Palestinians, especially in light of events such as the January 3, 2002 interception of the ship Karine-A, which was destined for Yasser Arafat and loaded with some 50 tons of military hardware from Iran, as well as a spate of deadly

Fast Figure

Mahmoud Abbas

Mahmoud Abbas (known also by the guerilla name of Abu Mazen) was born in 1935 in Mandate Palestine. He completed his doctoral dissertation in 1983 at Moscow's Oriental University and his dissertation was published next year in Jordan, titled *The Other Side: The Secret Relationship between Nazism and Zionism.* Abbas argues that the Nazi Holocaust had been exaggerated and that Zionists created the myth of six million murdered Jews to force the world to accept the establishment of a Jewish state in Palestine. Furthermore, Abbas says that Zionists collaborated with the Nazis to murder the Jews and that Hitler killed Jews only because David Ben-Gurion (Israel's first prime minister) provoked him into doing so by declaring war on the Nazis in 1942. As co-founder of Fatah, the ruling party in the PLO, Abbas has been in the Palestinian hierarchy for four decades and has served as the PLO executive committee chairman. According to Fatah operative Mohammed Daoud Oudeh, who masterminded the murder of 11 Israeli athletes at the 1972 Munich Olympics, Abbas financed and supported the operation. Portraying a distinguished and pleasant demeanor (in contrast to Yasser Arafat), Abbas played a visible diplomatic role in the Israeli-Palestinian peace process, both in unofficial talks with Israeli Labor and Pacifist movements in the 1970s and in the Oslo Accords of the 1990s. He was given the title of prime minister of the Palestinian Authority in 2003 after Arafat bowed to international pressure to relinquish control to those "uncompromised by terror." However, Abbas' own history is far from "uncompromised" and, as a figurehead without negotiating authority, he simply serves as Arafat's senior-most advisor.

homicide bombings that occurred around that time. At the same time, Bush felt obliged to honor the vital U.S. relationship with Saudi Arabia and support a Saudi peace proposal (endorsed by the Arab League) that called for Israel's withdrawal to pre-1967 lines and the establishment of a Palestinian state. Though Bush's support upset Jews and many Christians, he balanced his statements with a call for both a "secure Israel" and a "democratic Palestine," neither of which are possible with the Palestine Authority or in the present Arab world.

Fast Feature

The Two-State Solution

The Two-State Solution—that is, two peoples (Israelis and Palestinians) living side by side in peace and security—was first proposed in 1947 in the U.N. Partition Plan that was rejected by the Arab states. The Oslo Peace Process of the 1990s had this as its ultimate goal, although one of its architects, Prime Minister Yitzhak Rabin, stated that he never envisioned Oslo leading to the establishment of an independent Palestinian state, which he viewed as the first step toward the destruction of the Jewish state. Rather, he had intended only Palestinian autonomy in land shared by neighbors. The Saudi Peace Plan of 2002 revived the Two-State Solution by offering normalized relations to Israel with the Arab world in exchange for a withdrawal to the pre-1967 war lines and the establishment of a Palestinian State within these boundaries. The Road Map to Peace, begun at the Aqaba Summit in 2003, also made the Two-State Solution its primary objective. Advocates of the Two-State solution argue that a State of Palestine exists *de facto* by virtue of its established national identity in the international community by U.N. recognition of its claims of occupation and expulsion from its homeland in 1948 and 1967, and its continued struggle as a people group to gain independence. Opponents argue that no Palestinian people (as a nationality) existed prior to the establishment of the State of Israel, that return to ancestral land would have had been possible had violence been renounced, and that the Palestinian nationalism was created by foreign terrorist groups as a means to destroy the Jewish state. Jewish advocates will accept the Two-State Solution only with a guarantee of Israeli security. Jewish opponents contend that the parties pressuring the Two-State Solution are mainly pro-Arab, anti-Semitic, and hostile to Israel.

SECTION VIII

THE THREAT OF GLOBAL TERRORISM

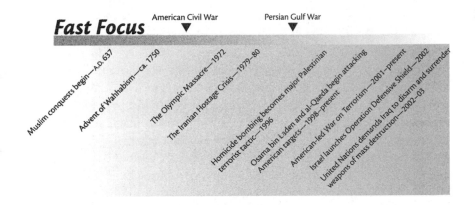

Fast Focus

American Civil War ▼

Persian Gulf War ▼

Muslim conquests begin—A.D. 637

Advent of Wahhabism—ca. 1750

The Olympic Massacre—1972

The Iranian Hostage Crisis—1979–80

Homicide bombing becomes major Palestinian terrorist tactic—1996

Osama bin Laden and al-Qaeda begin attacking American targets—1998–present

American-led War on Terrorism—2001–present

Israel launches Operation Defensive Shield—2002

United Nations demands Iraq to disarm and surrender weapons of mass destruction—2002–03

37

WHAT EVENTS HAVE CONTRIBUTED TO
THE RISE OF MILITANCY IN THE MIDDLE EAST?

The primary event that has contributed to the rise of militancy in the Middle East was the establishment of the State of Israel. Since the beginning of the Muslim conquests in the seventh century A.D., the Middle East has been exposed to ongoing militancy. Although Jews were often involved as a subjugated people in the countries conquered by Muslims, they were not the special focus of attack. This was because they were not rulers of the lands invaded by Muslims and generally did not hold places of power and therefore did not threaten the dominance of Islam or the Muslims' status as a superior religion. This was also the case in Palestine. The resident Jewish population was in the minority (although Arabs were also a minority), and Muslims were in control.

However, once Jewish immigration and settlement began, fear that the Jews would become a majority gave rise to the first waves of militancy by Arabs. This militancy was sustained through the period of the British Mandate with the hope of driving the Jews from Palestine so that the Pan-Arab state believed promised by the British could finally be realized. But the Jewish people declared their independence, established their Jewish state, and defeated the combined armies of the Arab world. This last event demonstrated Israel's military superiority, or rather, the Arab's military weakness, bringing on a collective shame that could be avenged only by removing Israel from the map of the Arab Middle East. In her book *From Time Immemorial,* Joan Peters draws a similar conclusion in her discussion about the rise of Arab militancy: "The Arabs believe that by creating an Arab Palestinian identity, at the sacrifice of the well-being and the very lives of the 'Arab refugees,' they will accomplish politically and through 'guerilla warfare' what they failed to achieve in military combat: the destruction of Israel—the unacceptable independent *dhimmi* state. That is the heart of the matter."[1]

Yasser Arafat, whose own revolutionary intrusion into the affairs of the Middle East has contributed to its militancy, affirmed this goal even during the Oslo Peace Process: "Peace for us means the destruction of Israel. We are preparing for an all-out war which will last for generations....We shall not rest until the day when we return to our home, and until we destroy Israel."[2] Israel made concessions to Arafat in the belief that he would control terrorism against Israel. However, it quickly became evident by the time of the second Intifada that his control was the *cause* of terrorism against Israel. The same militant agenda characterized Arafat's lieutenants, such as Faisal Husseini, who, until his death late in the spring of 2001, served as the administrator for Jerusalem Affairs. Husseini summed up the Palestinian strategy when he declared concerning the new Intifada, "We may win or lose," he said, "but our eyes will continue to aspire to the strategic goal, namely to Palestine from the river to the sea." Husseini, considered a moderate, envisioned a Palestinian state with boundaries from the Jordan River to the Mediterranean Sea with no Israel in between. The destruction of the Jewish state, as directed by the PLO charter, has ever been a foundational goal of Palestinian nationalism.

Another event that has contributed to the rise of militancy in the Middle East has been the involvement of the superpower states, especially

Great Britain and the United States, in the affairs of the region. In the early twentieth century, British colonialism brought the region into war and led to the division and domination of the conquered territory. During the rest of the twentieth century and now in the twenty-first century, the United States has sought to support or replace Arab regimes that posed a threat to its political and economic interests in the region. These foreign policies have had unintended consequences, often bringing into power despotic rulers or arming Islamic radicals who later threaten the very concerns their support was meant to protect. And by far, the most important aspect of superpower involvement has been the U.S. alliance with and aid to Israel. While this relationship has been vital to the United States, it has always been costly in terms of U.S. relations with the Arab world. This has been a special concern for Muslim militants, who view any Western presence in their part of the world as a secular corrupting influence and

Fast Feature

The Olympic Massacre

The 1972 Summer Olympics were held in Munich, Germany. They were the first Olympic Games held in Germany since Hitler's 1936 games, and the Germans wanted the Munich Games to erase the nightmare that had transpired through Hitler. Optimistic about the possibilities, they did not give enough thought to security. PLO terrorists, scorned by the Olympic committee's rejection of a Palestinian team, decided to crash the party. On September 5 at 4:30 A.M., eight Palestinians easily stole into the Olympic Village and fought with some of the Israeli Olympians. Two of the Israelis were killed before the terrorists were able to round up 11 of them as hostages. The Arab demands were simple: release 200 Arab prisoners from Israeli jails and guarantee them safe passage to Cairo, or the Israeli hostages would be killed. During the course of the incident, the German police fought with the terrorists numerous times, but were not able to save the Israelis. Eleven Israeli athletes, five PLO terrorists, and one German policeman were dead when all was said and done. The massacre was shown on television around the globe as the world was introduced to the horror of Palestinian terrorism.

suspect the United States of imperialistic motives or even a religious agenda (that is, a Christian crusade against Islam).

38

WHAT WAS THE SIGNIFICANCE OF THE IRANIAN HOSTAGE CRISIS TO TERRORISM?

In 1979 the Ayatollah Khomeini, spiritual leader and founder of Iran's Islamic Republic, overthrew the pro-Western Shah of Iran and brought Iran under the control of Islamic fundamentalism. The Ayatollah despised the West and sought to purge Iran of all Western influences. At the time, as many as 40,000 Americans lived in Iran. During the revolution, many Americans fled without incident. However, the Muslim fundamentalists protested the presence of a former Iranian premier in the United States and occupied the U.S. embassy in Tehran, taking over 50 American hostages. The former Iranian premier was believed to have stolen money and assets from Iran and the captors demanded that he be returned to Iran before the hostages would be let go. The United States rejected this demand and mounted a rescue operation in April 1980. The operation failed, and the situation continued to sour. Even after the Iranian premier died in mid-1980, the radicals of Iran refused to hand over the hostages until their stolen assets were returned. An agreement was finally reached in early 1980, but only after President Jimmy Carter had left office and would lose face by failing to have resolved the hostage crisis during his administration. By the time the crisis was over, the hostages had been held captive for 444 days. The significance of the Iranian hostage crisis was that it demonstrated for the first time the very real dangers of Islamic radicalism to Americans.

39

IS ISLAM A GLOBAL THREAT?

Islam has long been responsible for spreading terror throughout the Middle East. While it's true there are many sects of Islam, and some sects (such as Sufism, a nonliteral and mystical branch of Islam) oppose the fundamentalist form of Islam that is behind Middle Eastern terrorism,

Muslims and Arabs

Islam originated in Arabia, but about 80 percent of Islam's followers live outside the Arab region in the Middle East.

Islam has two main branches — the Sunni and the Shi'ite.

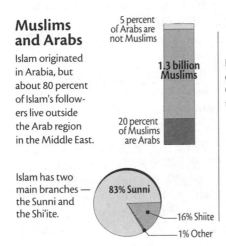

5 percent of Arabs are not Muslims

1.3 billion Muslims

20 percent of Muslims are Arabs

83% Sunni

16% Shiite

1% Other

The World's Fastest-Growing Religion

Islam is the world's fastest-growing religion, due to high birthrates and conversions. Given the current world population, more than 20 percent of all people follow Islam.

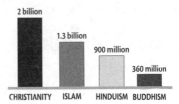

2 billion

1.3 billion

900 million

360 million

CHRISTIANITY   ISLAM   HINDUISM   BUDDHISM

Islam is the seed from which the flower grows, and it is only a matter of devotion to its doctrines in fundamental form (not reinterpreted in Western fashion) that separates a moderate from an extremist. One of the cardinal teachings of Islam is the Muslim's duty to destroy infidels (non-Muslims) and subjugate the *dhimmi* (tolerated minorities under Islamic rule, such as Jews and Christians).

Though Islam has spread through trade and missionary activity, its territorial and political gains were accomplished through the sword (*al-Harb*), and the concept of Holy War (*jihad*). Indeed, Allah requires Muslims to completely subdue the earth through military conquest. Accordingly, in Muslim thinking, the world is divided between *Dar al-Islam* (the "House of Islam") and *Dar al-Harb* (the "House of War"), that is, every part of the globe yet to be subdued politically and religiously by Islam. While there are some who have attempted to diffuse American sentiments against Muslims by saying that "Islam is a religion of peace," the concept of "peace" in Islam is not the same as that envisioned by others. In Islamic thought, peace is possible only where no further opposition to Islam exists. There can be a local and regional temporary "peace" where,

Fast Quote

The Coming Conflict

"The process of the revival of Islam in different parts of the world is real. A final showdown between the Muslim world and the non-Muslim world, which has been captured by the Jews, will take place soon. The Gulf War was just a rehearsal for the coming conflict....Muslims of the world, including those in the USA, prepare yourselves for the coming conflict."

*Dr. Israr Ahmed,
Amir of the Tanzeem,
Islami of Pakistan*

and for as long as, Islam has achieved and maintains domination. However, until the ultimate objective of total eradication or subjugation of the infidel is achieved, the command for *jihad* is a present and abiding obligation for every Muslim. Therefore, the political actions of any fundamentalist Islamic state are duty-bound to the religious rulings of Islam, which, in turn, are aimed at achieving the destiny of the religion.

As just stated, the global threat of Islam is the threat of global *jihad.* The average Westernized Muslim, and many moderate Muslim scholars, contend that *jihad* is misunderstood as "holy war" and that this is not its primary meaning, or even its necessary meaning. However, the Qur'an, in a number of places, appears to command "holy war." One of the most familiar of these is *Sura* 9:5, which, in part, says, "Fight and slay the pagans [idolaters] wherever you find them, and seize [capture] them, besiege them and lie in wait for them in every stratagem [of war]...." Moderate Muslims have said that non-Muslims do not understand that this command was meant to be temporary (for Muhammad's time) and referred only to defensive *jihad* (war fought to defend against attack).

However, leading Islamic scholars from Saudi Arabia and Al-Azhar University (Cairo), the highest centers for the study of Islamic law, contend otherwise. For example, Dr. Muhammad Said Ramadan al-Buti of Al-Azhar University has stated, "The *Sura* (9:5) does not leave any room in the mind to conjecture about what is called defensive war. This verse asserts that Holy War, which is demanded in Islamic law, is not defensive war (as Western students of Islam would like to tell us), because it would legitimately be an offensive war. This is the apex and most honorable of all Holy Wars."[3] Again, he declares: "Holy War, as it is known in Islamic jurisprudence, is basically an *offensive* war. This is the duty of Muslims *in every age* when the needed military power becomes available to them. This is the phase in which the meaning of Holy War has taken its final form. Thus the apostle of Allah said: 'I was commanded to fight the people until they believe in Allah and his message.'"[4]

Likewise, Saudi scholar Dr. Muhammad al-Amin has commented on *Sura* 9:5 as follows: "No infidel should be left on his land as it is denoted from the statement: 'I was commanded to fight the people until they believe in Allah and his message.'"[5] Summarizing the Islamic perspective on *jihad* and the interpretation of *Sura* 9:5, Islamic scholar Taqiy al-Din al-Nabahan has written,

Fast Fact

Official Palestinian Religion
The proposed Palestinian constitution declares Islam as the official Palestinian religion, even though 3 percent of Palestinians are Christian.

> So holy war continued as a means of spreading Islam. Thus, by holy war, countries and regions were conquered, by holy war, kingdoms and states were removed and Islam ruled the nations and peoples....The glorious Qur'an has revealed to Muslims the reason for fighting and the ordinance of how to war, and it declares that it is to carry the message of Islam to the entire world....Therefore, carrying the Islamic mission is the basis on which the Islamic state was established, the Islamic army was founded, and the holy war was ordained. All the conquests were achieved accordingly. Fulfilling the Islamic mission will restore the Islamic state to the Muslims.[6]

These statements by Muslim clerics and lawyers of the highest order confirm that the Islamic command for *jihad* is to be understood as both offensive in nature and unlimited in duration and obligatory for every Muslim throughout the world.

A final global threat within Islam is the growing nuclear capacity of some Islamic states, enabling them to wage *jihad* on a massive and global scale. One of the highest-ruling authorities for the Sunni Muslim sect, Sheikh Ala A-Shanawi, a member of the Islamic Ruling Committee in Al-Azhar, has declared:

> All Islamic nations are required to seize nuclear weaponry, giving the nation the utmost respect. We see how far behind our nation is as a result of not being prepared as well as it should be, while the enemy has equipped itself with the best weaponry there is, which it will use to harm and destroy Muslims....The founder of Islam, Muhammad, would have acquired a nuclear bomb to fight his enemies....The acquisition of modern nuclear weaponry is a religious obligation.[7]

If all Islamic nations are required to acquire nuclear weapons, and if even some of these Islamic nations are dominated by Muslim extremists (such as Saddam Hussein), we cannot help but acknowledge that Islam, with its commitment to *jihad,* poses a global threat.

40

WHAT IS WAHHABISM AND ITS RELATION TO TERRORISM?

Wahhabism is a radical sect of Islam founded by the eighteenth-century Arabian nationalist reformer Muhammad ibn Abdul Wahhab. Wahhab sought to reverse the century-old decline of the Muslim empire by removing the cultural pollution of Western influence and returning Islam to a past golden age in which the Qur'an was interpreted literally and fundamental Islamic law was practiced and strictly enforced. Based on a literal interpretation of the Qur'an, Hadith, and Sunna, Wahhabi theology promotes offensive *jihad* and promises *jihadic* martyrs heavenly rewards in paradise with celestial maidens. In 1744, Muhammad ibn Saud, the local ruler of Dariya, a town north of Riyadh, embraced Wahhab's teachings, and the two swore an oath of allegiance to spread this purified faith throughout Arabia. This was accomplished through Saud's tribal army and the Saud family, which continues to rule the kingdom of Saudi Arabia today.

In its purest form, Wahhabism is a death cult that has spearheaded the violent revolutionary overthrow of Islamic countries such as Afghanistan, whose local government was taken over by radical Taliban rule under *Shari'ah* (fundamentalist Islamic) law. Funded largely by petro dollars, Wahhabism has spent billions on the construction of mosques, schools, political institutions, and the like in an effort to export its teachings

Fast Figure

Muhammad ibn Abdul Wahhab
During the mid-1700s, as the world was caught up in nationalism, a man from Arabia took a personal journey that led him to believe that the Arabs were in need of an Islamic reformation. He wrote *The Book of the Unity* in the mid-eighteenth century, spelling out his fanatical interpretation of Islam. Much like the prophet Muhammad before him, Wahhab went from village to village preaching this fundamentalism but had little success until he met Muhammad ibn Saud, who was convinced the Wahhab was correct. The two men spread Wahhabism by the sword throughout Arabia. Today, the Saudi government no longer practices Wahhabism, bringing criticism from radical Muslims around the world that the Saudi regime is no longer devout.

throughout the Islamic world. Muslim American Stephen Schwartz, author of *The Two Faces of Islam: The House of Sa'ud from Tradition to Terror,* believes Wahhabism has been successful in influencing other Muslims from Shiites to secular leftists, and has even usurped the Chechen national movement, especially in its emphasis of martyrdom. For this reason Schwartz says, "Not all Muslims are suicide bombers, but all Muslim suicide bombers are Wahhabis."[8]

While the Saudi royal family continues to patronize Wahhabism, in the past it has expelled extremists such as Osama bin Laden because of his extreme criticism of the government for allowing U.S. military troops to be stationed in Saudi Arabia during the Gulf War (coupled with the revolutionary policies of his al-Qaeda terrorist organization). Nevertheless, the most authoritative and influential madrasas (religious schools) of Islam are in Saudi Arabia and daily indoctrinate young Muslims to hate and attack Western infidels. Saudi Arabia's support of and alliance with Wahhabism made it possible for 15 of the 19 al-Qaeda highjackers on September 11, 2001 to come from Saudi Arabia. Because of this connection, many political analysts believe that the real impetus behind Saudi Arabia's proposed "peace plan" is a bid to divert American and European attention from the Saudi kingdom's involvement in terrorism. Palestinian terrorists have also adopted the Wahhabi brand of Islam, and through the international terrorist activities of al-Qaeda (which has cell groups in some 60 countries), it today poses one of the greatest threats to the Middle East and the West.

Fast Figure

Abdul Aziz ibn Saud

The rival of Sharif Hussein, Saud conquered Arabia in the early 1900s. After Hussein's sons became monarchs in Iraq and Transjordan, his armed forces dwindled, which allowed Saud to move in and conquer Arabia. Due to his worries about Hussein's sons seeking revenge, he sought closer ties with Britain and the United States. Though Saud adhered to Wahhabism, he aggressively sought friendship with the West, which led to the development of the oil industry and great wealth for Saud's kingdom.

Fast Fact

Mistranslation and Martyrdom

"Pre-existing Christian Aramaic texts were misinterpreted by later Islamic scholars who prepared the editions of the Koran commonly read today....for example, the 'virgins' who are supposedly awaiting good Islamic martyrs as their reward in Paradise are in reality 'white raisins' of crystal clarity rather than fair maidens."

Alexander Stille, "Revisionist historians argue Koran has been mistranslated," San Francisco Chronicle *(March 2, 2002), p. A15*

Genealogy of the al-Qaeda

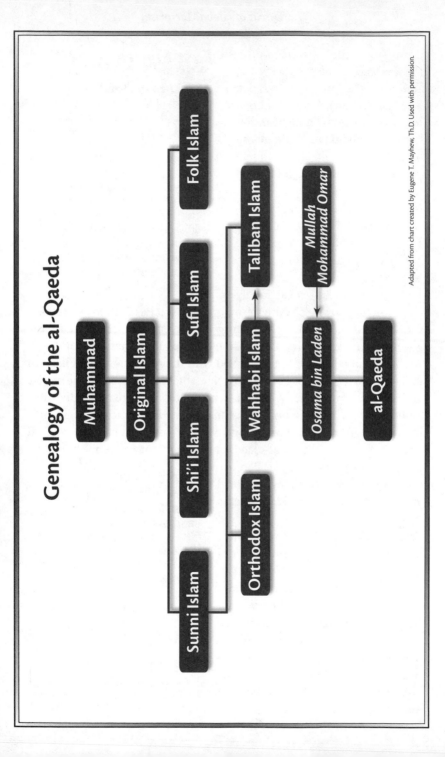

Adapted from chart created by Eugene T. Mayhew, Th.D. Used with permission.

The Worldview of Osama bin Laden: *Influences*

Ibn Taymiyyah (A.D. 1268–1328)
(theologian he quotes the most)

Wahhabism*
(foundation of his theology)

Muhammad Qutb
(Teacher of bin Laden at King Abdulaziz University).

Hasan al-Banna   Sayyid Qutb

FORMULATORS of his POLITICAL-RELIGIOUS WORLDVIEW

Mawlana Mawdudi

Osama bin Laden

B.rhanuddin Rabbani
Theology teacher, leader of Jamaat-i-Islami

Abdur Rab Rasool Sayyaf
Mullah of Itehar-i-Islami

AFGHAN MILITARY LEADERS in the ANTI-SOVIET JIHAD

Nabi Muhammadi   Yunus Khalis

Syed Ahmed Gailani   Ahmed Shah Masood

Sibghatullah Mujaddidi

Gulbuddin Hekmatyar

Abdullah Azzam   Hasan al-Turabi

MENTORS

Ayman al-Zawahiri

* "Osama's religious worldview was shaped by both Saudi Arabia's deeply conservative Wahhabi interpretation of Islam and by the revolutionary Islam that began to spread in the 1970s." —John Esposito, *Unholy War: Terror in the Name of Islam* (New York: Oxford University Press, 2002), p. 5.

Adapted from a chart created by Eugene T. Mayhew, Th.D. Used with permission.

41

WHO IS RESPONSIBLE FOR THE TERRORISM IN ISRAEL?

According to Dr. Ahmed Yousuf Abu Halabiah, the Rector of Advanced Studies at The Islamic University, the cause of terrorism in Israel is the Jews. As evidence for this claim he stated on Palestinian television on November 13, 2000, "The Jews are the Jews. There was never among them a supporter of peace. They are all liars....They are all terrorists. Therefore it is necessary to slaughter them and to murder them, according to the words of Allah....It is forbidden to have mercy in your hearts for the Jews in any place and in any land. Make war on them any place that you find yourself. Any place that you encounter them—kill them! Kill the Jews and those among the Americans that are like them."

The Israeli-Palestinian Declaration of Principles signed in September 1993 required the Palestinians to *renounce terrorism*. Yet statistics kept since the day of the handshake on the White House lawn—when the United States removed the PLO from its list of terrorist organizations— reveal that PLO terrorism actually *increased* against the Israelis during the "peace process" as opposed to the terrorist activity in the seven years before the declaration. And since the Palestinian Authority launched its new Intifada in September 2000, more than 700 Israelis have been killed in acts of terrorism. In addition, the Palestinian Authority oversees 11 Syrian-backed terrorist groups, including Hamas, Hizballah, and Islamic Jihad, which have carried out terrorist attacks on Israeli civilians. These acts most notably include homicide or suicide bombings in which a terrorist straps explosives on himself that are packed with nails and diseased matter (for greater collateral damage) and detonates himself (or is detonated remotely by others) in crowds of Israeli civilians. The Palestinian Authority has also terrorized and murdered fellow

Fast Quote

Confronting Islam

"Americans and Europeans and South Americans too need finally to recognize that Israel is the front line of Western Judeo-Christian culture in confronting Islam and its imperatives for war on and conversion of the infidel. Israel should be encouraged to fight and be helped in its fight until victory is achieved. Muslims understand only strength. To them, as to other dictators, concessions are a sign of weakness to be exploited. Peace will come only through strength. The sooner this lesson is learned, the sooner the blood of those thousands murdered September 11 will be redeemed."

Eugene Narret, author of Israel Awakened: A Chronicle of the Oslo War

Fast Feature

The Evolution of Palestinian Terrorism

The goal of the Palestinian National Committee is the destruction of Israel. The means to this end has been terrorism, and for this reason, the PLO was, until 1993 and its participation in the Oslo Peace Process, on the United States's list of terrorist organizations. Palestinian terrorism has evolved over the years and can be summed up in three periods: mob violence, airplane hijacking and hostage-taking, and homicide bombing. Each period has been more violent and hateful than the preceding one. Here are a few of the more infamous incidents involving Palestinian terrorism:

Period 1: Mob Violence

Goal: To keep the Jews from gaining autonomy in Palestine

- The 1920 Arab riots: Inspired by Jerusalem mufti Haj Amin al-Husseini, Palestinians attacked and looted Jewish businesses during the British Mandate years.
- The 1929 Arab riots: Rumors of Jewish plans to take the Temple Mount led to nearly a week of rioting throughout Palestine, in which the Jews experienced hundreds of casualties.
- The 1936–39 Arab riots: Hundreds of Jews were killed and wounded in a three-year riot directed by mufti Haj Amin al-Husseini.
- The 1948 Hadassah Hospital Massacre: A Palestinian force ambushed a convoy of nearly 100 Jewish doctors, nurses, and patients on the way to Hadassah Hospital, killing the majority of them.

Period 2: Airplane Hijacking / Hostage-Taking

Goal: To show the world that Israel should not be allowed to exist.

- September 6, 1970: Four airplanes from the Netherlands, Switzerland, Germany, and England were hijacked by Palestinian terrorists and forced to land in Jordan and Egypt. Hundreds were taken hostage, and all four planes were blown up on the ground. Seven known terrorists were set loose in exchange for

Continued on page 164

Fast Feature

Continued from page 163

the freedom of the hostages. None of the terrorists were ever brought to justice. (See also Black September, pages 100-01.)

- September 5, 1972: Eleven Israeli athletes were murdered by Palestinian terrorists at the Summer Olympics in Munich, Germany. (See also page 153.)

- June 27, 1976: Palestinian terrorists hijacked an Air France plane and forced it to land in Uganda. Ugandan dictator Idi Amin cooperated with and supported the terrorists, which complicated matters. They demanded the release of over 50 known Palestinian terrorists held in five different countries (including Israel) or the Jewish hostages would be shot. However, on July 3 and 4, Israel mounted a spectacular rescue operation in which a group of commandos stormed the airline terminal where the hostages were being held. By the end of the operation, all of the terrorists were killed and Israel had lost only four of the 105 Jewish hostages. Unfortunately, the Israeli commanding the operation, Yonatan Netanyahu (brother of Binyamin Netanyahu), was killed while leading the hostages to safety.

Period 3: Homicide Bombing

Goal: To kill as many Israelis as possible.

- March 4, 1996: Palestinian homicide bomber explodes at the Dizengoff Center in downtown Tel Aviv, killing 20 people and wounding over 75 others.

- June 1, 2001: A Palestinian Hamas terrorist homicide bomber blew up a discotheque in Tel Aviv, Israel, killing over 20 people and injuring 120 others.

- August 9, 2001: A Sbarro pizzeria in downtown Jerusalem was blown up by a Palestinian homicide bomber. Fifteen people were killed and over 100 were injured from the explosion.

Continued on page 165

Fast Feature

Continued from page 164

- March 27, 2002: A Palestinian Hamas homicide bomber killed 28 people and wounded 130 others at a hotel in Netanya, Israel. It is important to note that the attack was on a group of Israeli families at a Seder meal during the Passover holiday.

Palestinians who are suspected of collaboration with the Israelis.

Yasser Arafat regularly denounces the very terrorism he orders by defining his attacks on Israel not as "terrorism" but as "resistance to occupation." He defends his homicide bombers as "martyrs" or "freedom fighters." He further argues that his attacks are not on "civilians" because Israel has a reservist army and everyone serves. So even old people are "trained soldiers" and children are "soldiers in training." Thus, he believes he is not a terrorist by conventional definition. However, attacks on "soldiers" in their homes, in synagogues, at weddings and Bar-Mitzvahs, in restaurants with their families, at beaches, in night clubs, in shopping malls and outdoor markets, and while driving in their cars are not "resistance to occupation" or "freedom fighting," as the "soldiers" in these places are generally unarmed, pose no threat to Palestinians, and are involved in civilian affairs. Moreover, most Palestinian Authority attacks are intentionally

Fast Quote

Homicide Attacks Legitimized

One hundred and thirty Muslim clerics from 30 countries met in Lebanon to declare suicide attacks as legitimate and call for the elimination of the State of Israel: "Suicide operations against the Zionists are based on God's book, the Qur'an, and teaching of His Prophet, Muhammad, and will lead to Paradise."

Fast Quote

What Is Terrorism?

"[There exists a] false cliché that 'one man's terrorist is another man's freedom fighter.' Nevertheless, terrorism can be reasonably defined. It is the *deliberate and systematic* assault on civilians, on innocent noncombatants outside the sphere of legitimate warfare....In *thousands* of remorseless attacks, Arab terror organizations have deliberately and systematically sought out civilians as targets, attacking them in markets, airports, schools, universities, bus stops—even Olympic games, which have been declared off-limits to violence since ancient times."

Binyamin Netanyahu,
former prime minister of Israel

Fast Fact

The Jenin Incident

In March and April of 2002, when Palestinian homicide bombings seemed unstoppable, Israel launched Operation Defensive Shield in order to root out the terrorists and stop the homicide bombings. One of the refugee camps they visited was in the village of Jenin, known to some as the homicide-bombing capital of the occupied territories. A horrific fire-fight ensued between Palestinian terrorists and the Israel Defense Forces, ending in the destruction and bull-dozing of much of the camp as well as the deaths of 52 Palestinians and 23 Israeli soldiers. Much like in 1948 at Deir Yassin, the Palestinians claimed a massacre took place and resulted in the deaths of hundreds of innocent civilians. The incident ended in controversy as the world was horrified at the sight of the ruins of Jenin; however, looks can be deceiving. Recent evidence, including information from the Arab press, shows that many of the houses were booby-trapped with explosives so that no Israeli soldier who took part in the raid would survive entering them. Some terrorists even bragged that they set up the Israelis and were out to kill as many as possible. Even after the fighting had been long over, the Palestinians took advantage of a curfew rescinded by the Israelis to give the Palestinians time to buy food, and instead they used that time to booby-trap areas of the camp. Israel was severely condemned for the incident at Jenin, yet few people really know what happened there.

indiscriminate, aiming to cause panic and fear by their randomness and high casualty count. This, by any definition, is a characteristic of terrorism.

Israeli forces, by contrast, do not attack Palestinians offensively, but respond with reprisals to Palestinian Authority attacks. When this occurs, Israel Defense Forces soldiers' targets are carefully defined and limited to the houses of known or suspected terrorist ringleaders. They are also instructed to fire only upon clear threats to their safety, which are usually armed individuals or those making menacing gestures that, from a distance, can only be interpreted as engagement. As an example of the caution exercised by the Israel Defense Forces, in a deployment to Jenin to capture terrorists who had bombed Israeli civilians, 13 of the soldiers were killed by a nine-year-old boy wired with explosives who was detonated from a distance. The restraint of the soldiers, who watched the boy walking towards them but would not shoot, cost them their lives. Such restraint should be weighed against the Palestinian Authority's claims that the Israel Defense Forces, in the same reprisal against Jenin, committed a massacre, murdering more than 500 Palestinians. The official count, as reported by independent investigators, was 64.

Fast Feature

Palestinian Terrorist Groups Outside Israel

- *Hamas*—The leading terrorist organization in Palestine. It was created in the 1980s before the Intifada and regularly calls for the destruction of Israel. The PLO/Palestinian Authority is its secular rival and the Hamas sees them as traitors to their cause. Much like the Palestinian Authority, Hamas runs kindergartens, an Internet site, and provides other social services to the Palestinian people. As more and more Palestinians become frustrated with Arafat and the dying peace process, Hamas gains more support and more legitimacy with the Arab people. There are two main branches of Hamas: the military wing and the Majd wing, which punishes any Palestinians it deems as collaborating with the Jews. It was Hamas that introduced homicide bombings as the weapon of choice against Israel.

- *Islamic Jihad*—Formed in Egypt in 1979 and inspired by the Islamic revolution in Iran, the group seeks to create an ultraradical Palestinian state that will replace Israel. Even more radical than Hamas, Islamic Jihad opposes all secular influences and even attacks other Arab governments, including Egypt and Jordan. Though not as popular with the Palestinian people as Hamas is, the two groups cooperate closely to bring about the one goal they have in common: the destruction of Israel.

- *Hizballah*—A radical Islamic organization that works out of Lebanon and is funded primarily by Iran and Syria. The organization is much like Hamas—it runs hospitals, charity networks, and other social services for Palestinians and the Lebanese. However, its primary goal is the destruction of Israel and the United States. Despising any Western influences, it is also like Islamic Jihad in that the organization seeks to set up an Islamic fundamentalist state to replace Israel. Throughout Israel's occupation of Lebanon, Hizballah was a constant threat to the Jewish state. Even though Israel left Lebanon in 2000, Hizballah continues to attack Israel at the Lebanese-Israeli border.

Major Terrorist Organizations

Location	Name	Facts
Founded in Kuwait. Bases in Tunisia, Lebanon, West Bank, and Gaza Strip. Most important group within PLO.	**Fatah (Branch: Al-Aqsa Martyr's Brigade)**	Headed by Yasser Arafat. Name means "conquest." Contains special units: Tanzim, Force 17, Hawari Special Operations Group.
The West Bank and Gaza Strip.	**Hamas**	Palestinian outgrowth of the Muslim Brotherhood; targets Israeli civilians and military.
Beirut, south Lebanon; with cells in Africa, Asia, Europe, the Americas.	**Hizballah**	Opposes peace negotiations, anti-Israel, anti-West, allied with Syria and Iran.
Israel, Jordan, Lebanon; headquartered in Syria.	**Palestine Islamic Jihad**	Seeks destruction of Israel, anti-U.S., opposed to moderate Arab governments.
Based in Iraq; supported by Iraq and Libya.	**Palestine Liberation Front**	Split into pro-PLO, pro-Syrian, and pro-Libyan factions. PLO faction led by Muhammad Abbas.
Supported by Syria and Libya. Operate in Syria, Lebanon, Israel, West Bank.	**Popular Front for the Liberation of Palestine**	Founded by Jerusalem businessman George Habash. Cooperates with Hamas and Islamic Jihad. Attacks Israelis and moderate Arabs.
Headquartered in Damascus, Syria, with bases in Lebanon, ties with Iran.	**Popular Front for the Liberation of Palestine—General Command**	Founded by Ahmed Jibril, a former Syrian army captain. Guerrilla operations in southern Lebanon, attacks in Israel.
Global reach (in some 60 countries), operates out of Afghanistan under the Taliban regime, where training camps are maintained.	**al-Qaeda**	Founded by Osama bin Laden, seeks to destroy Israel and U.S., establish global caliphate (theocratic state under Islamic law) through offensive *jihad.*
Cairo, with cells in Yemen, Afghanistan, Pakistan, Sudan, and Lebanon.	**al-Jihad**	Close partner with bin Laden; seeks to overthrow Egyptian government; anti-U.S. and Israel.

42

WHY WAS THE UNITED STATES ATTACKED ON SEPTEMBER 11, 2001?

During the past two decades, Muslim terrorists have attacked and murdered thousands of people, and bombed and destroyed buildings, planes, and vehicles all over the globe, including Kenya, Algeria, Indonesia, Tanzania, Egypt, Iran, Sudan, Libya, Yemen, Afghanistan Syria, Lebanon, Israel, Jordan, France, and in South America. During this period, Muslim terrorists especially focused their attacks on Western targets such as U.S. embassies and their personnel. Over the past decade, these attacks have become increasingly domestic. In January 1993, Pakistani Mir Aimal Kasi shot five CIA employees outside an agency headquarters, killing two. The next month the World Trade Center in New York was bombed, killing six and causing 1,000 to suffer smoke inhalation. Four men were indicted and 118 were found to be potential unindicted co-conspirators.

That same summer, sheikh Omar Abdel Rachman and nine of his followers were arrested for planning a "Day of Terror" in New York to bomb the United Nations, the Lincoln and Holland Tunnels, the George Washington Bridge, and a Federal Office building. In March 1994, Rashid Baz attacked a bus carrying 15 Hasidic Jews on the Brooklyn Bridge. In February 1997 a Palestinian terrorist opened fire on the Empire State Building observation deck, and in July of that same year, police foiled a plot by Ghazi Abu Mezer to bomb the New York subway system. These acts indicated a growing presence of Islamic terrorist organizations operating in the United States. By 1994, former CNN reporter Steve Emerson had documented al-Qaeda, Hamas, Islamic Jihad, Muslim Brotherhood, Hizballah, and other terrorist groups in over 30 U.S. cities.

The U.S.-led invasion of Iraq in 1991 and the stationing of U.S. troops in Saudi Arabia was a pivotal event for Wahhabi Muslims such as Osama bin Laden. He and his brand of radicals viewed the incursion of the corrupt West (the Great Satan) into the previously undefiled lands of Islam (and especially Saudi Arabia, keeper of the sanctity of the holy mosques in Mecca and Medina) as a renewal of the unforgotten and unforgiven Christian Crusades (from the tenth to the twelfth centuries A.D.). In bin Laden's eyes, not only did the sacred lands of Islam have to be cleansed from

Terrorist Organizations in the U.S.A.

Seattle, WA
- Algerian Armed Islamic Group
- Al Gama'at al Islamiyya

San Francisco, CA
- Abu Sayyaf

Santa Clara, CA
- al-Qaeda
- Hamas

Los Angeles, CA
- Hamas
- Al Gama'at al Islamiyya
- Algerian Armed Islamic Group

San Diego, CA
- Algerian Armed Islamic Group

Tucson, AZ
- al-Qaeda
- Hamas

Denver, CO
- al-Qaeda

Oklahoma City, OK
- Hamas (Groups and Conventions)

Kansas City, MO
- Hamas

Dallas, TX
- Hamas

Arlington, TX
- al-Qaeda

Houston, TX
- Hamas
- Muslim Brotherhood
- al-Qaeda

Chicago, IL
- Hamas
- Islamic Jihad

Plainfield, IN
- Muslim Brotherhood
- ISNA

Columbia, MO
- al-Qaeda
- Algerian Islamic Salvation Front
- Hamas

Detroit, MI
- al-Gama'at al Islamiyya
- Muslim Brotherhood
- Hizballah
- Hamas

Cleveland, OH
- Muslim Brotherhood
- Islamic Jihad

Charlotte, NC
- Hizballah

Raleigh, NC
- Islamic Jihad

Orlando, FL
- al-Qaeda

Tampa, FL
- Islamic Jihad

Ft. Lauderdale, FL
- al-Qaeda

Boca Raton, FL
- al-Qaeda

Philadelphia, PA
- al-Gama'at al Islamiyya
- Hamas
- Hizballah
- Al Muhajiroun

Boston, MA
- al-Qaeda

New York, NY (metro)
- Al Gama'at al Islamiyya
- Hamas
- Al Muhajiroun
- Jamaat e-Islami
- National Islamic Front

Laurel, MD
- al-Qaeda

Potomac, MD
- Hizballah

Washington, DC
- Hamas
- Hizballah

Herndon, VA
- al-Qaeda
- Islamic Jihad

Springfield, VA
- Hamas

Adapted and used with permission from Steve Emerson, *American Jihad* (New York: Simon & Schuster, 2002), pp. 178–79.

Western pollution, but Allah's honor had to be avenged upon America and the West. The superpower status wielded by the United States is also an affront to the superior status conferred on Muslims in the Qur'an and a forceful opposition to the fulfillment of the Islamic command to subjugate the non-Muslim world to Islam. The US alliance with Israel (the Little Satan) was also a stated cause for the attack.

On the evening of the initial U.S. bombing of Kabal, Afghanistan, Osama bin Laden proclaimed: "They came out to fight Islam in the name of fighting

Fast Figure

Osama bin Laden

Currently the world's most-wanted man, bin Laden is the leader of al-Qaeda, the world's most deadly terrorist network. The organization is funded by bin Laden, who is said to have inherited millions of dollars from his wealthy Saudi family. He adheres to Wahhabism and his goal is to re-establish the Islamic empire and expand its influence and power around the world. Bin Laden has been behind some of the world's most heinous terrorist attacks, including the 1998 U.S. Embassy bombings in Kenya and Tanzania and the September 11, 2001 attacks on Washington, D.C. and New York City. Large numbers of people were casualties in each of these attacks.

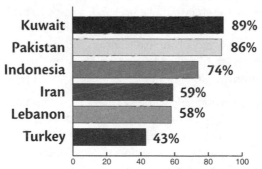

Islamic Views

Sixty-one percent of Muslims polled say Arabs were not involved in the September 11 attacks. Breakdown by country:

Country	Percentage
Kuwait	89%
Pakistan	86%
Indonesia	74%
Iran	59%
Lebanon	58%
Turkey	43%

Source: Gallup Poll of 9,924 adults in Islamic nations conducted in December and January, 2002.

terrorism. I say these events have split the whole world into two camps—the camp of belief [Muslims] and disbelief [non-Muslims]…. There will be no peace in the West until there is peace in Palestine." However, there is no evidence prior to 9/11 that Osama bin Laden championed the Palestinian cause. His justification for *jihad* on the West on the basis of Israel's occupation of Palestine was a play to the Muslims who identify more passionately with the problems of Palestinians than with Wahhabi concerns for Islamic purity. Ultimately, the U.S.-led War on Terrorism and its invasion of Afghanistan forced al-Qaeda and other Muslim terror organizations to regroup and develop new strategies of attack and has provoked a greater determination to wage a final *jihad* against the West.

Fast Feature

Al-Qaeda

Al-Qaeda is a militant guerrilla Islamic terrorist organization established by Osama bin Laden in 1987 to continue the Islamic resistance movement against the Soviet occupation of Afghanistan that began in the late 1970s. It developed as an offshoot of the original resistance force, the Makhtab al-Khidamat, which recruited, trained, and financed Islamic terrorists from the outset of the Soviet-Afghan conflict. Its success in this conflict led to its establishing governmental control over the country through the Taliban, a group of Islamic clerics and students who destroyed ancient Buddhist statues and imposed *Shari'ah* (a body of legal tradition which informs the Islamic community of the faithfulness Allah requires of it) on the entire population. Funded partly by bin Laden, son of a multimillionaire Saudi family, the organization has also received funds from the Islamic world, charitable front organizations in the United States and around the world, and during the Afghan resistance, even from the U.S. government (to prevent a Soviet buildup in the region).

Adopting the revolutionary Islamic perspective of Wahhabism, the ultimate goal of al-Qaeda is to depose Israel and the West, as well as moderate Islamic regimes (which it believes have compromised the standards of Islam), and establish a global Islamic empire under *Shari'ah*. Active in some 60 countries, including the United States, Al-Qaeda has planned or claimed involvement in terrorist attacks around the world, including the 2001 attacks on the World Trade Center and the Pentagon in Washington, D.C.

THE IRAQI CONFLICT AND ITS AFTERMATH

43

WHAT WAS THE EVIDENCE AGAINST IRAQ
FOR WEAPONS VIOLATIONS?

Despite a tenuous report to the United Nations by chief weapons inspector Hans Blix, it was acknowledged that Saddam Hussein had reneged on 18 Security Council Resolutions and had failed to comply proactively and completely with UN Resolution 1441, which called for him to disarm. The evidence justifying this verdict and compelling a U.S.-led invasion of Iraq to forcibly disarm Saddam was presented in brief by U.S. Secretary of State Colin Powell as well as by Iraqi defectors and British lawmakers, such as Baroness Emma Nicholson, a member of Britain's House of Lords and the European Parliament. As the founder of a humanitarian aid foundation after the Gulf War, she oversees a staff of 270, nearly all Iraqis, and gave evidence to Blix of genocide committed by Saddam as well as previously unknown locations where weapons of mass destruction were hidden.[1]

Under Saddam Hussein's regime, Iraq had been a state that both supported and sponsored terror. Iraq has trained hundreds of terrorists in hijacking, sabotage, and murder. Captured Taliban fighters confessed that Saddam Hussein supplied chemical weapons

Fast Figure

Saddam Hussein

After years of regime changes, Iraq found its first true leader in the ruthless and violent Saddam Hussein. A top Iraqi leader since 1968, he seized and retained total power in 1979 by destroying any dissension, real or imagined, and sought to expand his influence through the production of weapons of mass destruction. After two wars and a decade of U.N.-imposed sanctions, Hussein remained in power until 2003, when the U.S.-led coalition invaded Iraq with the goal of regime change.

training to al-Qaeda and consulted with Osama bin Laden. Like Osama bin Laden, Saddam had a reputation for mass destruction. In 1988–89, Hussein is said to have been responsible for the deaths of between 70,000 and 150,000 Kurds in northern Iraq, killing some 5,000 in just 15 minutes' time with mustard and sarin nerve gas. Those who survived exposure to these toxins have since acquired horrible physical deformations and genetic changes that are untreatable and will be passed on to successive generations. It is said that every conversation in any major city in northern Iraq includes references to family or friends killed in one of Saddam's many purges.

Saddam also is accused of forcibly relocating some 180,000 Marsh Arabs from southern Iraq by draining the marshlands in which they lived. After the Gulf War, Saddam allowed 500,000 Iraqi children to die of malnutrition while he continued to build immense personal palaces and erect enormous war monuments. Throughout his rule he ruthlessly assassinated family members and murdered thousands of Iraqi civilians.

Moreover, Laurie Mylorie's book *Study of Revenge: Saddam Hussein's Unfinished War Against America,* reported that Saddam was the sponsor of the 1993 attack on the World Trade Center. Saddam's agent, Ramzi Yousef, stated that his mission was to kill 250,000 people. In addition, the government of Kuwait has sought to try Saddam for war crimes and crimes against humanity, presenting testimony and photographic evidence of over 1,000 Arabs tortured and murdered by Saddam's SID (Special Intelligence Division). This pattern of terrorist behavior by a brutal dictator like Saddam was clearly a threat to the Middle East and to the West, and could not be ended except by regime change.

After the Gulf War, UN Resolution 1441, by a unanimous vote of 15 member nations, required Iraq to disarm and destroy its weapons of mass destruction, including chemical and biological weapons. UN weapons inspectors were shown gyroscopes found hidden beneath the Tigris River and quantities of de-weaponized anthrax, but tended to disregard the evidence. Yet every time they thought they had reached a "bottom" in uncovering evidence of hidden weapons, another bottom even further down appeared. One example of this was Saddam's "super-gun," a giant rocket launcher designed to fire missiles equipped with chemical and biological warheads to a range of 600 miles, which the inspectors subsequently dismantled. In a surprise visit during the mid-1990s, inspectors also discovered programs that had run computer simulations of long-range missile attacks. As a result of these disclosures, Saddam expelled the inspectors, claiming they were CIA spies, and he renewed hostilities against the United States and Allied flyovers, and continued to violate the no-fly zones in northern and southern Iraq.

In 2002, inspectors were allowed to return, but with limited access to sites. In December 2002 Iraq submitted to the United Nations a weapons declaration of 12,000 pages that was said to be a "complete disclosure." In his report on January 27 and March 3, 2003, Hans Blix gave a tentative confirmation that a materials breach had occurred in Iraq's lengthy report. Examples of omissions included 6,000 warheads unaccounted for and several caches of prohibited weapons discovered by the inspectors in an abandoned warehouse. These caches consisted of empty chemical warheads designed to fit rockets and dispense deadly sarin gas or other toxic agents. Also omitted from disclosure were tons of bacteriological and nerve agents, such as mustard gas, anthrax virus, and botulinum toxin covertly produced and turned into weapons in the 1980s. U.S. soldiers who fought in the 1991 Gulf War have since suffered from "Gulf War Syndrome" as a result of fallout from Iraqi chemical dumps that were destroyed by the allies.

Fast Quote

Bush on Iraq's Weapons
"We will not allow the world's most dangerous regime to threaten us with the world's most dangerous weapons."

George W. Bush

After the Gulf War, chemical and biological weapons production continued full-scale, as exposed by Saddam's son-in-law (whom Saddam later executed), and the CIA has disclosed that it believes Saddam was also close to genetically modifying his biological weapons to enhance their devastation potential. In addition, dried anthrax (such as that found in letters mailed to U.S. officials in October 2001, which caused a number of deaths), smallpox, and camel pox (similar to smallpox) viruses are believed to have been developed by Saddam. A smallpox weapon alone is the biological equivalent of a nuclear bomb, the virus having claimed over 500 million lives during the twentieth century. In addition, one pound of anthrax can decimate the population of a large city. Saddam had enough stockpiles of anthrax to kill every person on earth three times over.

According to unconfirmed reports, beginning in 1998, Saddam attempted to purchase uranium from Africa and enrich it in order to obtain a fusion weapon. He had also acquired aluminum tubes used to make centrifuges and electronic switches for detonating implosion bombs. In January 2003, about 3,000 pages of material related to uranium enrichment was uncovered in the home of an Iraqi physicist. This gave evidence that Iraq was not only withholding information on its nuclear capability, but was in production of nuclear devices. Because of this evidence, Saddam refused to allow inspectors to enter the private homes of Iraqi scientists (where documentary evidence might be hidden) or to even interview them in private. U.S. intelligence has confirmed that Saddam's agents told the scientists what to say and that Saddam had threatened to kill any scientist (and the family of any scientist) who cooperated with the inspectors. Worse still, Saddam initially would not allow U-2 spy planes to do flights over Iraq to search for weapons facilities, as required in the UN resolution. Nevertheless, a U.S. satellite was able to photograph a compound in northern Iraq that was suspected of being a facility for the production of chemical and biological weapons.

It is established fact that Iraq has been aggressively developing a nuclear weapons program for at least 15 years. Several Iraqi scientists who defected to the United States have revealed details to U.S. intelligence about Saddam's continued nuclear program. One of these Iraqi defectors, Khidir Hamza, who for several decades helped build Iraq's nuclear weapons programs, has confirmed this with his testimony.[2] Nicknamed "Saddam's bombmaker" (after the title of a book he coauthored), Hamsa revealed that Iraq accelerated its secret nuclear program after the Israeli attack on Iraq's Osirak reactor, going from 500 to 7,000 workers in a time frame of five years. After the Iran-Iraq war, Iraq perfected the barriers that made it possible to diffuse and enrich uranium, so Iraqis already have a workable design for nuclear weapons. According to Hamza, Iraq needs two to three years to enrich its uranium, unless a country like Russia gives it to them. Then Iraq will have enriched uranium immediately. He also believes that Saddam had the components hardened for a bomb of smaller design to make a flight for delivery to a target.

Some critics (including the CIA) believe Hamsa does not have accurate information (he defected in the late 1980s), or may be a fraud (he didn't direct the nuclear program).[3] How-

Fast Fact

The Bombing of the Iraqi Nuclear Reactor

Arab fear of Israel's secret nuclear weapons program led many Arab nations to develop nuclear arsenals of their own. One of the first to do so was Iraqi dictator Saddam Hussein. When Israel learned of Saddam's nuclear capabilities, realizing it would be an eventual target, it planned an air attack to destroy Saddam's Osirak nuclear reactor before it reached completion. The successful attack took place in June 1981. Israel was reprimanded by the United Nations, but when the Persian Gulf War commenced, the world would have Israel to thank for stopping Saddam from becoming "unstoppable."

ever, even if he is wrong in his current assessments, he did have direct contact with Saddam and makes it clear that Saddam's intentions were to be a nuclear power in the region. Other Iraqi defectors have stated that Saddam had a number of mobile laboratories that produced weapons of mass destruction in the sub-basements of his palaces and in the backs of recreational vehicles, weapons of mass destruction hidden in an underground complex, and five bunkers beneath Iraqi sands dunes (stocked with warheads) in tunnel complexes beneath the sewers of Baghdad. Much of this evidence was provided by Israeli intelligence officials who debriefed Saddam's senior bodyguard, Abu Hamdi Mahmoud, who had personally visited these sites. A number of the mobile laboratories were believed to be secretly producing nuclear weaponry, and Saddam had hidden chemical and biological military agents in dual-use facilities where legitimate pharmaceuticals and chemicals were supposedly produced. One typical example is a castor oil plant, which could easily be converted to produce the deadly toxin Risin, which is extracted from the mash of castor beans.

Fast Fact

Iraq's Nuclear Capability

In 1974 the French supplied the nuclear reactor and fuel for Iraq's Osirak reactor (bombed by Israel in 1981), and in 1989 German scientist Carl Schaub taught the Iraqis how to build centrifuges (for refining uranium to fuel nuclear reactors).

Fast Feature

The Ba'ath Party

Building on the philosophies and rivalries within the Arab nationalist movement is the Ba'ath (Renaissance) Party, a very radical and militant political system in the Middle East. Originating in Damascus during the 1930s, Ba'athists took control of both Syria and Iraq in later decades. Their doctrines follow the same lines as Egyptian president Gamel Abdul Nassar's Pan-Arab vision, in which the entire Arab world was to unite under the Egyptian banner. Ba'athists view the individual Arab nations as a temporary arrangement until they can be replaced by a united Arab state. The Ba'ath party has been deeply split since the 1960s, with both Syria and Saddam Hussein's Iraq vying for position of ruler of the Arab world. With the overthrow of Hussein in 2003, only Syria remains under the influence of Ba'ath politics.

The U.S. government has stated that it has detailed evidence of Saddam's weapons violations, but has also said that revealing these details would have compromised the top-secret intelligence-gathering methods used to obtain the information, placing the United States at a military disadvantage. Despite these claims, former U.S. allies such as France and Germany refused to support the U.S.-led coalition strike on Iraq based on the evidence at hand. Many feel this reaction is suspect, given the fact that these same countries helped supply nuclear technology to Iraq. Still, the abundance of evidence available to the world led most countries to accept the charge of material breach, which they believe justified disarming Saddam.

Fast Feature

Iraqi Weapons of Mass Destruction Discovered and Destroyed (1991–1998)

- 2,850 tons of mustard gas
- 5.5 tons of sarin and VX nerve gas
- 3,000 tons of precursor chemicals
- 40,048 filled and unfilled chemical munitions
- 2,210 gallons of anthrax
- 5,000 gallons of botulinum toxin
- Uranium enrichment facilities fissile material
- 125 al-Samoud 2 Missiles (disclosed in 2003, a portion of which were destroyed)

Iraqi Weapons of Mass Destruction Unaccounted for Before the 2003 War in Iraq

- 48 SCUD missiles and SCUD launchers
- 3.9 tons of VX nerve gas
- 790 tons of sarin gas
- 5,300 gallons of botulinum toxin
- 2,200 gallons of anthrax
- 31,858 filled and unfilled chemical munitions
- 550 artillery shells loaded with mustard gas
- Design plans for nuclear weapons
- Approximately 600 tons of mustard gas and nerve agents
- Thousands of tons of precursor chemicals

44

WHY DIDN'T THE UNITED STATES REMOVE SADDAM HUSSEIN FROM POWER DURING THE GULF WAR?

The failure to remove Saddam Hussein from power in 1991 has been called the biggest mistake of the Gulf War. Indeed, Saddam's remaining in power allowed him to proclaim an Iraqi victory in the Gulf War and to persist in his belligerency toward the United States and Israel while secretly continuing his weapons programs. A number of reasons have been given for the U.S. withdrawal from Iraq in 1991 even though the United States had the capability to topple the Iraqi government and American ground troops were advancing upon Baghdad without opposition.

The official explanation is that the U.S. mission was simply to force Saddam's withdrawal from Kuwait, and once that objective was accomplished, there was no longer any reason to continue hostilities. Given the damage inflicted during the war, the UN sanctions and inspectors in place, the no-fly zones, and the U.S. troops remaining stationed in adjoining countries, it was believed by the United States that Saddam's regime could be held in check.

There's also a theory that the U.S. government had planned to remove Saddam Hussein from power but learned that he had planned to use biological agents in warheads against U.S. forces if they entered Baghdad. Not wanting to suffer the political fallout that might have resulted from higher casualties among U.S. troops, then-President Bush ordered a withdrawal before Saddam could make good on his threat.

An Israeli theory is that the United States feared that had the war continued, Israel, despite its initial restraint, would eventually retaliate with a nuclear bomb against Baghdad. In order to avoid a war between Israel and Iraq with weapons of mass destruction—which could have escalated into an all-out war in the region—a compromise was reached. The United States and Israel pulled back and Saddam was permitted to stay in power.

Yet another view is that the Saudi government compelled the United States to stop short of invading Baghdad because the Saudis did not want the United States to bring down a fellow Arab regime.

Each theory has its advocates, and it's possible the scenarios presented in these theories each may have contributed in some way to the ultimate decision to withdraw from Iraq and leave Saddam Hussein's dictatorship intact.

45

WAS THE U.S.-LED WAR WITH IRAQ ABOUT IMPERIALISM AND AN ATTEMPT TO CONTROL MIDDLE EAST OIL?

Far from maintaining imperialistic ambitions, a study of U.S. history reveals that America, in its victories in foreign wars, has retained less land than any other conqueror. In fact, the United States, more than any country in the world, has supported self-rule and freedom in the lands it has liberated, and has stated categorically that this is its goal in Iraq and other regions of the Middle East. While U.S. troops have been, and will remain, stationed in parts of the Middle East, the United States's intention is to remain only so long as is necessary until a democratic regime is established, as was the case with the overthrow of the Taliban regime in Afghanistan.

It is widely believed throughout the Middle East that the U.S. government's chief ambition in Iraq and the Middle East is to gain control of the region's oil. The Arab press referred to the Gulf War in 1991 as the "War for Oil," and continues to speak about the U.S. goal in the Middle East as trading "blood for oil." It is thought by Arab analysts that the road to the Middle East runs through Baghdad and that control of Iraq's oil reserves (second largest in the world) by the United States is a first step toward controlling oil production in Saudi Arabia (largest in the world). They see this as part of a grand scheme to reconstruct the Middle East, suggesting that the events of September 11 were embraced as a means to this end. It is also claimed that President George Bush and Vice-president Dick Cheney's links with the oil industry and desire to help American oil companies is the reason for the American attack on Iraq. This view argues that U.S. control of Iraqi oil will give American companies better leverage in getting subcontracting projects in the country and will prevent Baghdad from resuming full oil production. Iraq has proven reserves of 112 billion

Fast Quote

U.S. Wants to Control Oil?

"The United States is talking of war with Iraq not because Baghdad has allegedly amassed weapons of mass destruction but to control the country's huge oil reserves....They want an excuse to reconstruct the whole of the Middle East. [Iraqi president] Saddam Hussein is the first one. Last year it was Osama [bin Laden], this year it is Saddam, next year it will be somebody else."

Indian defense analyst
K. Subrahmanyam

barrels of crude oil; however, under UN sanctions, it is permitted to produce only 3 to 3.5 million barrels of oil a day as part of an oil-for-food program. Lifting the sanctions could throw the global oil market into a tailspin if full-fledged production was resumed. Such a move would significantly affect U.S. interests in the price of crude oil and could threaten American oil companies' deep-water exploration.

There are other concerns that influence this foreign opinion regarding the United States's involvement in Iraq. The change of regime in Iraq has jeopardized oil contracts with other countries—countries such as India, France, Russia, China, Italy, Vietnam, and Algeria, which had signed or sought to sign agreements to develop Iraqi oil fields, rebuild refineries, and undertake exploration activities. If Saddam's regime had survived and production had continued, new Iraqi oil wells would have been drilled by the Russian, Chinese, and French companies, as well as Iraqi companies. No such guarantees exist for these countries now that Saddam has been deposed and a new government friendly to the West may possibly be formed.

However, the facts of American diversification in oil importation argue against the conclusion that the United States seeks to control Middle East oil for its own consumption. Currently, the United States imports only 10 percent of its oil from the Middle East, with domestic oil production supplying about 50 percent of total oil consumed in the United States, and Canada, Venezuela, Mexico, and several African countries providing the rest of the needed oil. Also, an imbalance in oil production is not a major motive for the United States, as oil is commonly traded on the market, and market conditions are expected to take care of any imbalance.

The United States's primary concern in the Middle East is national security, and therefore it has a vital interest in *who* controls the oil in the Middle East, since a monopoly of control by a despotic regime that sponsors terror (such as Iraq or Iran) would result in an imbalance of power, destabilize the region, and ultimately export terror through weapons of mass destruction to the United States. The Gulf Cooperation Council states (comprised of Saudi Arabia, Kuwait, Oman, Qatar, the United Arab Emirates, and Bahrain), Iran, and Iraq jointly possess 64 percent of the world's proven oil reserves, with Saudi Arabia alone controlling 27 percent. The United States entered the Gulf War against Iraq because Saddam Hussein had seized Kuwait's oil fields and was thought to be planning to invade the oil fields in Saudi Arabia. Had this occurred, Saddam Hussein would have controlled a majority of the world's oil reserves with an almost limitless source of income to help finance his "Mother of All Battles" against the West. The United States contends that Saddam's agenda to control this oil remained unchanged and that his links with terrorist organizations, such as al-Qaeda, as well as his own illegal weapons program, proved him a threat to the entire region. As for U.S. intentions, U.S. Secretary of State Colin Powell has affirmed that once the United States had removed Saddam from power, "Iraq's oil will be held in trust for the Iraqi people."

46

DID THE UNITED STATES HAVE ANY GOALS BEYOND DISARMAMENT IN IRAQ?

The United States's first goal regarding Iraq was to effect Iraq's compliance with UN Resolution 1441 and disarm Saddam Hussein. A second goal, in order to prevent a return to past problems, was a change of regime. The primary purpose of introducing a regime change in Iraq was the liberation of the Iraqi people from a tyrannical dictatorship that had brutalized its citizenry for almost half a century. As one of the leaders at the central mosque in Suleimaniyah, the regional capital of Iraq, declared, "I welcome even the Jew Sharon if he can liberate us from Saddam!"[5] However, the regime change will take time, and it is estimated that 150,000 troops (a large percentage of whom are reservists) will have to remain in Iraq to maintain order so that the new government would have a chance to form. This will prove a costly venture on several fronts and is likely to strain U.S. relations with a number of Arab states that are already anxious for the American forces to withdraw.

47

HOW WERE THE U.S. PLANS AGAINST IRAQ TIED TO A LARGER MIDDLE EAST PLAN?

While the first concern of the United States was to disarm Saddam's regime by force, other concerns were to change the Iraqi regime and democratize the country so it can become an example to other rogue states in the Middle East that have, or are attempting to, acquire weapons of mass destruction. The removal of Saddam's regime demonstrated what can happen to these other states and hopefully will serve as a deterrent to terrorism. This, it is believed, will open a new path for peace in the Middle East and inspire democracy throughout the Arab world. In particular, the overthrow of Saddam's regime is seen as a major step toward resolving the Israeli-Palestinian conflict. Indeed, both the Madrid Peace Conference and the Oslo Peace Process began as a result of the weakening of Iraq through the Gulf War in 1991. In regard to the present-day possibilities, President Bush has stated, "Israel, as the terror threat is removed and security improves, should support the establishment of a viable Palestinian State and end its settlements."[6] This statement assumes that the fall of Saddam's government will affect funding for terror attacks against Israel and permit Palestinian reformists, whom Israel will accept as peace partners, to take control of the Palestinian Authority and work with the Israelis on a two-state solution.

However, as long as the Palestine Liberation Front receives Arab support, and as long as there are sources that finance homicide bombings, there will continue to be many avenues of funding for Palestinian terrorism. For example, Syria and its client state Lebanon are hosts to the militant Palestinian groups Hamas, Hizballah, Islamic Jihad, and the Popular Front for the Liberation of Palestine, while Iran and North Korea, the two remaining countries in President Bush's "Axis of Evil," have ties with some of these militant Palestinian groups or have sold armaments to Palestinian terrorists. Moreover, numerous other terrorist organizations, including al-Qaeda, have ties with militant Palestinian organizations and influence much of the Palestinian population. This was made clear when Palestinian citizens in general applauded the attack on America on September 11 and the loss of the U.S. space shuttle Columbia (which was seen as a symbol of cooperation between the United States and Israel).

Consequently, many Arabs, as well as Western political analysts, dread what could happen in the postwar Middle East. As Saudi Arabia's foreign minister prince al-Faisal whined, "The consequences of war are going to be tragic."[7] Some Arabs are convinced that a war will breed regional instability, spark new anti-American hostilities, and infuse terrorist ranks with fresh recruits eager to spread terrorism on a grander scale. In addition, Iraq, as well as most of the countries in the Middle East, are deeply tribal, vengeful, and embittered. The vacuum left by Saddam's departure could result in power struggles between Kurdish, Shi'ite, and Sunni factions, leading to long-term civil strife or the division of the country. Whatever the case, the greater goals of regime change and democratization of Iraq in the aftermath of the war will require both time and careful management in order to avoid a return to a dictatorship, which is the status quo in the Middle East.

48

WILL MUSLIM STATES IN THE MIDDLE EAST ACCEPT DEMOCRACY?

The United States' desire is to help promote democracy in Iraq and bring about the rebuilding of the Iraqi government under national leadership (much like the United States did in Japan and Germany after World War II). After this is accomplished, it is hoped that Iraq will be a model of democracy to the rest of the region. However, the greatest obstacle faced is the fact that not one of the 22 Arab states in the Middle East has ever been a democracy. The reason for this is hotly debated, with one school of thought pointing to sociological and political causes and the other to religious causes. On the one hand, it is said that democracy has been linked in the Arab mind with Western militarism and imperialism, and so a fear of the West has forced an isolation from Western values in the East. On the other hand, it is noted that the religion of Islam unites the Arab states. Even though Turkey practices democracy, it is largely secular, achieving its form of government only by renouncing and even banning certain forms of Islamic practice. At least nine other Islamic countries outside the Middle East, many which are of Third World status, do practice democracy; however, these are also farther from the hub of the Islamic world. Although this may argue against the Islamic religion being the sole determining factor, it does not rule it out as the principal factor. It is a fact that the Arab states that are governed most strictly by Islamic law are also the most despotic. While the Qur'an may contain principles upon which a democracy might be built, Islam itself is built upon the life and teachings of Muhammad, whose pattern of rule was dictatorial. Islamic law, interpreted for the masses by Imams (spiritual clerics), requires strict conformity in every realm of life (social, economic, judicial, and religious).

Thus, even though sociological and cultural factors have a significant impact on the East's view of democracy, they are not inseparable from the worldview of Islam. For example, in her book *Islam and Democracy: Fear of the Modern World*,[8] Fatima Mernissi observes that democracy has always been viewed by the East as a humanistic idea propagated in the West by secular schools. Such principles as individual autonomy, freedom of thought, the right to freedom of action, and tolerance are democratic

Fast Quote

Every Arab Country a Monarchy/Theocracy, Dictatorship

"Virtually every Arab country is a monarchy, theocracy, or military dictatorship. Freedom of speech, property rights, free elections, and the separation of church and state are almost nonexistent. Speaking out against the rulers or against the Moslem religion leads to imprisonment or death. All attempts to start competing political parties are ruthlessly crushed."

Edwin Locke, Dean's Professor of Leadership and Motivation, University of Maryland

concepts not practiced under Islamic law. For this reason, when Western colonization ended after World War II, the newly independent Muslim states fought against the advances of Enlightenment philosophy and banned Western humanism as foreign and imported. Arab countries preferred the security of past tradition within the boundaries of Islamic law.

For this reason, the virtues of democracy common to the West have not simply been tried and found wanting by the East; rather, they have been found unwanted and left untried. The culture and values of western democracy, while envied economically by the East, have been despised socially and religiously. Historically, Israel has been the only democracy in the Middle East, and because Israel is viewed as an enemy by almost every Muslim state, democracy has long been identified with Americanism and Zionism. As a result, any imposition of democracy on a Muslim state (such as Iraq), even as a model, by the United States (the ally of Israel), will be viewed negatively in the region. In addition, Robin Wright, author of *Sacred Rage: The Rise of Militant Islam*, observes that the longer the United States and its Western allies maintain a presence in a Muslim country like Iraq (for the purpose of making a transition to a democratic regime), the more its actions will be viewed as neo-colonialism. The original U.S. plan estimates a direct U.S. presence for one to two years of between 125,000 and 200,000 troops, much longer than it is believed most Iraqis (as well as other Arab states) will tolerate.

The U.S. plan, however, is not to impose democracy, but to let a free Iraqi people decide their direction. As President Bush explained: "The United States has no intention of determining the precise form of Iraq's new government. That choice belongs to the Iraqi people."[9] However, according to Benazir Bhutto, former prime minister of Pakistan, the problem with this approach is that while the Muslim people want democracy, the Muslim rulers do not. This is understandable, since Muslim states are dictatorships, a system that benefits the rulers but not those who are ruled. Rarely, if ever, have the Muslim people been able to decide their destiny. Islamic law rejects democratic principles, and Muslim rulers, who are generally expected to conform to Islamic law, have themselves been born and bred in dictatorial regimes and will have to continue to align themselves with Islamic dictatorial regimes in the region. Moreover, Muslim officials will not "take orders" from Americans (who are viewed by their religion as infidels), and thus "lose face" before their people and other Muslim rulers.

There is a possibility that even if a form of democratic rule is adopted in Iraq, it will not prove to be a boon to the people, but rather, lead to greater bondage. Under the democratic process, it is likely that fundamentalist Muslim Iraqis could vote a Taliban-styled government into power. Ironically, then, the people's adoption of democratic freedom of choice could result in their losing freedom of choice with the imposition of Islamic law.

So, while a liberated Iraq has freed the Iraqi people from a tyrant who ruled by the means of force and fear, and may present an opportunity for democracy in an Arab state, there are formidable difficulties to overcome because other Muslim rulers are not likely to welcome such a form of government.

49

WHY DID SADDAM HUSSEIN WANT TO ATTACK ISRAEL?

In the Gulf War, Saddam Hussein promoted himself as the leader of the Arab world against the "Zionist entity" (the term used by Iraqi officials for Israel). He depicted himself as a reincarnation of Nebuchadnezzar, the "first Iraqi ruler to destroy the Jews" (in 586 B.C.), and believed that by championing the cause of the Palestinians and attacking Israel, the mutual enemy of the Arab world, he could deflect the anger over his invasion of Kuwait, sever the U.S. coalition with the Arab states, and head an Arab alliance against the West in what he proclaimed as "the Mother of All Battles." Saddam was thwarted in this attempt by Israeli restraint but continued to use the Israeli-Palestinian conflict, and especially the American support of Israel, as a rallying point for Arab support in his fight against the United States. To this end he embraced Yasser Arafat and the Palestinian Intifada, and financially encouraged the homicide bombings against Israeli civilians.

Saddam Hussein began to develop his weapons of mass destruction, and especially his nuclear weapons program, because of Israel's nuclear capabilities and with the express purpose of destroying Israel. This was admitted by Tariq Aziz, the Iraqi defense minister, to Richard Butler, a former UNSCOM executive chairman: "In one of my private conversations with Tariq Aziz, he chose to tell me, not as a result of questioning by me, that Iraq had developed biological weapons—to deal with the Zionist entity. He could not say the word 'Israel.' He made it very clear that the justification for Iraq's manufacturing of biological weapons was to deal with the Jews. It was a statement of a genocidal character."[10]

In the U.S.-led war against Iraq, strategic analysts thought that Saddam's strategy would be to make Israel a target. Besides hoping to gain an Arab alliance, his plan would be to strike Israel with biological weapons that would cause massive human casualties. At the same time,

Fast Feature

Saddam Hussein and Israel

During the Gulf War, Saddam Hussein claimed he was the new Nebuchadnezzar who was destined to destroy Israel in "the Mother of All Battles" and attempted to influence the Arab world to join him in his attack on Tel Aviv. That attack failed, but Palestinians still chanted "Our beloved Saddam, strike Tel Aviv!" Iraq's military announced a willingness to carry out a missile attack on Israel in cooperation with the Palestinians as part of an all-out Arab war. Moreover, Saddam said he had raised a 6.5 million volunteer "Jerusalem Liberation Army." Iraq had also called on Islamic countries to impose an oil embargo on the United States and other allies of Israel. Qusai Hussein, the son of Saddam Hussein and the commander of the Republican Guards, once said, "The Jews know their doom will come from Babylon!"

Fast Quote

Saddam's Attack on Israel

"We have to expect Saddam to lash out at Israel, if for no other reason than when Saddam does believe that his days are finally over, and that the United States is about to evict him from power and he believes this will lead to his own demise, he is going to try to secure his place in the history books as being the great Arab leader who launched some massive blow against Israel with his dying breath."

Kenneth Pollack, Middle East Expert

Iraqi agents in the United States were thought likely to launch similar attacks against U.S. cities, and Iraqi soldiers were likely to do the same against American ground troops. The resulting high civilian death toll, they believed, would create a backlash of popular opinion in both Israel and the United States against the U.S. invasion, demoralizing U.S. troops and forcing a U.S. withdrawal. Ultimately, Saddam's desire was to leave a legacy that would establish him in the eyes of the Arab world as the successor of Nebuchadnezzar.

50

WHAT EFFECT WOULD THE AFTERMATH OF THE U.S.-LED WAR AGAINST IRAQ HAVE ON ISRAEL?

Israel's domestic decisions have, of necessity, been based on security concerns. Therefore, as President Bush noted in his 2003 State of the Union message, peace would be considered only in the context of "a secure Israel." For this reason, as the United States anticipated war with Iraq, reporter Joe Klein observed that "a stronger Israel is very much embedded in the rationale for the war with Iraq."[12] Indeed, the U.S. administration believes that the path back to the peace process depends on the removal of Iraq from the equation of the Middle East conflict. It was hoped that the end of Saddam's rule would undermine Iranian, Syrian, and Lebanese terrorist organizations as well as diminish Jordanian influence, and tip the balance of power in Israel's favor, strengthening its position in dealing with the Palestinians. Even before the war, Palestinians feared that "if the balloon goes up over Iraq, Sharon will use that as cover to come in and get rid of Arafat."[13]

The most optimistic postwar scenario envisioned Islamic terrorism reduced, or better, going into temporary retirement, and Yasser Arafat removed from power, permitting Palestinian reformists to negotiate with the Sharon government on some modified version of the Saudi

Peace Plan. Other analysts proposed a more pessimistic scenario. The unpredictable consequences of the war could inflame the already vehement Islamic radicals to call for an all-out *jihad* against the "Zionists and Crusaders" until they are once more expelled from Muslim lands. The Palestinians, aided by these militant factions, would press forward with their Intifada, trapping Israel between a collapsing economy and a growing and ever more violent Palestinian population. Israel would act in the interest of its security and seek to kill or exile Arafat and other militant Palestinian leaders in neighboring Lebanon and Syria.

In fact, the aftermath of the war contained a bit of both of these scenarios. Saddam loyalists continued daily resistance against American and Allied forces in Iraq, leading the U.S. Administration to announce an extension of its military presence for 5-10 more years, even while Arab countries demanded an immediate withdrawal of all U.S. troops and al-Qaeda threatened new attacks on U.S. cities. The Saudi Plan gave way to the Road Map for Peace in the Middle East, brokered by the quartet (U.S., UN, E.U., and Russia) and saw the Israelis and Palestinians begin the first steps toward new negotiations at the Aqaba Summit in Jordan. While an initial wave of new Palestinian terrorism in Israel sought to derail implementation of the Road Map, the Palestinian militant groups that launched the attacks were persuaded to join a cease-fire between the Palestinian Authority and the Israelis and a general truce opened the door to the possibility of the Palestinian Authority fulfilling the Road Map prerequisite of "cessation of hostilities."

Fast Quote

Israel After Saddam

"If it wasn't for Iraq, Israel's 1948 War of Independence would have been totally different....The Iraqis pushed everyone to invade, and they themselves sent a whole division. Even so the advent of Saddam represented a quantum leap. Saddam has threatened in the past to incinerate and obliterate Israel from the face of the earth....Whatever comes after Saddam, Jerusalem hopes Iraq will be taken out of the Mideast battlefield for the first time in Israel's history." [14]

Isabel Kershner

Yet the region remains in tension, the Arab world continues in a state of belligerency against a Jewish state, and the Arab street has increased its anti-American rhetoric. The single prospect of hope at the moment appears to be the Road Map and the significant pressure exerted by the international quartet to force parties to conform to the plan's timetable. However, the concessions demanded by the Road Map call for Israel to return to its pre-1967 war boundaries (considered indefensible) with an armed Palestinian population with international recognition living next door. It is the outworking of this scenario that will fill the headlines of our newspapers and news programs in the days ahead, creating new facts for the future on the Middle East conflict.

SEEKING A SOLUTION

It is my hope that the facts presented within this book have provided you with a clearer understanding of the conflict in the Middle East. Yet the purpose has not been merely to inform, but to impress upon readers the urgency of seeking a solution to the regional conflict between the Jews and Arabs and the potential global conflict between the East and the West.

At present, the situation in Iraq has offered the possibility of introducing the principles of democracy to the future government of the country with the hope of also influencing the region away from the traditional forms of dictatorships and theocratic states. However, the western democracies still are contending with enforcing control in Afghanistan and Iraq, while facing new challenges from Iran and North Korea as well as continuing to hunt for al-Qaeda cells and fight the War on Terrorism. Meanwhile, anti-Semitism has returned in force in Europe and hatred of the West, and particularly the United States, has risen to unprecedented levels in the Middle East. In addition, all attempts to implement the Road Map to Peace, beginning with the Israelis and Palestinians, has faced significant roadblocks, resulting in more map than road.

Ultimately, the story told at the beginning of this book about the scorpion and the crocodile remains unchanged. The crocodiles continue to take chances with the scorpions in hope that the river might be crossed, and the scorpion, despite every pledge to the contrary, still stings. And, as of yet, no one has made it to the other side.

While there are some who believe (including myself) that the only permanent solution is spiritual and awaits the coming of the Prince of Peace, we also believe that a temporary political solution is possible and should be the fervent prayer of people of faith. If through prayer and the political process the scorpion could be stopped from stinging, or at least the crocodile could be made safe from the scorpion's sting, perhaps both parties could finally make it across the river.

INDEX TO SIDEBARS

Fast Figures

Fast Quotes

NOTES

INTRODUCTION

1. Mitchell G. Bard, *The Complete Idiot's Guide to Middle East Conflict*, 2d ed. (Indianapolis: Macmillan, 2003), p. 339.

SECTION I

1. Quoted from *Palestine: History, Case and Solution* as cited in the newspaper *Al Qaida*, June 21, 2001.
2. Dr. Kamel el Baker as cited in D.F. Green, ed., *Arab Theologians on Jews and Israel: Extracts from the Proceedings of the Fourth Conference of the Academy of Islamic Research*. 3d ed. (Geneva: Editions de l'Avenir, 1976), p. 59.
3. See the final program of action of the World Conference on Racism, Racial Discrimination, Xenophobia and Related Intolerance posted at www.unhchr.ch/html/racism/.
4. As cited by Mubeer Rizeq, "Coming days will be harder—military intelligence chief on the future of the Intifada," *The Jerusalem Times* (September 14, 2001).
5. Although Herzl proposed Uganda as a temporary refuge to relieve present Jewish persecution at the Sixth Zionist Congress (1903), he conceded this was not the ultimate aim, and the Seventh Jewish Congress (1905) rejected the proposal in favor of the original goal of Palestine.
6. Joseph Heller, "Zionism and the Jewish Problem," Symposium on *The Future of the Jews*, ed. by J.J. Lynz (London: Lindsay Drummond, 1945), p. 72.
7. Carl Voss, *The Palestine Problem Today: Israel and Its Neighbors* (Boston, MA: Beacon Press, 1953), p. 13.
8. As cited by Abba Eban, *Heritage* (1984), p. 330.
9. Found in "The Year the Arabs Discovered Palestine" by Daniel Pipes, *Jerusalem Post*, September 13, 2000 at www.danielpipes.org/article/352.
10. As cited in the *Jerusalem Post* (November 2, 1991) and by Clarence Wagner, "40 Significant Facts About Israel's History" (Jerusalem: October, 2000), 3:3.
11. Quoted in the newspaper *Al-Nahar Al-Arabi* (December 26, 1981) and as cited by Binyamin Netanyahu, *A Place Among the Nations*, p. 147.
12. Quoted in *New Republic* (1974) as cited by Ramon Bennett, *When Day and Night Cease*, p. 211.
13. Tareq Y. Ismael, *The Arab Left* (New York: Syracuse University Press, 1976), pp. 12-13.
14. Mitchell G. Bard, *The Complete Idiot's Guide to Middle East Conflict* (Indianapolis: Alpha Books, 1999), p. 122.
15. Ibid., p. 115 (sidebar).
16. Ibid., p. 118.
17. Ibid., p. 119.
18. Ibid.
19. See Sidney Zion, "The Palestinian Problem: It's All in a Name," *New York* magazine (March 13, 1978), pp. 42-45.
20. As cited in Bard, *The Complete Idiot's Guide*, p. 159.
21. Personal conversation with Ory Mazar at Kibbutz Kalia, Dead Sea, Israel, September 12, 2002.

SECTION II

1. S.D. Goiten, *Jews and Arabs: Their Contacts Through the Ages* (New York: Schocken Books, 1964), pp. 121-22.
2. Stanley A. Ellisen, *Who Owns the Land?* (Portland, OR: Multnomah Press, 1991), p. 157.

3. As cited by Eliyahu Tal, *Whose Jerusalem?* (Tel Aviv: International Forum for a United Jerusalem, 1994), pp. 100-01.

4. As cited in Abba Eban, *My Country: The Story of Modern Israel* (New York: Random House, 1972), p. 33.

5. This estimate is given in Stanley Ellisen, *Who Owns the Land?,* p. 153.

SECTION III

1. Daniel Pipes, "The Origins of the Palestinian Arabs," at www.us-israel.org/jsource/History/palarabs.html.

2. See David Jacobson, "When Palestine Meant Israel," *Biblical Archaeology Review* 27:3 (May/June 2001): 43-47.

3. As cited by Eliyahu Tal, *Whose Jerusalem?* (Tel Aviv: International Forum for a United Jerusalem, 1994), p. 93.

4. As cited by Clarence Wagner, "40 Significant Facts About Israel's History," Bridges for Peace Teaching Letter (October 2000), 3:3.

5. As cited in Avner Yaniv, *PLO* (Jerusalem: Israel Universities Study Group of Middle Eastern Affairs, August 1974), p. 5.

6. Quoted in the article "Is Jordan Palestine, or Not?" *Dispatch from Jerusalem* (Fall 1993).

7. Yasser Arafat speaking to Orina Fallacei and quoted in *The New Republic, The Jerusalem Post,* International Edition (Friday, September 11, 1992).

8. Tad Szulc, "Who are the Palestinians?" *National Geographic* (June 1992).

9. As cited in "The Arab Case of Palestine: Evidence Submitted by the Arab Office, Jerusalem, to the Anglo-American Committee of Inquiry, March 1946," in *The Israel-Arab Reader,* ed. Walter Laqueur (New York: Bantam Books, 1969), p. 92.

10. Trude Dothan, "The 'Sea Peoples' and the Philistines of Ancient Palestine," *Civilizations of the Ancient Near East,* ed. Jack M. Sasson (Peabody, MA: Hendrickson Publishers, 2000), 1:1271.

11. See Jonathan N. Tubb, *Canaanites,* Peoples of the Past series (Norman, OK: University of Oklahoma Press, 1998), pp. 145-46. Tubb sees a Neo-Punic artistic tradition continuing until A.D. 200, but agrees that the Canaanite influence ended at Carthage.

12. For this list see DeHass, *History,* p. 258, and John of Würzburg in Reinhold Rohricht edition, pp. 41, 69.

13. Ernst Frankenstine, *Justice for My People* (London: Nicholson & Watson, 1943), p. 127.

14. As cited by Gil Hoffman, "Netanyahu: Palestinians are 'foreign workers,'" *The Jerusalem Post* (July 15, 2001), p. 3.

15. As cited in Rachel Ehrenfeld, "Where Does the Money Go? A Study of the Palestinian Authority" (New York: American Center for Democracy, October 2002), p. 4.

16. MEMRI (www.memri.org): *Kuwait Daily:* "Arafat deposited $5.1 million from US aid into personal account."

17. Rachel Ehrenfeld, "Where Does the Money Go?" p. 15.

18. Roger David Carasso, "Palestinians (Western Palestinian Arabs)," 1994 at www.carasso.com/roger/Israel/palestine.html.

19. Joseph Farah, *From Arab America* (February 22, 2002).

20. This statistic was reported on July 25, 2002 by the Department for Humanitarian Aid and SHA.

21. As cited in Murray Dixon, *Whose Promised Land?* (rev. ed.), Heinemann History Project (Auckland: Octopus Publishing Group, 1996), p. 88.

22. As cited at www.pmo.gov.il/english/nave/violence-5.html.

23. As cited in *Levitt Letter* 24:11 (November 2002): 4.

24. "Principles Guiding Israel's Policy in the Aftermath of the June 1967 War" Jerusalem (August 9, 1967), as cited in Yehuda Lukacs, ed., *The Israeli-Palestinian Conflict: A Documentary Record 1967–1990* (New York: Cambridge University Press, 1992), p. 171.

25. *Levitt Letter,* p. 4.

26. Yasser Arafat, as reported to the Norweigen Daily *Dagen*, February 6, 1996 and cited by Arutz 7 (February 7, 1996).

27. As cited in *Al-Misri*, October 11, 1949.

SECTION IV

1. As reported to me by Ory Mazar, who was present at Deir Yassin and participated in the transfer of these Arabs. Conversation at Kibbutz Kalia, September 9, 2002.

2. Mitchell G. Bard, *The Complete Idiot's Guide to Middle East Conflict* (Indianapolis: Alpha Books, 1999), p. 163.

3. Mitchell G. Bard, *Myths and Facts: A Guide to the Arab-Israeli Conflict* (Chevy Chase, MD: American Israeli Cooperative Enterprise, Inc. 2001), p. 63.

4. This speech by Nasser was made on August 31, 1955 and recorded in *Middle Eastern Affairs* (December 1956), p. 461.

5. Voice of the Arabs broadcast (May 18, 1967), as cited in Bard, *The Complete Idiot's Guide*, p. 225.

6. Syrian defense minister Hafez Assad (May 20, 1967), as cited in Bard, *The Complete Idiot's Guide*, p. 225.

7. Ehud Ya'ari, "Syria on the Boil," *The Jerusalem Report* (January 27, 2003), p. 31.

8. Palestinian Authority daily newspaper *Al-Hayat Al-Jadida*, December 1, 1997. In this regard it should be noted that Louis Rene Beres, professor of International Law, Department of Political Science, Purdue University, has reported that the formation of a Palestinian state poses a threat to Israel's nuclear infrastructure, leaving Israel "weakened" in the eyes of other Arab powers and vulnerable to attack.

SECTION V

1. Ariel Sharon, "Towards a National Agenda of Peace and Security," address to AIPAC Policy Conference (Washington, D.C., March 19, 2001), p. 1.

2. David Bar-Illan, "Errors in Arabizing Jerusalem," *The Jerusalem Post International Edition*, November 27, 1993, p. 13.

3. Correspondence between Wickley in the Jerusalem office to Rose in the foreign office in London, April 7, 1955, Public Record Office, Foreign Office 371/121850.

4. As cited in Bernard Wassertein, *Divided Jerusalem: The Struggle for the Holy City* (London: Profile Books, Ltd., 2001), p. 189.

5. Interview with Adnan Husseni by Ulf Carmesund, September, 1991. As cited in his book *Two Faces of the Expanding Jewish State: A Study on How Religious Motives Can Legitimate Two Jewish Groups Trying to Dominate Mount Moriah in Jerusalem* (Uppsala, Sweden: Uppsala University, 1992), pp. 86-87.

6. Found in "Jews Lay Foundation for Temple as Clashes Erupt," anonymous, on the website of DAWN, the most widely circulating English newspaper in Pakistan, at www.dawn.com/2001/07/30/top15.htm

7. As cited in Mitchell G. Bard, *The Complete Idiot's Guide to Middle East Conflict* (Indianapolis: Alpha Books, 1999), p. 410.

8. As reported by Arutz 7 news, July 26, 2000.

9. From the Friday, May 15, 1998 broadcast as cited in *Dispatch from Jerusalem* (July-August 1998), p. 19.

10. Remarks of then-Prime Minister Binyamin Netanyahu at the National Unity Coalition for Israel, Washington, D.C., December 7, 1996.

11. Shelomo Dov Goitein, "The Historical Background of the Erection of the Dome of the Rock," *Journal of the American Oriental Society* 70:2 (April-June 1950), p. 107.

12. Ya'qubi (writing in A.D. 874) in G. Le Strange, *Palestine Under the Moslems*, reprint of the 1890 edition (Beirut: Khayats, 1965), p. 116. While repeated by later Muslim authors and accepted by most Western historians, the account suffers by virtue of the fact that no other contemporary historians are aware of Ya'qubi's story, but instead offer entirely different explanations.

13. Miriam Ayalon, "Islamic Monuments In Jerusalem," in *Jerusalem: City of the Ages*, p. 82.

14. *Al-Muqaddasi: Description of Syria, including Palestine*. Translated from the Arabic and annotated by G. Le Strange. Palestine Pilgrims Text Society 3, reprint of 1896 edition (New York: AMS Press, 1971), pp. 22-23, as cited in F.E. Peters, *Jerusalem*, p. 198.

SECTION VI

1. As cited in Mitchell G. Bard, *The Complete Idiot's Guide to the Middle East Conflict*, 2d ed. (Indianapolis: Macmillan, 2003), p. 203.

SECTION VII

1. For the full report by Lamia Lahoud, see *The Jerusalem Post* (March 4, 2001).

2. Recorded on May 10, 1994 and reported by Arutz Sheva offshore radio.

3. As cited in *Dispatch from Jerusalem* 18:4 (November-December 1993): 8.

4. As cited in *The Washington Post* (October 20, 2000), p. A33.

SECTION VIII

1. Joan Peters, *From Time Immemorial* (San Francisco: Harper & Row, 1984), pp. 391-92.

2. Yasser Arafat, *El Mundo* (Venezuela, February 11, 1980), as cited in Ramon Bennet, *The Great Deception: Philistine* (Jerusalem: Arm of Salvation, 1995), p. 100.

3. Dr. Muhammad Said Ramadan al-Buti, *Jurisprudence in Muhammad's Biography* (7th ed.), pp. 323-24.

4. Ibid., p. 134.

5. Dr. Muhammad al-Amin, *The Method of Islamic Law* (no page number in original).

6. Taqiy al-Din al-Nabahan, *The Book of the Islamic State* (Jerusalem, 1953), pp. 113, 117.

7. Reported in World Tribune.com and cited in the article "The Islamic Mindset" at hallindsey oracle.com (January 27, 2003): 1.

8. As cited in Ira Rifkin, "Blame It on the Wahhabis," *The Jerusalem Report* (January 27, 2003), p. 46.

SECTION IX

1. See Edith M. Lederer, "British Lawmaker Claims Iraq Evidence," *Yahoo! News* (February 4, 2003), p. 1.

2. See "Querying Saddam's Bombmaker," A Question and Answer Session with Dr. Khidir Hamsa, Carnegie Endowment (November 23, 2000).

3. For details of the accusation, see www.tokyotightwad.com/sanctions.html#2 (p. 3).

4. Quote taken from the program "Saddam's Arsenal," aired on The History Channel (February 26, 2003).

5. *Wall Street Journal* (March 5, 2003), p. A14

6. President George Bush in a speech to the American Enterprise Institute, February 26, 2002.

7. As cited by Johanna McGeary in "Looking Beyond Saddam," *Time* (March 10, 2003), p. 33.

8. Fatima Mernissi, *Islam and Democracy: Fear of the Modern World*, trans. Mary Jo Lakeland (Cambridge, MA: Perseus Books, 1992).

9. As cited in the Associated Press story by Ron Fournier, "Iraq war tied to Mideast peace," *San Antonio Express-News* (February 27, 2003): 1A.

10. As cited by the Jerusalem Center for Public Affairs, Daily Alert (jcpa.org/daily), February 6, 2003, p. 1.

11. From the program "Saddam's Arsenal," aired on The History Channel (February 26, 2003).

12. Joe Klein, "How Israel Is Wrapped Up in Iraq," *Time* (February 10, 2003), p. 27.

13. Quote from an unnamed senior U.S. official cited in "Will Arafat Step Aside?" *Time* (February 24, 2003), p. 16.

14. Isabel Kershner, "When He's Gone: Israel and a Post-Saddam Iraq." *The Jerusalem Report* (March 10, 2003), p. 15. The quote cites, in part, the words of Amatzia Baram of Haifa University.

About the Author

Randall Price is recognized as an expert on the Middle East and holds a master of theology degree from Dallas Theological Seminary in Old Testament and Semitic Languages, a Ph.D. from the University of Texas at Austin in Middle Eastern Studies, and has done graduate study at the Hebrew University of Jerusalem in the fields of semitic languages and biblical archaeology. He is Research Professor of Biblical Studies and Archaeology at Oregon Theological Seminary, Professor of Archaeology and Biblical History at Trinity Southwest University, and Adjunct Professor of Old Testament at Baptist Bible Seminary.

As President of World of the Bible Ministries, Inc., a nonprofit organization dedicated to reaching the world with a biblical analysis of the past, present, and prophetic Middle East, Dr. Price speaks to international audiences through conferences and lectureships each year. He also serves as director of the Qumran Plateau excavation project in Israel, is a certified pilgrim tour guide in Israel, and through his tour company World of the Bible Tours has directed 65 tours to the Bible lands. Dr. Price has authored or coauthored some 20 books on the subjects of biblical archaeology and biblical prophecy, and is a contributor to the *New Eerdmans Dictionary of the Bible*.

He has appeared on numerous television documentaries, including the "Ancient Secrets of the Bible" series, *Encounters with the Unexplained*, the "Thief in the Night" series, "Uncovering the Truth about Jesus," and "The Search for Jesus Continues." He has been the executive producer and on-screen host of five video productions based on his books, and is featured regularly on television and radio talk shows. Dr. Price and his wife Beverlee have five children and reside in Texas.

Free Newsletter About the Middle East

If you enjoyed the information in this book and would like to stay updated on current events in the Middle East, you can do so with our bimonthly newsletter *World of the Bible News & Views*. To receive a complimentary subscription, please make your request through our website or send it to our ministry address below.

A catalog of our books, publications, videos, and CD products can be found online at our website **www.worldofthebible.com**, or you may request a printed copy from our office.

Dr. Randall Price is available as a conference or pulpit speaker and also conducts annual tours to the Bible lands. To contact him about speaking to your group or for information on his tours, please call (512) 396-3799.

Communicating the facts of the past,
present, and prophetic world of the Bible

Dr. Randall Price is the founder and president of World of the Bible Ministries, Inc., a nonprofit corporation that seeks to provide accurate information about the biblical world and the modern Middle East. For information about our various ministries, please contact us at:

World of the Bible Ministries, Inc.
P.O. Box 827
San Marcos, TX 78667-0827

(512) 396-3799/Fax: (512) 392-9080
http://www.worldofthebible.com

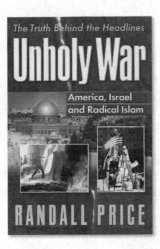

- **Who are the terrorists, and what are their goals?**

- **What is all the fighting about in the Middle East?**

- **Why is the Israeli-Palestinian conflict so key?**

- **Where does America fit into the picture?**

For years the Middle East conflict has seemed a distant problem, appearing no closer than the newspaper headlines. But recent catastrophic events have changed all that. What was once a faraway conflict has now spread to America and the rest of the Western world.

How did all this come about? Why has terrorism spilled over to America? These are the questions people are asking—and it's difficult to get answers because of the many misunderstandings about the Middle East, the Israeli-Palestinian problem, terrorism, and the Islamic religion.

Randall Price provides clear, concise answers to all these questions and more in *Unholy War*. His exceptional expertise on the Middle East and his intimate knowledge of Judaism, Islam, and the modern-day controversies make this an ideal reference for understanding the complex issues behind today's news headlines.

Available at your local bookstore, or from
World of the Bible Ministries, Inc.
P.O. Box 827
San Marcos, Texas 78667-0827

Books by Randall Price

Unholy War
Why does strife continue in the Middle East? How is it connected to terrorist attacks on Western nations? Dr. Price provides a concise, fascinating look at the problems and the players in the Middle East.

Secrets of the Dead Sea Scrolls
Discover the new technology that helps translators with previously unreadable Scrolls fragments, supposedly "secret" Scrolls, the debate about who owns the Scrolls, and the newest efforts to find more. Includes never-before-published photos. *(Video also available.*)*

The Stones Cry Out
Recently uncovered ancient artifacts shed light upon the lives of the patriarchs, the Ark of the Covenant, the fall of Jericho, and more. A fascinating survey of the latest finds in Bible lands, with more than 80 photographs affirming the incontrovertible facts that support biblical truth. *(Video also available.*)*

Jerusalem in Prophecy
Jerusalem has an incredible future in store, and it's at the very center of Bible prophecy. This book reveals what will happen, who the key players will be, and what signs indicate we're drawing close. *(Video also available.)*

The Coming Last Days Temple
The Bible says there's a new Temple in Jerusalem's future, but the current Israeli-Arab conflict makes that seem unlikely. Some claim the prophecies of Jerusalem's future are merely symbolic—but are they? Does the Bible give evidence that we can expect a literal Temple? Dr. Price surveys the preparations now being made for the next Temple, and offers a fascinating perspective on how they fit with biblical prophecy. *(Video also available.)*

In Search of Temple Treasures*
Does the Ark of the Covenant still exist? Why is it so important? *In Search of Temple Treasures* takes you on a remarkable expedition into the Ark's mysterious past, its explosive significance today, and its implications in the timing of last days' events, providing a factual inside view of one of history's most fascinating quests. *(Video also available.*)*

---

* These items available only through World of the Bible Ministries, Inc.